100 CLASSIC COASTAL WALKS IN SCOTLAND

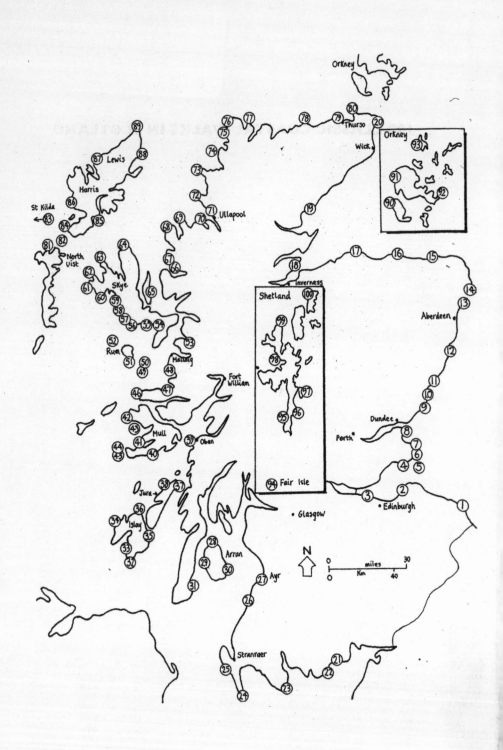

100
CLASSIC
COASTAL WALKS
IN SCOTLAND

ANDREW DEMPSTER

MAINSTREAM
PUBLISHING

EDINBURGH AND LONDON

This edition, 2011

First published in Great Britain in 2011 by
MAINSTREAM PUBLISHING COMPANY
(EDINBURGH) LTD
7 Albany Street
Edinburgh EH1 3UG

ISBN 9781845965860

The information in this book is believed to be correct as at March 2011
but is not to be relied on in law and is subject to change. The author and publishers
disclaim, as far as the law allows, any liability arising directly or indirectly
from the use, or misuse, of any information contained in this book.

Grateful acknowledgement is made to the Society of Authors as the literary
representative of the Estate of John Masefield for permission to reproduce lines
from 'Sea Fever' by John Masefield on p. 5 and to Carcanet Press Limited
for permission to reproduce lines from 'Hallaig', taken from
From Wood to Ridge/O Choille gu Berradh (Carcanet, 1999)
by Sorley Maclean on p. 252

A catalogue record for this book is available
from the British Library

Printed in Great Britain by
Clays Ltd St Ives plc

7 9 10 8

I must go down to the seas again, for the call of the running tide
    Is a wild call and a clear call that may not be denied;
        And all I ask is a windy day with the white clouds flying,
            And the flung spray and the blown spume, and the sea-gulls crying.

'Sea Fever', John Masefield

CONTENTS

2. The West Coast 1: Solway Firth to Mull

3. The West Coast 2 and North Coast: Ardnamurchan to Dunnet Head

4. The Outer Isles: The Outer Hebrides, Orkney and Shetland

INTRODUCTION

The lure of coastal walking

According to the British Cartographic Society, the coastline of the whole of Britain is 11,073 miles long. This is longer than those of countries such as Italy, France or Spain, all bigger in area than Britain. Scotland has the lion's share of this staggering figure, the mainland alone having nearly 7,000 miles. Including its countless islands, the estimated mileage of Scotland's coastline rises to over 10,000 miles, enough walking to last a lifetime – but why walk a coastline?

Scotland boasts not only the finest mountains in Britain but also a truly magnificent and rugged coastline. For many walkers, there is a close connection, or kinship, between these two wild domains. The heady intoxication derived from striding out along a narrow mountain ridge is akin to that of following the snaking edge of a craggy, cliff-girt coastline.

On days when the weather dictates low-level walking rather than battling gales on mountain summits, coastal routes can come into their own. A bracing stroll along an exposed, dramatic clifftop when buffeting winds and strong currents are pounding Atlantic waves against a fractured rock face, creating billowing white foam and sea spray, is an addictive experience.

Of course, coastal walking is much more than just a bad-weather alternative to hillwalking – it has a magical lure of its own. As a race, the British have a close affinity with the sea and all things nautical. We all live within 70 miles of the coast, and our love affair with the seaside is well established and strong.

The iconic image of two silhouetted figures strolling across a vast expanse of lonely sands as the sun sets over a silken sea strikes a chord deep within us. There is something about the tempestuous turbulence of the ocean that incites passion and romanticism and stares into our very soul. The intensity of emotion and raw sense of simply being alive elevate coastal walking to a higher, more captivating sphere.

Listening to the gentle lapping of wavelets on a Hebridean shore, searching for shells on some remote beach, exploring a wild rocky headland, discovering a hidden cave – all these and more possess the potential for reconnecting the child and the wild in all of us. The invigorating sea air and the tangy brine are not only a pick-me-up for the body but also a tonic for the soul.

The exploratory nature of much coastal walking in Scotland tends to stretch out the time required to complete a route. The time spent observing, photographing, exploring, rock scrambling and simply standing and staring can grow out of all proportion to the actual time spent walking, but it is what gives the pursuit its great allure. Becoming absorbed and captivated by the coastal landscape is what this book is all about – the walks are a means to that end. To give an example, on a visit to Shetland several years back I visited the small island of Noss in order to complete the classic walk around its dramatic coastline (see Route 97). The highlight of this route is the awesome cliff and stack scenery round the highest point of the island, at the Noup of Noss. The real distraction, however, was the charming antics of our most colourful and endearing bird specimen – the puffin. The time spent just sitting, observing and photographing these comics of the coastline was the true highlight of the walk and gave a penetrating insight into and a cogent connection to the natural world. The complete four-mile circular route took nearly four and a half hours: that is, an average speed of less than one mile per hour!

The ingredients of a classic coastal walk: choosing the routes

What constitutes a classic coastal walk? What are the ingredients that transform a relatively mundane walk into a memorable and inspirational experience? These questions have been partially answered in the first part of this introduction and the aim here is to offer a more practical basis as to how the 100 routes in this book were finalised.

One of the first conditions imposed on the routes is that they all are completable in a day. This, of course, has nothing to do with their classic status or otherwise – indeed, many serious walkers would argue that the only real classic coastal walks in Scotland are the multi-day routes such as the Fife Coastal Path, the Moray Coastal Trail and the new Ayrshire Coastal Path. Ultimately, the logical conclusion would lead to only one classic walk – a walk round the entire coastline of Scotland! (See Appendix for more on this.) By far the majority of walkers look to day walks as their staple 'meat and drink'; therefore that is what is offered in this book. The obvious corollary of this is that many of the walks can be linked into longer excursions if so wished.

Coastal walks tend not to fall into tidy 'watertight' lists in the same way that mountain walks do, where there exist definitive lists of Munros, Corbetts and Grahams, for example. The criteria for defining a mountain as a Munro or Corbett or whatever are fairly specific and subject to rules of height, drop and so on (e.g., a Munro is a Scottish mountain over 3,000 ft in height; a Corbett is a Scottish mountain over 2,500 ft in height but less than 3,000 ft, and it must also have at least 500 ft of reascent on all sides; a Graham is a Scottish mountain over 2,000 ft in height but less than 2,500 ft, and it must also have at least 500 ft of reascent on all sides; and a Marilyn is any British hill having at least 500 ft of reascent on all sides). A coastal walk, on the other hand, can begin or end anywhere and be of any length. This inherent vagueness produces an enormous challenge in the choice of specific routes, and obvious subjectivity must enter into the final selection.

An interesting question to pose is this: if another author had produced a similar book to this, completely independently, would they have come up with the same choice of routes? The answer would obviously be a definite 'no'. On the other hand, it is highly unlikely that there would not be a great deal of overlap between the two sets of routes. The exact beginning and end points of many routes would vary enormously, but the highlights would undoubtedly be repeated in both works. For instance, such notable features as Dunnottar Castle, the Duncansby Stacks, the Carsaig Arches, Crail, Culzean Castle, Sandwood Bay, Rubha Hunish, Dunnet Head, Cape Wrath, St Kilda, the Old Man of Hoy, Hermaness, Fair Isle and many more would be bound to feature prominently in both books, although specific walk details may be slightly different.

A glance at the above list gives an inkling as to some of the ingredients that produce a classic walk. These are dramatic coastal features (such as stacks and natural arches), headlands, castles or other features of historical interest, fine beaches, islands and picturesque villages. Other factors to add in are wildlife and, of course, weather.

Islands in particular exude their own unique and individual charm and, as such, are featured frequently in this book. It should come as no surprise that, considering the many hundreds of islands off Scotland's west and north coasts, over half the routes described are island walks. There is an enormous satisfaction to be found in the complete circumnavigation of an island on foot, and many smaller Scottish islands are ideal for this treatment: for example, Ulva (off Mull), Noss (Shetland), Isle of May, Fair Isle and so on. Many larger islands, such as Skye and Mull, contain a vast amount of coastal walking potential, and Skye alone has 11 classic routes.

Peninsulas and headlands, though part of the mainland, can possess certain island qualities. Walking round the tip of a wild and exposed headland also has the feel of reaching a sharp mountain summit, and headlands form the highlight of many of the described routes.

Scotland's coastline is crammed with ruined fortifications, Clearance settlements, archaeological sites and other points of historical significance. If historical interest was the only factor to be considered in selecting a walk, there would still be an abundance of suitable venues and places to visit.

Again, if fine sandy beaches are your thing then there are many to choose from. Locations such as Lunan Bay, Forvie Sands, Sandwood Bay, Tentsmuir and Morar are just the tip of a very large iceberg.

The upshot of all this is that there are simply too many wonderful places to walk on Scotland's coastline, but the hundred routes contained here possess a blend of some, if not all, of the above features.

One point not yet mentioned is the existence of paths. The majority of the described routes are on well-established footpaths or tracks, but a few involve wild, pathless walking, beach walking or rock scrambling and some may include sections of all these. The existence of footpaths has influenced the choice of routes to some extent, but often the main attraction of a walk can be to remove oneself from the beaten track and reach more remote and wild places. Obviously, not all the routes in this book will suit all walkers. Some are suited to families, some to reasonably fit walkers and some to hardened backpackers; but whatever your age, fitness and inclination, you should discover many ideal and pleasurable excursions.

Logistics

By their nature, coastal walks are generally linear A-to-B excursions and therefore do not readily lend themselves to a natural and easy return to the starting point. However, having said this, well over half the routes described here are circular walks, including not only the circumnavigation of smaller islands but also headlands and many general coastal routes with interesting inland return options. Only a minority of walks will require some forethought as to how to return to the point of departure. What follows is a selection of possible ideas for dealing with this 'return' problem.

> **Use of two cars:** Perhaps the most obvious, but extravagant, solution is to leave a second car at the end point of the walk, but this entails a second driver. This option is obviously not available if you are a lone walker.
>
> **A helpful partner:** This option relies on having a non-walking member of your group to drive to the end point and wait patiently until you arrive or to begin walking from the end point to meet you en route.
>
> **Use of a bike:** This healthy option is ideal if you are a lone walker and there is a scenic road or track route between the start and end points of the walk. It is positively recommended on several routes in this book (e.g. Dunnet Head – see Route 80). The question of whether to drive to the end point and leave the bike there before returning by car to the start or leaving the car at the end point and cycling back to the start is entirely up to the individual. Some people may not be entirely happy about leaving a bike for several hours, but there are usually suitable locations in bushes and woods or deep heather in which to hide one. Never leave a bike in a prominent open position, even if it is locked.
>
> **Use of public transport:** Unfortunately, public transport such as buses or trains cannot be readily relied upon in more remote parts of Scotland, but several of the walks included are ideally suited for this option (e.g. Portknockie to Portsoy on the Moray coast – see Route 16).
>
> **Use of a taxi:** This option should really only be considered

as a last resort, but it is in any case only suitable if you are ending the walk in a populated area.

Use of private transport: If you are staying in a hotel, hostel or guest house, there is sometimes a 'pick-up' service offered by the owners, usually for a small fee, and this is worth investigating.

The two-party option: If you are walking in a large group and have access to two cars, the group can be split into two, with each half starting the walk at opposite ends. Upon meeting up (possibly for lunch) in the middle, car keys can be exchanged, enabling each party to drive back to a suitable rendezvous point.

Walk back by the same route: This is the simplest option and involves no cars, bikes, buses or other companions. It also allows you to observe sights from the opposite direction. However, for longer routes it is not viable and, unless you are ultra fit, should only be considered for shorter walks of less than seven miles. A return walk is usually more satisfying if accomplished by a different (or partly different) route to that of the outward journey, and these options are included in the route descriptions whenever possible.

Safety

Walking a section of coastline may seem like a fairly safe pastime, but walkers should be aware of inherent dangers and treat the coast with respect. Cliff edges are generally unfenced and can become loose and highly eroded. The coastline is often a windy environment and the combination of gusty winds and clifftop walking can be potentially dangerous, especially if you have small children.

Several of the walks in this book are not passable at extremely high tides, and this is mentioned in the route assessment or description where applicable. If you are in doubt as to the state of the tide, play safe and do not allow yourself to become stranded. Most tourist information centres possess tide tables that can be consulted before attempting a route.

In more remote parts of Scotland, and especially on islands such as Shetland, St Kilda and Handa, you will very likely be dive-bombed by large birds called great skuas, or bonxies. These are birds with attitude that fiercely defend their nesting territory by swooping from behind to fly low over the heads of intruders in their domain. The smaller Arctic terns use much the same tactic. If caught out by either, get away from their nesting area as quickly as possible. It is a good idea to carry a walking pole on such occasions, keeping it vertical above your head. Do not wave the pole about or attempt to hit the birds with it!

When attempting any of the longer, more remote routes in this book, remember to leave word of your route and estimated time of completion with a responsible person, and carry a mobile phone if you have one. This is especially important if you are a lone walker. Remember that in Scotland the weather can change from sunshine to wind-driven rain and low cloud within hours, so you should carry a rucksack containing waterproofs, a hat, gloves and some food and drink. A torch is also a useful item if you intend to visit any caves en route.

The sketch maps accompanying each route are not intended to be used 'in the field' and on most of the routes you would be advised to have the necessary Ordnance Survey Landranger 1:50,000 map, which will give you a better idea of terrain and topography. A compass is not really necessary except possibly on some of the more hilly routes, such as Hoy, in Orkney, and Skye, where mist can be a problem.

Finally, never be afraid to turn back if adverse circumstances prevail, such as poor weather, tidal conditions or tiredness. You can always return on another day. Above all – enjoy!

MAP SYMBOLS

Cliffs

Rocky Foreshore

Sandy Beach

Road

Vehicle Track -----

Path -·-·-·

Un-made route ·······

Parking P

Start/Finish Point O

Route regions

For ease of use and convenience, the one hundred walks have been classified into four distinct geographical areas. These are:

1. The East Coast: St Abb's Head to Duncansby Head (Routes 1–20)
2. The West Coast 1: Solway Firth to Mull (Routes 21–45)
3. The West Coast 2 and North Coast: Ardnamurchan to Dunnet Head (Routes 46–80)
4. The Outer Isles: The Outer Hebrides, Orkney and Shetland (Routes 81–100)

Each of the Regions 1 to 3 also includes islands easily reachable from that region. For instance, the Isle of May is included in Region 1, as it is reached from Anstruther on the east coast.

The islands of Arran, Islay, Jura and Mull are included in Region 2 as well as several smaller islands, such as Davaar, Holy Isle, Kerrera, Iona and Ulva.

The islands of Rum, Eigg, Canna, Skye, Raasay and Handa are included in Region 3, which also contains the highest number of routes (35).

Route descriptions

Each walk is summarised by a short introductory assessment offering a brief overview, indicating, for instance, difficulty, terrain, quality, suitability for children and any other relevant factors. This is followed by a note on distance, time and the number of the relevant Ordnance Survey Landranger map. Distances are classified as one of either 'linear', 'return' or 'circular'. A linear distance is one-way only, a return distance includes walking back by the outward route and a circular distance includes walking back by a different route.

The timings provided never give an exact number of hours but a range, such as three to five hours. This should generally cover the range of times required to complete the routes by walkers of different speeds, from fast to slow, and also includes time for exploration and stops.

The main route description gives a detailed account of the route as well as offering information on any points of interest, such as rock formations, beaches, historical and archaeological sites and so on. Other relevant information is also given, such as ferry details where necessary. For smaller, more remote islands, a 'Getting to . . .' panel has been included, giving fuller details of ferry operators and timings.

Many of the route descriptions also include possible extensions or interesting alternatives to the main route, offering a more ambitious schedule for stronger walkers. Conversely, ideas for shorter walks may be incorporated.

Finally, many of the route descriptions end by stating a recommended pub. At the end of a long coastal ramble there is nothing nicer than relaxing in a cosy tavern, perhaps by a log fire, and enjoying that all-important pint of real ale while avidly discussing the highlights of another classic coastal walk.

I

The East Coast:

ST ABB'S HEAD TO DUNCANSBY HEAD

1

The East Coast:

ST ABB'S HEAD TO DUNCANSBY HEAD

ST ABB'S HEAD

The spectacular cliffs of St Abb's Head and Pettico Wick provide a perfect focus for an exhilarating walk through a National Nature Reserve that boasts one of the largest concentrations of breeding seabirds on the east coast of mainland Britain. The route is suitable for children provided they keep clear of cliff edges.

Distance: 4 miles/6 km (circular)
Time: 2–3 hours
OS map: 67

THE ROUTE DESCRIBED BEGINS AND ENDS AT THE NATIONAL Trust car park near Northfield Farm, where there is a visitor centre. This is just off the B6438 road between Coldingham and St Abbs. The route is a popular one and is well waymarked.

From the car park, walk downhill past the row of cottages that have been converted into a visitor centre, toilets, coffee shop and craft shop. Follow the path running parallel with the road and then turn left at a high wall. After going through a gate, reach a picnic table perched at the edge of a cliff with stunning views across Starney Bay to White Heugh and the Wuddy. Continue delightfully along the clifftop path to the rocky promontory of White Heugh, which is a prelude to the sheer cliffs and inlets further on. From here, there is a fine view looking back to the quaint village and harbour of St Abbs.

Descend to Horsecastle Bay, where there is a gate at the bottom of Kirk Hill. Beyond the gate the path continues along the base of Kirk Hill, but it is more interesting to bear off to the right to reach the cliff edge once again. This option offers a grandstand view of St Abb's Head with its attendant lighthouse and foghorn perched on the very edge of the cliff. When visibility is poor, the foghorn echoes eerily around the

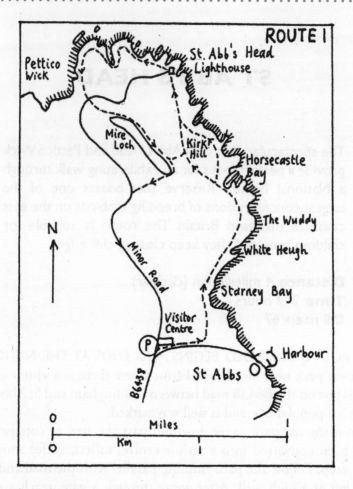

cliffs and the lighthouse is one of the main markers on the approach to the Firth of Forth.

Rejoin the main path, which leads up to the lighthouse and the end of a minor tarmac road. Many people believe this to be the end of the coastal walk and continue happily down the road to Mire Loch, but the climax is still to come! In fact, the greatest concentration of St Abb's Head's 50,000 or so seabirds is on the superb cliffs and sea stacks to the north-west of the lighthouse, where there exist perfect nesting sites for kittiwakes, guillemots and razorbills. Gannets do not breed here, but many pass over en route to the Bass Rock. Take plenty of time to savour the awesome, dizzying situations and to observe at close quarters the high-rise living of thousands of cliff-dwelling birds.

A little further round the cliffs from the lighthouse and before a long narrow inlet is Nunnery Point, the site of what was originally believed to be a seventh-century nunnery but now reckoned to be that of a more recent medieval construction.

Descend to Pettico Wick by an obvious grassy gully to reach a small harbour. From here, leave the road and follow a grassy path along the left (north) side of Mire Loch, a peaceful freshwater loch offering a complete contrast to the wild coastline.

Guillemot

This artificial loch was constructed in 1901 primarily for trout fishing and is home to swans, mallards and tufted ducks. The crags above the loch contain some rare plants such as spring sandwort and soft clover. Wheatears nest in rabbit burrows on the lower slopes. Mire Loch lies on a geological fault separating much older heavily folded rock from the younger volcanic rock of St Abb's Head.

At the southern end of Mire Loch, it is easy to rejoin the outward route by heading left, but you can complete a pleasant round in less than a mile by crossing the dam and then following a Land Rover track uphill to the road that leads back to the car park.

The pretty village of St Abbs should not be missed, and the harbour is still used extensively for fishing. The village is named after St Aebba, who founded a church here in the seventh century. The present church and harbour were constructed by one of the Usher brewing family, who ironically declared that there should be no public house here – sadly his declaration is still in force, so don't expect a post-walk pint!

Cliff and sea stacks, St Abb's Head

Route 2

ABERLADY BAY TO YELLOW CRAIG

A long and varied coastal walk taking in some fine bays and isolated sandy coves, followed by a more rural inland route along the recently established John Muir Way (see Appendix). The route can easily be shortened if so wished, and this may be preferable if you are not a strong walker or if young children are involved.

Distance: 12 miles/19 km (circular)
Time: 4–5 hours
OS map: 66

THE ROUTE IS SITUATED WEST OF THE POPULAR HOLIDAY TOWN of North Berwick and begins at the small parking area on the A198 at Aberlady Bay. The coastal part of the walk ends at Broad Sands, just west of North Berwick, and if transport can be arranged the return route following the John Muir Way could be omitted.

An alternative start point is the large parking area at Gullane Bay (known as Gullane Bents), which would reduce the coastal part of the walk to 3.5 miles.

If you start at the Aberlady Bay parking area, walk across the wooden bridge going over the estuary and salt marsh to enter the Aberlady Local Nature Reserve, the first of its kind to be established in Britain, back in 1952. The area encompasses one of the largest naturally developing dune systems in south-east Scotland and is an important breeding site for many varieties of birds. The path is well made and passes through the middle of the site to the left of Gullane links rather than sticking rigidly to the coastline. After entering a copse of hawthorn bushes you emerge at a small loch where you are likely to spot swans and tufted ducks. If you are really lucky you may see a red-throated diver, which offshores here in early spring before departing to more northerly breeding sites.

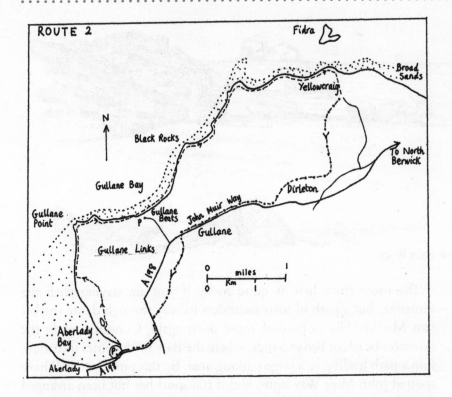

As you continue on through open grassland, you will doubtlessly be accompanied by a skylark high above spilling out its sylvan song. At an obvious track junction, take the left fork, which leads in less than half a mile to the dunes and Gullane sands.

A fine beach walk then leads to the igneous rocky outcrop of Gullane Point, where oystercatchers are common. Before Gullane Bay, pass some peaceful little sandy coves and enjoy the view out over the Forth Estuary to the Kingdom of Fife. Arthur's Seat is plainly visible to the far left while the prominent little pair of East and West Lomond lie straight across.

Gullane Bay provides another fine beach walk prior to rejoining the coastal path before Black Rocks, where you pass the ruin of an old chapel. Beyond is another idyllic little bay, which is usually deserted, unlike Gullane Bay. A succession of beautiful little coves and rocky nooks follows until the coastline makes a turn eastwards. The lighthouse ahead looks like part of the mainland but is actually on the small rocky islet of Fidra.

The Bass Rock

The route from here is quite rocky if you are staying with the shoreline, but a path of sorts meanders its way through dense thicket past Marine Villa to become more open again. Continue on to the extensive beach of Broad Sands, where the Bass Rock comes into view. Join a path leading to a large parking area. By this point you will have spotted John Muir Way signs, and if transport has not been arranged then this route provides the best return to the starting point.

The return route does not really require any description as the way is extremely well waymarked through Dirleton and Gullane.

SOUTH QUEENSFERRY TO CRAMOND

A charming and peaceful walk from the Forth Rail Bridge in the historic village of South Queensferry through the Dalmeny Estate to the outflow of the River Almond near Cramond village. Unfortunately the little ferry across the river to Cramond is no longer operating, but this is still a fine walk. A good bus service links Barnton and Queensferry.

Distance: 4.5 miles/7 km (linear)
Time: 2–3 hours
OS map: 65

SOUTH QUEENSFERRY'S HERITAGE OF NEARLY FOUR CENTURIES of famous architecture and its notable geographical site as the original ferry terminus across the Forth have endowed it with a uniquely Scottish charm. Hemmed in between the great rail and road bridges, it is an ideal location from which to view those structures. The famous Hawes Inn, which was featured in Sir Walter Scott's *The Antiquary* as well as being woven into Robert Louis Stevenson's *Kidnapped*, lies under the rail bridge.

Parking is plentiful just before the rail bridge, and this marks the start of the walk. As you walk under the massive ramparts of the rail bridge, it is sobering to think that of the four and a half thousand souls who built the bridge nearly 60 died and many hundreds were seriously injured in its construction – no health and safety rules then!

Take the tarmac road forking off to the left, where you will notice a sign for cyclists (NCN route 76). This is roughly the same as the walkers' route. Go through a gate next to a cottage, which marks the start of the Dalmeny Estate, and follow the pleasant track through wooded rural countryside with fine views of the Forth Estuary to your

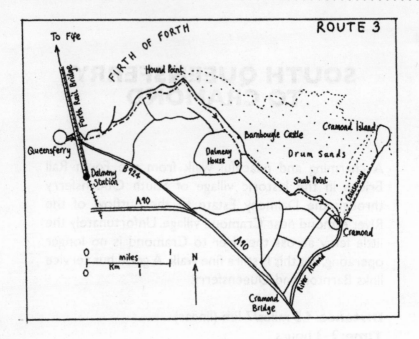

left. Numerous opportunities exist to gain access to the shoreline, and the little promontory of Hound Point is an ideal spot for the first stop, having a small bench and great views across to Fife and Inchcolm Island.

The route beyond is clear, on a track and sometimes tarmac, passing the large, occupied seventeenth-century Barnbougle Castle jutting out seawards on a small promontory. A short distance further on, you will pass the elegant Gothic Revival mansion of Dalmeny House, built in 1815 by the fifth Earl of Rosebery. Still the family's home, it is partly open to the public during the summer.

Follow the sign saying 'Shore-walk', which leads along the edge of the private golf course to the waterfront. There is a fine beach further on almost totally covered in shells, offering a good view back to Barnbougle Castle. Continue along the shoreline before climbing steeply up to the path again at Snab Point. Some distance beyond here is the little rocky promontory of Eagle Rock, so called because of a much-worn Roman carving of an eagle to be found there. In AD 142, a Roman fort was built in Cramond to supply the soldiers building the Antonine Wall between the Forth and the Clyde.

The Hawes Inn, South Queensferry

Finally, reach Cobble Cottage, the little cottage at the mouth of the River Almond, where you can look directly across to the quaint whitewashed cottages of Cramond. You will also have noticed Cramond Island, a tidal island connected to the mainland by a causeway. If the tide is well out you may just be able to ford the Almond nearer to its outflow to the sea, but don't bank on it!

Either return by the same route or, if taking vehicular transport back to Queensferry, follow the dirt track up from Cobble Cottage, which arrives in just over a mile at Cramond Bridge, where a bus will take you back to South Queensferry for a well-earned pint!

Recommended pub: The Hawes Inn, South Queensferry

Route 4

THE CHAIN WALK

The Chain Walk is unique in being the only chain-assisted coastal scramble in the UK. At only half a mile it is the shortest route in this book, but for novelty and situation it earns its classic status. The route is only suitable for those with some scrambling ability and a good head for heights. Many older children will revel in the exposed situations!

Distance: 0.5 miles/1 km (linear)
Time: 1–2 hours
OS map: 59

THE CHAIN WALK IS SITUATED IN EARLSFERRY, JUST WEST OF ELIE in the Kingdom of Fife, and forms an alternative part of the well-known Fife Coastal Path, which follows the clifftop high above the shoreline scramble described here.

After entering the quaint fishing village of Elie, take the road signposted 'Earlsferry golf course' and park at the links. The sandy bay at Earlsferry can be reached via a track through the golf course, and care should be taken due to low-flying golf balls! At the beach, turn right to follow the signposted Fife Coastal Path. The Chain Walk itself runs along the base of the cliffs about half a mile distant. It should be noted at this point that if there is a very high tide then the Chain Walk may be impracticable or even impossible.

Continue on to the start of the Chain Walk, where a flight of stone steps leads up to a cliff-face on which there is a sign indicating the start of the route. The sign also gives warning of steep cliffs, falling rocks and incoming tide.

Follow the cliff round into a deep channel and scramble up to a flattish area of rock where the first of many chains and incut steps is situated. It is worth pointing out that if the tide is more in than out

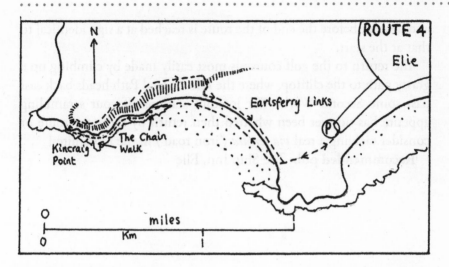

then this first part of the route can be the most intimidating. Climb the broad incut steps using the chain as a handrail and then sidestep along a series of ledges and footholds for about 10 m using a chain above. If the tide is in, you will be glad of the chain. If not, the channel can be easily crossed on large, smooth boulders.

On the opposite side of the channel, scramble onto an obvious detached rock that is about half a metre away from the main cliff. At this point, you need to step out onto a foothold on the cliff and grab the chain before making one or two tricky moves to become established on the wide ledge, which leads round to safer ground further to the left. If all this sounds suicidal, don't despair: it is easier to do than to describe! This is probably the hardest part of the whole route.

Beyond this point, it is mainly walking and easy scrambling until a beautiful and secluded shingle beach is reached. This is most noteworthy for the unusual curved, columnar basalt rock formations at its far end. The hexagonal columns are reminiscent of the Isle of Staffa. At the end of the beach, climb a short cliff via stone steps and a chain and continue on up a footworn slope of loose grit to reach the first steep descent. This is made fairly easy by initial wide steps and subsequently by a chain and incut holds on the vertical part.

Another narrow channel similar to the one at the start soon follows, and the head of this channel contains a small cave worth a quick look. Beyond here, there is a second small cove with a chain-assisted ascent and descent before the end of the route is reached at a sign identical to that at the start.

The return to the golf course is most easily made by climbing up a grassy path to the clifftop, where the Fife Coastal Path heads back east past some Second World War lookout stations. If your scrambling appetite has not yet been whetted then return by the same route or consider tackling a real *via ferrata* ('iron road') in the Dolomites!

Recommended pub: The Ship Inn, Elie

ISLE OF MAY CIRCUIT

For small-island and bird enthusiasts, this grand walk around the 'jewel of the Forth' cannot be bettered. The island is also steeped in fascinating archaeological and historical interest, which together with its rugged, picturesque coastline have made it a magnet for tourists for many years. The walking is easy and entirely on set paths, which should be adhered to at all times.

Distance: 2.5 miles/4 km (circular)
Time: 2–3 hours
OS map: 59

THE ISLE OF MAY IS THE LARGEST OF THE FIRTH OF FORTH islands, being just over a mile long and about a quarter of a mile wide. Since 1956 the island has been a National Nature Reserve, and it is owned and managed by Scottish National Heritage, who also coordinate internationally important scientific studies on sea birds and seals during spring, summer and autumn. The name May possibly derives from Old Norse for 'gull island' or from the Gaelic word *magh*, meaning 'a plain'.

Archaeological remains show that the Isle of May was occupied 5,000 years ago. Earliest recorded history tells of the missionary St Adrian, who settled here around AD 860 but was massacred along with his fellow monks by the Vikings some ten years later. Since then, the island accrued sacred status and became a centre of pilgrimage, rather like Iona on the west coast. King David I of Scotland founded a monastery on the island dedicated to St Adrian, and later a Benedictine priory was established.

Scotland's first lighthouse was built on the island in 1635. It was basically a square stone tower with a large metal basket on the roof where a coal fire was burned every night. The fire used between one

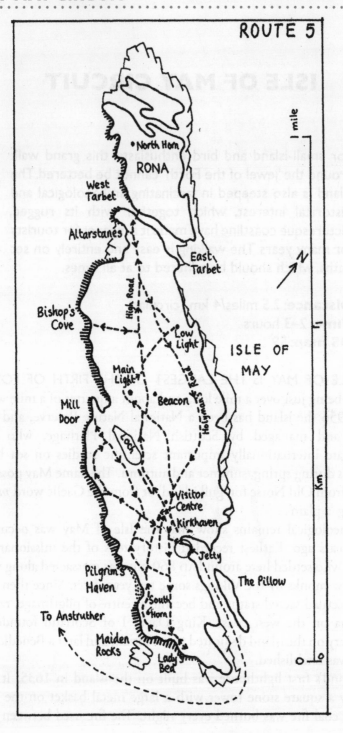

ROUTE 5

RONA

• North Horn

West
Tarbet

Altarstanes

Bishop's
Cove

High Road

Low
Light

ISLE OF
MAY

East
Tarbet

Main
Light

Beacon

Holyman's Road

Mill
Door

LOCH

Visitor
Centre

Kirkhaven

Jetty

Pilgrim's
Haven

The Pillow

To Anstruther

South
Horn

Maiden
Rocks

Lady
Bed

N

1 mile

Km

and three tons of coal every night! The designer of this 'beacon tower' was drowned while on a visit to the island, and the blame for this tragedy was placed on several innocent old ladies of Pittenweem who were subsequently burned as witches.

The lighthouse that stands today is a fine though rather out-of-place building totally dominating the whole island. It was built in 1816 by the grandfather of Robert Louis Stevenson and is now fully automated.

The island's strategic position at the entrance to the Forth Estuary has resulted in many naval battles, and wreckage from warfare and other tragedies is scattered throughout the east-coast shallows, making it a mecca for diving clubs.

Landing on the island is at the southern anchorage of Kirkhaven, which is the far (southern) end of the island. This gives ample opportunity to observe the high western cliffs from the seaward side, and the boatman will no doubt sail in close (sea conditions permitting) to observe a sample of the 200,000 seabirds that live here. The main cliff residents are guillemots, gulls and razorbills. Look out also for seals and the many points of interest such as Bishop's Cove and Pilgrim's Haven. Kirkhaven lies at the end of a narrow creek between the island and a rock skerry known as the Pillow.

On arrival, as well as being greeted by a cacophony of noise from terns, gulls and oystercatchers, you will be met by the current warden, who will welcome you to the island and offer some useful advice and information, including the exact time of the boat's departure – very important! The main piece of advice when walking round the island is to stay on the paths at all times. This is to ensure that your feet do not collapse a puffin burrow, which could result in the death of a chick. In the main, the paths are of short grass and marked by small, blue painted posts. Normally, no guidance is given as to whether to make a clockwise or anticlockwise circuit of the island, and besides, the path system is not quite as simple as that.

A good idea is to first head for the south of the island to the area known as Lady's Bed, where you are sure to see plenty of puffins. Continue along the path around South Horn, following the cliff edge to Pilgrim's Haven, and opt for left forks in the path, which lead you along the cliffs to various viewpoints. In early summer, the ground is awash with carpets of white sea campion and the cliffs are dotted with colourful clumps of pink sea thrift. Most of the paths and tracks have delightful names such as Prior's Walk, Palpitation Brae and Holyman's Road, reflecting the history of the island.

Getting to the Isle of May

Anstruther Pleasure Cruises sail from Anstruther Harbour from April to September on the *May Princess*. The crossing time is just under one hour with typically two to three hours ashore, depending on sea and tide conditions. Landings cannot be guaranteed. There is only one sailing per day and tickets are available from the kiosk at Anstruther Harbour about an hour before sailing.

> Tel: 01333 310103 (24-hour information line)
> Tel: 01333 310054 (booking)
> Email: info@isleofmayferry.com
> Tel: 01333 311073 (Anstruther Tourist Information)

An information booklet with a detailed map is issued to all passengers when purchasing tickets. For this reason, a detailed route description is not really necessary and most visitors to the island will wish to go their own way and do their own thing. However, the accompanying text gives a few pointers and some useful advice.

At the viewpoint at Mill Door you will need to double back to the visitor centre along the path above the manmade freshwater loch before heading along Fluke Street and Palpitation Brae to the main lighthouse in the centre of the island. During your walk, you will discover many plaques offering interesting snippets of historical information. Continue north along High Road and you will reach the bridge to the adjacent island of Rona; however, you will not be allowed to cross over to it, as public access to Rona is prohibited. A return to the visitor centre can be made by the Low Road past the island's second lighthouse (now a private residence and bird observatory) and Holyman's Road.

Although the total distance walked is less than 2.5 miles, time should be allowed for bird-watching, photography and simply standing

The Isle of May

and staring. As with many coastal walks, time can soon run away all too quickly, but being on an island it is essential that you don't miss the boat!

Route 6

THE EAST NEUK OF FIFE: ELIE TO CRAIL

The East Neuk of Fife is the classic section of the celebrated Fife Coastal Path, an 80-mile walk between the Forth and Tay bridges (see Appendix). Described by James II as 'a fringe of gold on a beggar's mantle', the East Neuk has also been compared to a string of pearls joined together by the Fife Coastal Path, the pearls being the picturesque and quaint fishing villages lining the route. This is a charming and memorable walk with few or no difficulties. A good bus service connects all the villages.

Distance: 11 miles/18 km (linear)
Time: 5–7 hours
OS map: 59

IN ELIE, TAKE THE ROAD TO THE HARBOUR THAT IS SIGNPOSTED 'Award Beach' and 'The Ship Inn'. A sharp left turn up a narrow street followed by a right turn takes you to a large parking area with information boards and the start of the described walk. It is also possible to park in the harbour area, but payment is required. From the car park, the little Stevenson lighthouse at Elie Ness is prominent as you look south. On a clear day, you should also spot Berwick Law, the Bass Rock and the Isle of May.

Leaving the car park, you should soon spot the Fife Coastal Path marker post with its distinctive 'wavy lines' logo. This bypasses the little headland of Fife Ness, and rather than going left (east) it is worth taking the grassy path out to the lighthouse and also to the little stone tower known as the Lady Tower. This tower was built in the eighteenth century as a changing room for Lady Anstruther when she swam in the sea. Allegedly, she would send her bellman around the streets of

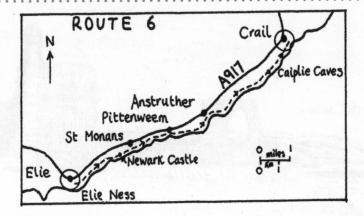

Elie warning people to stay indoors, as she disliked being seen in her bathing costume!

The path from the tower is clear, as it stays close to the shoreline, and at low tide it may be preferable to walk along the sandy beach. About a mile from the tower are the remains of Ardross Castle, built by the Sheriff of Fife, husband to one of Robert the Bruce's sisters. Less than a mile further along the coast are the more substantial remains of Newark Castle, perched high on a rocky promontory. Just before you climb up to the castle, you should notice a large wooden marker post advising as to the safety of adopting the low-tide route to St Monans. If the sea is up to the post then the alternative route is recommended. The route description following is the low-tide route.

Beyond Newark Castle, the path continues to a beehive-shaped doocot before dropping down to an eroded section of coastline. The top of the next rise offers a fine view of St Monans, with its church dominating the immediate foreground. The low-tide route follows a stone ledge above a retaining wall and traverses round the right side of the church, crossing a small pier and stream to emerge on the other side of the church. This now joins the high-tide route as it snakes its way up some stone steps and along a narrow walkway hemmed in between private properties and gardens. Turn right at the obvious junction and walk down the street to the picturesque harbour.

Beyond the harbour area, turn left up Forth Street then right along Rose Street, following the signposts for the windmill. At the windmill, there are information boards describing the salt pan industry, which was established here in 1771 when the windmill was a working part of

Newark Castle

the process. Foundations of the old salt pan houses are clearly visible, and it is worth taking time to read the fascinating history.

The path continues on pleasantly towards Pittenweem, climbing up steeply to a children's play park. Notice the old outdoor sea swimming pool, which has long since gone into decline. Just beyond the small shelter, the path forks off to the right, winding round the hillside and descending to sea level at Pittenweem's west shore. Follow the footpath past the picturesque stone cottages to the harbour area. It is worth making a small diversion to the left up Cove Wynd to view St Fillan's Cave, the alleged home of the seventh century's St Fillan. The name Pittenweem means 'land by the cave' – 'weem' is derived from *uaimh*, which is Gaelic for 'cave'.

Head east along the road and up the hill before more coastal path signs take you along the back of some houses and down steps to the golf course. From here to Anstruther via the headland of Billow Ness is easy and pleasant walking. If the tide is out, you can drop down to the beach and make your way to the main esplanade following the large stone sea wall across low rocks and sand. Alternatively, reach the main harbour area via Shore Street and Crichton Street.

Anstruther is the 'capital' of the East Neuk and boasts the Scottish Fisheries Museum, a tourist information centre and the official best fish and chips restaurant in Scotland! Like all the East Neuk villages, the harbourside houses boast some of the finest indigenous architecture in Scotland, reflecting so much of our character and lifestyle.

Caiplie Caves

Continue along the winding street to the peaceful and picturesque harbour at Cellardyke, originally built by the Dutch several centuries ago but since extended and strengthened. This old harbour is a pleasant contrast to the hustle and bustle of Anstruther.

Beyond Cellardyke, the path winds its way past a caravan park and an extensive pig farm to the vicinity of Caiplie Farm. A short distance beyond on a raised beach are the Caiplie Caves, a weird sandstone upthrust weathered and eroded by waves thousands of years ago into a contorted mass of almost organic-looking stacks and arches. The caves have a long and interesting history going back to 2000 BC, and Greek and Latin inscriptions have been found, along with crosses carved by medieval monks. Today all you are likely to find are the names and initials of local children!

From here, a mile of pleasant walking takes you to the last of the Neuk villages of Crail and the end of the walk. As you enter the village by the coastal path there is a superb view of Crail Harbour, arguably the most picturesque of all the harbours. The path follows the top of a cliff before descending to the harbour past a series of unique stone houses full of colour and character. Crail is a fitting end to a superb walk.

Recommended pub: The Ship Inn, Elie

Route 7

CRAIL TO ST ANDREWS

This is a lengthy and varied walk along the wildest part of the Fife Coastal Path. Unlike the East Neuk section (see Route 6), the route does not pass through any villages or towns and is altogether a more serious proposition. You will need to be self-sufficient with food and drink. A shorter alternative is to walk from the parking area near Kingsbarns to St Andrews, a distance of seven miles.

Distance: 13 miles/21 km (linear)
Time: 6–8 hours
OS map: 59

CRAIL HARBOUR IS PROBABLY THE QUAINTEST AND MOST picturesque of all the East Neuk harbours and marks the start of the long trek to the university town of St Andrews. If you cannot park a car at the harbour, there is plenty of space in the main street higher up.

Leave the harbour and wander up the street until you see the sign for Castle Walk, a short, high-level route giving great views across the Forth Estuary to the Bass Rock and the Isle of May. King David I built a castle here in the twelfth century but has since long gone. Beyond Castle Walk, drop down to the seafront and enter an extensive caravan and holiday-chalet park before reaching the Kilminning Coast Wildlife Reserve. The prominent stack known as Kilminning Castle was used for target practice by aircraft in the Second World War by bombarding it with bags of flour!

Fife Ness is the point where the direction of the walk changes from north-east to north-west and has little to commend it other than the Craighead Links golf course and the coastguard lookout station. The coastal trail passes below the modern lighthouse and a wooden bird hide used to track passing migrants. Further on, it is worth stopping

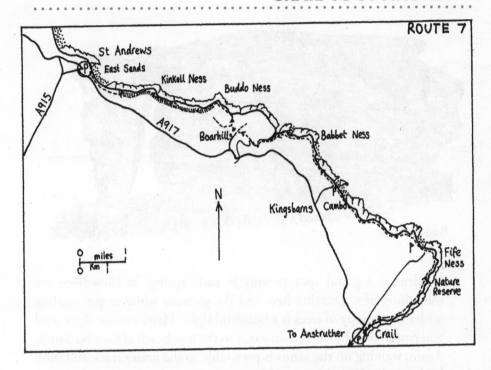

ROUTE 7

to read the information signs indicating the location of an old eighteenth-century tidal mill, a highly unusual construction. As you approach the golf course, you will pass a small cave known as Constantine's Cave, where King Constantine I was allegedly killed after a battle in AD 874.

Beyond here, if the tide is low it is advisable to walk on the beach, not least to avoid serious injury from low-flying golf balls but also because, at the time of writing, there were several signs indicating path erosion. Indeed, for the next few miles there are signs telling the walker to 'keep to the beach for the next half-mile'. The one at the end of the golf course beyond a series of steps has the added instruction 'If high tide, wait until tide recedes before continuing'. However, it is better to use common sense and climb the grassy slopes and follow the fence rather than wait for several hours! Interestingly, beyond the flat grassy area (where livestock are sometimes present) there is another sign near a stone wall indicating a 'high-tide route', a route not mentioned by the sign at the end of the golf course. Confused? So was the author!

Ahead you will notice a large bank of trees at Cambo, which is reached by following the edge of a new links golf course. Cambo

Buddo Rock

Gardens is a grand spot to visit in early spring, as snowdrops are something of a speciality here and the glorious white carpet nestling under the canopy of trees is a beautiful sight. Here, various signs send you past a toilet block and onwards to the fine beach at Cambo Sands. Again, walking on the sands is preferable to the grassy track and soon leads to the Kingsbarns parking area, the only place on the route accessible by car.

At Kingsbarns there is another golf course and, beyond, a sign indicating that the seven-mile section from here to St Andrews is 'rough and remote coastal terrain'. This is all relative, however; compared with some of the big routes on Skye's west coast, this is a stroll in the park! The route stays to the right of a fence on slabby stones before you 'follow beach until next marker'. The sandy beach at Airbow Point provides excellent walking before you are forced back onto the path by rocks at Babbet Ness. There is another idyllic little beach about half a mile along from here, with a lonely ruined house standing on the skyline just beyond. A wide grassy track winds its way past the ruin and in several hundred metres leads to the outflow of the Kenly Water, the only major river to be crossed en route. Before the metal bridge was built upstream, the route crossed the river and continued along the coast, and, indeed, if the water is low this is entirely possible. However, the current prescribed route of the official Fife Coastal Path follows the path upstream for over half a mile to cross the river by a bridge. In only a few hundred metres you will need to turn sharp right at a gate before a private house and go down some steps to reach a lovely winding path following the meandering river through a peaceful wooded section, which is a pleasant change from the ever-present sea on your right. Pass some ruins on your left and cross a wooden bridge over a side stream before reaching the metal pedestrian bridge. Cross the bridge and pass a farmhouse on your right to enter a tarmac road, where you turn left. A short distance further on, take a right turn (which should be signposted) along a wide track leading to some farm buildings at Boarhills. Again, a signpost directs you to turn left then immediately right along another track. Finally, another sign leads you right after 200 m to rejoin the coastline in a quarter of a mile. This point is just over a mile further along the coast from the river outflow.

Continue along the grassy path to pass the unusual rock formation known as Buddo Rock, a sculpted sandstone monolith about 10 m high with a natural arch at its seaward side. It is similar in appearance to the rock formations comprising Caiplie Caves (see Route 6) and has a large fissure on the landward side through which it is possible to enter and walk up for several metres. By stepping over a gap, it is possible to make a scrambling ascent to the top if you are feeling adventurous.

Beyond Buddo Rock, the character of the walk changes as the path clings to an extensive vegetated cliff and climbs a long series of steps to a golf course, crossing a gorge by a wooden bridge. The path follows the clifftop before descending to the shoreline once again. Much of the path around here is, at the time of writing, in a state of repair and re-routing but generally easy to follow. Just before the final major headland at Kinkell Ness is another curious rock formation known as the Rock and Spindle, which is worth a short detour from the path. Another long series of steps takes you back to the clifftop and along Kinkell Braes, with the dreaming spires of St Andrews now dominating the view ahead. Finally, follow the marked route through the caravan site and make the final gradual descent to the East Sands of St Andrews, completing a long but memorable walk.

Recommended pub: The Whey Pat, St Andrews

Route 8

TENTSMUIR POINT

Famed for its breadth of wildlife and wonderful stretch of sand and natural forest, Tentsmuir Point National Nature Reserve is the focus of a beautiful and easy walk with every chance of spotting seals and a vast array of seabirds and is ideal for children. There is currently a £1 charge for taking a car into the reserve.

Distance: 6 miles/10 km (circular)
Time: 3–4 hours
OS map: 59

TENTSMUIR POINT LIES NORTH OF THE EDEN ESTUARY, JUST north of St Andrews in Fife and close to the Leuchars airbase. The area became a National Nature Reserve in 1954, and due to its vast range of wildlife and dynamic landscape it is now a Site of Special Scientific Interest (SSSI). It has even received a prestigious European accolade, having been designated a Natura 2000 site.

Tentsmuir is easily reached by car from Leuchars by following the signs to Kinshaldy Beach and Tentsmuir Sands past the old church. The minor road makes a sharp right-hand turn before entering Tentsmuir Forest, and a mile further on there is a barrier requiring the payment of a pound before further progress can be made. A second barrier to the right opens automatically on exit. Note that parking is only allowed at the official parking area about a mile ahead and not on the side of the road. The parking area itself is not a tarmac monstrosity but completely natural, with plenty of space to park under the tall pines. There are a few picnic tables, a children's play area and an information point.

Begin the walk by heading east, that is the opposite direction from where you entered the car park, past a row of wooden posts and following a wide path onto the sand dunes. The dunes soon develop

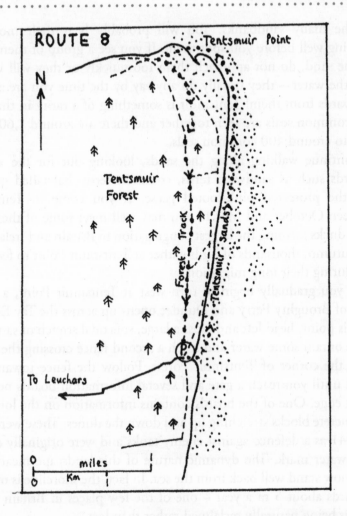

ROUTE 8

N

Tentsmuir Point

Tentsmuir
Forest

Forest Track

Tentsmuir Sands

To Leuchars

P

miles

Km

into a vast expanse of firm sandy beach where you turn left and simply follow the shoreline north. It is about three miles to Tentsmuir Point from here. During a good spell of weather, and especially at weekends, there are bound to be many people about, but the further north you walk the less busy it becomes and you will have more chance of spotting wildlife.

There are numerous sandbanks along this stretch and great care should be taken not to become stranded or cut off from the main section of sands. About a mile and a half from the start, you should reach a line of posts forming a fence that crosses the beach. Beyond this is the usual location for spotting seals both in the water and resting on the many sandbanks. You will probably hear their mournful whining well before you spot them. If you see a group of them lying on the sand, do not approach them too quickly or they will waddle into the water – they usually do anyway by the time you are around 100 yards from them! Tentsmuir is something of a rarity in that grey and common seals are seen together and there are around 1,600 grey seals to around 400 common seals.

Continue walking along the sands, looking out for the various seabirds such as sandwich terns, common terns, bar-tailed godwits and the protected pink-footed geese. If you come to Tentsmuir between October and March, you may well meet some of the 1,200 eider ducks forming the largest congregation in Britain and Ireland. In the autumn, thousands of birds gather at Tentsmuir Point to feed and rest during their long migration.

As you gradually begin to turn west at Tentsmuir Point, a grand view of Broughty Ferry and Dundee opens up across the Tay Estuary. At this point, head left and cross a large, soft tidal stretch of sand that may contain some water and reach a second fence crossing the beach from the corner of Tentsmuir Forest. Follow the fence towards the forest until you reach a gate and several information boards near the forest edge. One of the boards contains information on the long row of concrete blocks stretching up and down the dunes. These were built in 1941 as a defence against enemy tanks and were originally on the high-water mark. The dynamic nature of this landscape means that they now stand well back from the sea. In fact, the shoreline is moving seawards about 5 m a year – one of the few places in Britain where land is being naturally reclaimed rather than lost.

Take a short path through the dunes towards the forest and turn left to follow a track with the forest on the right and a fence on the left. Pass a gate and information board on your left and continue until you reach a gate crossing the path with a stile to its right. Cross the stile and continue along a grassy path in a forest clearing until it bears right towards a kissing gate. Go through the gate and straight on for

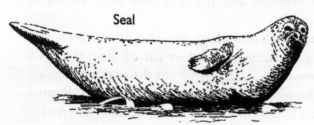

Seal

about 30 yards, where you will find a junction with a wide track. Turn left here. This point is about two miles from the car park.

In a short distance you will pass a turf-roofed nineteenth-century icehouse, which was stocked by ice blocks dragged from ships moored in Tayport Harbour and used to store locally caught salmon. It is now home to a colony of bats. As you follow the track through the forest, notice that the trees are not a regimented Sitka spruce variety but natural Scots and Corsican pine and home to a variety of wildlife, such as red squirrels and roe deer, which you may be lucky enough to spot. Finally, reach the car park to complete a most satisfying walk.

Route 9

THE SEATON CLIFFS WALK: ARBROATH TO AUCHMITHIE

A highly scenic and varied clifftop walk on an excellent path, with numerous opportunities to explore the many coastal features such as caves, sea stacks and natural arches. This is an ideal route for older children provided they keep a sensible distance from cliff edges.

Distance: 3 miles/5 km (linear)
Time: 2–3 hours
OS map: 54

SEATON CLIFFS WERE FORMED FROM SANDS DEPOSITED OVER 350 million years ago when Scotland was part of an arid continent close to the equator. As the continent drifted northwards, the mountains of red sandstone gradually eroded to leave the worn residue we now call Seaton Cliffs. Through subsequent ages, the erosive influence of pounding waves has worked on the weaknesses in the cliffs to form coves, caves, sea stacks and arches, which now provide nesting sites for the likes of herring gulls and fulmers.

The low sandstone cliffs winding north from Arbroath are the jewel of the Angus coast, a snaking ribbon of red between arable farmland and sea. The Arbroath to Auchmithie trail, which follows the top of these cliffs, is part of the Whiting Ness to Ethie Haven SSSI.

On arrival at Arbroath, follow the signs to Victoria Park and the cliffs, perhaps paying an initial visit to the tourist information centre at the harbour where an excellent leaflet describing the walk can be found. On a Saturday, this is not open until 11 a.m. There is ample parking on the wide promenade at the start of the cliffs from where the tarmac footpath leads up a short distance to the clifftop.

The first main coastal feature is evident after only a few hundred metres and is a natural arch known locally as the Needle E'e. Formed

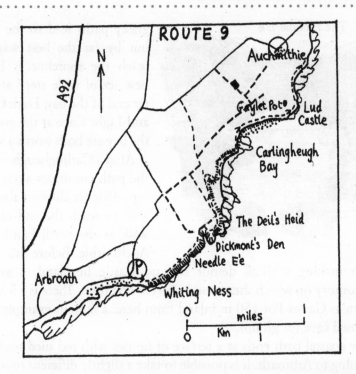

by a collapsed sea cave when the sea level was several metres higher, the landform can be reached via careful footwork on a loose path. Several hundred metres further on is Dickmont's Den, an impressive geo or narrow inlet around which the path makes a dog-leg. A seat at the head of the geo makes a grand stop.

Perhaps the most well-known feature is the Deil's Heid (Devil's Head) occurring a short distance further on, which is a sea stack formed of Lower Devonian sandstone. The best view of this is from a grassy promontory where there is a seat just before the stack, which also gives superb views of the distant cliffs beyond Carlingheugh Bay, a sample of the delights yet to come.

Just beyond the Deil's Heid, it is possible to descend via a rough grassy path to the shingle beach, where you can hunt out the deep cleft of Mason's Cave, the arch known as Castle Gate and some weird wind- and water-sculpted rocks known as the Sphinx and the Camel's Humps.

Before Carlingheugh Bay, the path makes a detour inland round the head of a shallow gorge to cross a stream by a plank. By now, the path has been relegated from its tarmac status to mud and gravel. Several

The Needle E'e

grassy paths lead to the bay, but by far the best way to reach the shoreline is by a new set of wide steps at the far end of the bay. Dark Cave and Light Cave at the end of the bay are both worth a visit.

After Carlingheugh Bay, the path continues along the top of higher cliffs for about a mile to reach the end of the walk at the small hamlet of Auchmithie. Before this, it is worth making a small detour to Lud Castle headland, a grassy promontory on which there stood a fort at one time. There is a feature known as Gaylet Pot 150 m inland from here, a famous example of a collapsed cave (or gloup).

The coastal path ends at a terrace of houses with red tiled roofs. If returning to Arbroath, it is possible to take a slightly different route by following the track to the road then turning left opposite a children's playground along a vehicle track to the vicinity of Windyhills House. Turn left, then right to follow another track eventually leading to a gate going into the tree-lined gorge and plank stream crossing mentioned earlier.

Extension

For those hardy walkers whose appetite has only been marginally whetted, it is quite possible to continue the extra three or four miles along the coastline to Ethie Haven at the south end of Lunan Bay. There is a path for most of this optional part.

Recommended pub: The But 'n' Ben, Auchmithie

LUNAN BAY

Lunan Bay is undoubtedly one of the finest unspoilt beaches on the east coast of Scotland. The walk about to be described covers the full 2.5-mile stretch of 'singing sands' and a contrasting clifftop section at the southern end. Lunan Bay was voted best beach in Scotland in 2000.

Distance: 6 miles/10 km (return)
Time: 3–4 hours
OS map: 54

LUNAN BAY LIES ABOUT SEVEN MILES NORTH OF ARBROATH and is easily reached by turning off the A92 road at Hawkhill. There is a car park at Lunan just beyond the farm and equestrian centre. Follow the boardwalk through the dunes to reach the extensive sands of Lunan Bay.

The first part of the walk follows the sands north to the distant cliffs and returns by the same route and can be omitted if so wished. However, if the tide is well out it is worth wandering along to inspect a curious shallow double-entranced cave and a natural arch. Unless you don't mind removing shoes and getting wet feet, it is not possible to walk the whole length of Lunan Bay along the sands, due to the outflow of the Lunan Water. Instead, return to the car park and walk back past the farm, then turn left at the junction past a church and over a stone bridge (crossing the Lunan Water). Continue along the road and look out for a path on the left climbing up to the brooding ruin of Red Castle, which offers a superb view of the bay. Red Castle was built in the twelfth century by King William 'the Lion' to deter beach invaders.

A steep path leads back down to the beach, and from here enjoy grand beach walking for over a mile to the ramshackle collection of wooden holiday chalets at the southern end of the bay. Keep an eye out for great grey shrikes and red-backed shrikes, which reside here throughout the summer. Lunan Bay is also noted for its semi-precious stones and agates.

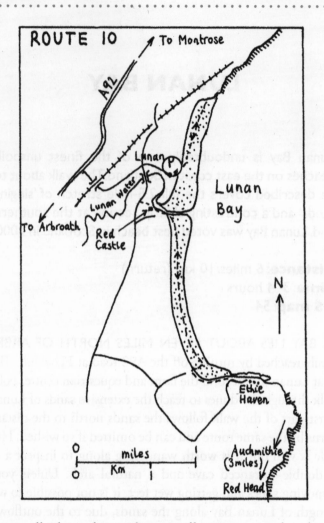

As you walk along the sands you will notice a tiny hamlet perched in a cove a short distance beyond the bay. This is the quaint fishing village of Ethie Haven and can be reached by following a good clifftop path then a vehicle track descending to the village. At the end of the tiny hamlet, it is possible to climb back up to the clifftop path by a steep grassy path, using a thick hawser rope to aid the ascent.

If you are inclined, it is worthwhile continuing along the path that winds its way along the cliffs to Red Head, passing a ruined chapel. This path eventually leads to Auchmuthie and the end of Route 9. Return to the car park by the same route.

ST CYRUS NATIONAL NATURE RESERVE

This is a scenic walk, with much variation possible, through the St Cyrus National Nature Reserve lying at the north end of Montrose Bay. The route involves dune and beach walking and also a clifftop trail leading to an isolated fortified ruin overlooking the North Sea. This route is ideal for children.

Distance: 3 miles/5 km (circular)
Time: 2–3 hours
OS map: 45

THE NATIONAL NATURE RESERVE AT ST CYRUS WAS ESTABLISHED in 1965 to protect the location's fine sand dunes, cliffs, salt marsh and wildlife, and it also serves as a base for local salmon fishermen, whose buildings, stakes and nets are visible behind the dunes. Towering cliffs form a natural backdrop to the reserve and there is a tranquil 'away from it all' feeling to the area nestling serenely under the cliffs.

The start of the walk is at the reserve's visitor centre, where there is a car park and toilets. This is reached by turning off the A92 road north of Montrose under a viaduct. From the visitor centre, head north-east along the road, then turn off on the coastal path to the right as the road swings round. Walk along the track through dunes and gorse bushes, passing the Nether Kirkyard cemetery on your left – a grand spot for 'guddling among the graves'.

The track continues pleasantly behind some old fishermen's cottages and onwards to the end of Montrose Bay below a line of steep cliffs. At this point, you will probably have noticed several cliff paths climbing upwards; take the last of these, which zigzags up on

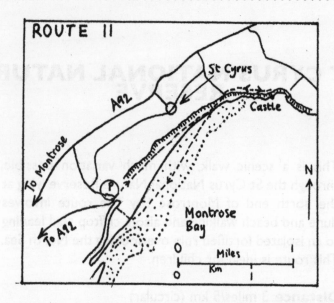

steps to a cottage perched on the cliff edge. Turn right and meander along the clifftop path for about half a mile until you are looking down on a small ruined fortification clinging to a rocky outcrop. The castle can be reached by following the edge of the narrow grassy

The Nether Kirkyard cemetery

spur, though great care is needed and it is not recommended for those with a fear of heights. The castle itself can only be reached by climbing up a wedged boulder and up onto a rocky platform that is the top of a separate crag just feet away from the grassy spur. In between there is a dizzying drop to the churning sea, a hundred feet below. From this point, there is a marvellous view southwards of the line of sand and dunes stretching far into the distance. It is interesting to note that it has taken only 7,000 years for the beach and dunes to develop whereas the rocks of the cliffs can be dated back 375 million years.

A return can be made similar to the outward route, but it is more interesting to vary the walk by going through the drive in front of the cottage mentioned earlier and taking the next path dropping down to the shoreline. Look out for a plaque on the right recording the path's construction back in 1882.

The final leg back to the visitor centre can also be varied by walking along the beach and then crossing the long wooden bridge over the salt marsh, which leads directly to the car park.

Route 12

STONEHAVEN TO DUNNOTTAR CASTLE

The historic ruin of Dunnottar Castle perched high on dramatic sea cliffs provides a fine focus for this short and easy walk from Stonehaven. En route to the castle and beyond, there are two fine shingle coves to explore, and this is an ideal walk for children. Payment is required for entry to the castle.

Distance: 3 miles/5 km (return)
Time: 2–3 hours
OS map: 45

THE WALK BEGINS IN MARKET SQUARE IN THE CENTRE OF Stonehaven, where there is a car park. Walk down Market Street following the Dunnottar Castle sign and reach the beach in just a few minutes. Continue along the waterfront on a boardwalk for a short distance until a sharp right leads to the quaint old harbour area of Stonehaven. This is a pleasant and peaceful spot with a plaque giving information about the harbour.

Follow the signpost pointing right and take the path leading up behind some houses and then steeply upwards to a viewpoint giving a fine bird's-eye view of the harbour and Stonehaven beyond. From here, follow the road uphill then take the path on the left at a bend in the road. Against the skyline you will see the war memorial, which is worth a short visit.

Continue past Strathlethan Bay, from where Dunnottar Castle can be seen on the skyline. At the bay of Castle Haven, it is worth descending a steep path to the shingle beach and walking along the shoreline until you come across a path leading directly up to the castle itself. When observed from higher up, Dunnottar Castle has a look of utter impregnability. It sits commandingly on an enormous flat-

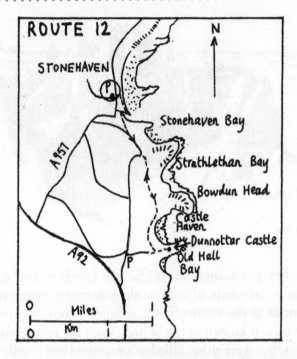

ROUTE 12
STONEHAVEN
N
Stonehaven Bay
Strathlethan Bay
Bowdun Head
Castle Haven
Dunnottar Castle
Old Hall Bay
A957
A92
P
Miles
Km

topped crag with sheer cliffs facing the North Sea on three sides and a deep ravine known as St Ninian's Den on the fourth. In fact, it is only on closer inspection that access to the castle can be seen to be possible by way of a break in the cliff-face. A path leads up to this break, goes under an arch and leads by way of steps round to a small payment booth. There is a nominal payment of around £5 for entry.

As you walk round the extensive ruins of this extraordinary fortification, consider the fact that Dunnottar is more than just one of the most photographed castles in Scotland: it is also a microcosm of much of Scotland's turbulent history. The crag has been fortified since at least the seventh century, and St Ninian founded a church on the rock. Both church and castle have since co-existed together.

The castle has been the scene of some notable gruesome events. In 1297, William Wallace burned alive an English garrison that had taken refuge in the church. In 1652, Oliver Cromwell attempted to steal the Scottish crown jewels placed in the castle for safe-keeping and wrecked the library and the chapel in the process, to no avail. (In fact, the regalia were no longer in the castle, and the manner of their disappearance remains one of the most romantic episodes in Scottish

Dunnottar Castle

history.) A few years later, in 1685, one hundred and sixty-seven Covenanters – members of a Scottish movement sworn to uphold Presbyterianism as the country's sole religion – were imprisoned in a damp stinking cell known as the Whig's Vault for two months. Some tried to escape but were either killed or recaptured and cruelly tortured; the remainder were given a last chance to recant or face transportation to the American plantations. In the seventeenth century, the seventh Earl Marischal held Dunnottar against a siege by Montrose, who in anger and revenge set fire to Stonehaven!

If you can pull yourself away from the fascinating history of Dunnottar you may wish to descend to the little cove north of the castle called Old Hall Bay. A fine view of the castle and crag can be gained from the headland just beyond, and a good path leads to this point from the main path leading to the car park.

Return to Stonehaven by the outward route or walk up to the car park and follow the B road to the right, which leads in less than a mile to the harbour viewpoint.

Recommended pub: The Market Bar, Stonehaven

FORVIE NATIONAL NATURE RESERVE

This is a coastal walk that includes everything: a river estuary, remarkable sand dunes, a huge expanse of sandy shore, clifftop trails and a vast variety of flora and fauna. The route combines several of the waymarked trails and returns by an old established route across the dunes. It is great for children and shorter options are possible.

Distance: 7 miles/11 km (circular)
Time: 3–4 hours
OS map: 38

FORVIE NATIONAL NATURE RESERVE LIES SOME 16 MILES NORTH of Aberdeen and just north of Newburgh at the estuary of the River Ythan. It is one of the largest untouched dune systems in Britain and extends nearly four miles north-east from the Ythan Estuary to the old fishing village of Collieston, where there is a visitor centre.

The walk begins at the substantial parking area at the north side of the bridge over the River Ythan on the A975 road to Peterhead. There is an informative leaflet on the reserve, published by Scottish Natural Heritage, available at the parking area – failing that, you should be able to pick one up at the visitor centre in Collieston.

Leave the car park and turn right down a good track through an avenue of trees. Ignore the track going left a short distance later and continue onwards with the River Ythan on your right. About a mile from the start, the path moves inland across the dunes to your left. At the time of writing, this route followed the blue markers of the 'Estuary Trail'. To your right is an area of restricted access that is closed between April and August to protect breeding terns. Four species of tern breed here: sandwich, common, Arctic and little tern. The Arctic tern (or

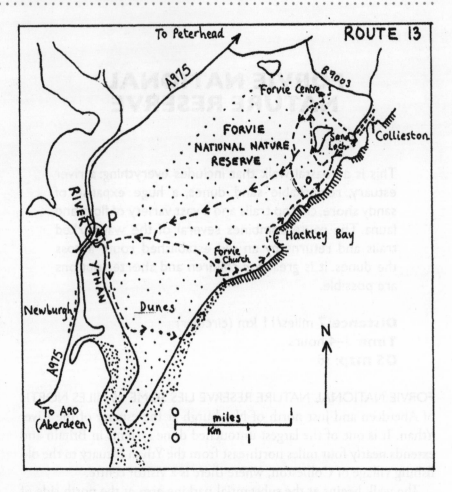

ROUTE 13

To Peterhead

A975

B9003

Forvie Centre

FORVIE
NATIONAL NATURE
RESERVE

Sand
Loch

Collieston

RIVER

Hackley Bay

Forvie
Church

Newburgh

YTHAN

Dunes

A975

N

To A90
(Aberdeen)

P

miles
Km

tirrick) travels an amazing 20,000 miles from the Antarctic just to breed here, which in a typical Scottish summer might seem like a waste of time!

The dunes around here are some of the largest in Britain, forming around 2,000 years ago and gradually shifting north to Collieston by the year 1700. The path becomes increasingly sketchy as you near the sea, but the smell of salt and seaweed soon lures you out of the dunes and onto a vast promenade of flat sand backed by sea and sky. Turn left here and follow the firm sand northwards for nearly a mile until you reach Rockend, the obvious rocky area below a line of low cliffs. At this point, turn left on a distinct sandy track after first crossing a small stream. In a few hundred yards you leave the blue Estuary Trail markers and instead embark on the 'Coastal Trail', which is indicated by red markers and moves off to the right (north). You will soon reach the ruins of Forvie's twelfth-century kirk, built on the site of an earlier chapel possibly dating back to the eighth century.

Until the Middle Ages there was a thriving community here, forging a life from farming and fishing, until advancing sands forced the hardy villagers to beat a retreat and leave the land they had laboured for centuries to tame. The whole area is like another Pompeii, with sand taking the place of volcanic ash, but over a much longer timescale. The complete settlement of Forvie had vanished under sand by the fifteenth century, but a few buildings, like Forvie kirk, have subsequently been uncovered.

Beyond the ruin, the path turns right and meanders its way delightfully along the clifftop to the pleasant, sheltered Hackley Bay, just beyond Hackley Head (or Forvie Ness). A new path and steps lead down to this fine sandy bay, but the main trail follows the clifftop around the bay. If you wish to descend to the sands you must return by the same route, as the path on the north side is currently closed for repair. At the right time of year, this clifftop trail is carpeted with varied wild flowers, such as sea thrift, sea campion, kidney vetch and northern marsh orchid. The top layer of red boulder clay is also ideal for cowslips, primroses and butterworts.

Continue along the clifftop trail, which tends slightly more inland before reaching the village of Collieston after about a mile. The route turns left at this point, but it is worth going straight ahead through the gate and following the path to the village, which has an interesting old harbour and a viewpoint. The visitor centre is unfortunately outwith the village on the B9003 road, but it would be possible to rejoin the walk from there if so wished.

Terns

From Collieston, return to the gate and continue to follow the trail round the left (west) side of the freshwater Sand Loch. The trail here doubles as the Coastal Trail and 'Moorland Trail' indicated by green markers. Just beyond the loch, there is a sign for the visitor centre, less than half a mile away off the main trail. From this point, you are now entirely on the Moorland Trail as it heads south through the dunes.

Although the map gives the impression that this is just one huge swathe of sand, the dunes have gradually, over the centuries, become stabilised and capable of supporting a wide variety of plants, such as heather, crowberry and marram grass. Forvie is home to the country's largest population of eider ducks, and several thousand regularly nest among the heather and the long grass.

About half a mile from Sand Loch, the Moorland Trail makes a sharp turn towards the coast. At this point, leave this trail and follow another, older path heading south-west through the centre of the dune system. There is a marker post at this point. This older trail is marked on the OS map but not on the map on the information leaflet. You should spot a triangulation pillar off to the right marking the 57-m high point of the reserve.

A mile and a half later, reach the main track of the Estuary Trail, where you turn right, then right again at the T-junction to finally return to the car park.

SLAINS CASTLE AND THE BULLERS OF BUCHAN

This walk is short but takes in some of the most dramatic cliff scenery in Britain. Add to this a huge, mysterious castle, an enormous rock arch and the 'monstrous cauldron' of the Bullers 'Pot' and you have the ingredients for one of the finest walks in this book. There is easy scope for extension if so wished. This route is not suitable for young children.

Distance: 4 miles/6 km (circular)
Time: 3–4 hours
OS map: 30

THE STRETCH OF COASTLINE FROM CRUDEN BAY TO BODDAM, just south of Peterhead, is a rugged, windswept edge of granite cliffs, narrow inlets, caves and natural arches, and the full eight-mile walk would be the obvious extension to the route about to be described. A clifftop path exists for the whole way and a main road is never more than half a mile from the cliff edge.

There is a parking place on the A975 at a bend in the road, just north of Slains Castle (GR 102370). From here, ignore the waymarked path and walk south down a muddy track, the entrance to which is blocked by large boulders to prevent vehicular access. However, walkers can easily pass them! This leads directly to Slains Castle, which is visible from the car park. The gaunt, brooding ruins of the castle have a distinctive Gothic feel, and allegedly Bram Stoker drew inspiration from them for his novel *Dracula*. Indeed, he began writing the famous novel while on a visit to Cruden Bay in 1895, and early drafts had the vampire coming ashore at Slains Castle! As you explore the extensive ruins, containing turreted towers, dark dungeons and gloomy rooms, it is easy to see how he obtained his inspiration. It is

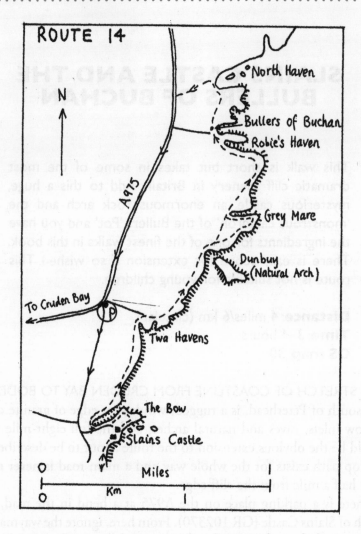

ROUTE 14

N ↑

North Haven

Bullers of Buchan

Robie's Haven

A975

Grey Mare

Dunbuy
(Natural Arch)

To Cruden Bay

Twa Havens

The Bow

Slains Castle

Miles

Km

not easy to understand, however, why this superb castle has not had the tourist treatment of, say, Dunnottar Castle near Stonehaven (see Route 12). A grand view of the whole castle can be had by continuing south along the coast and walking out to a prominent headland with a series of hillocks. This area is a paradise for rock scrambling and exploring, and you may just spend an hour here without realising it.

From the vicinity of the castle, walk round a long, narrow sea inlet and become established on the coastal path heading north. The path is well defined but often narrow and muddy in places. Looking back gives a good view of the castle. Also, if you drop low enough, it is possible to observe a

Slains Castle

double rock arch known as the Bow. However, it is half a mile further on where there is one of the finest rock arches in Britain. The massive granite islet of Dunbuy initially looks like a prominent headland that could be accessible by easy scrambling. On closer inspection, however, it is clear that it is separated from the mainland by a narrow horseshoe-shaped sea inlet. The first view of this enormous arch is truly awe-inspiring. On a more practical note, the arch has been formed by the sea eroding away the softer rock embedded in the prevailing pink granite.

Dunbuy hosts a huge gull colony, and the raucous screeching of thousands of nesting gulls assaults the senses, accompanying the visual assault of the arch itself. This is a place to stand (or sit) and stare on a fine sunny day. As you walk round the cove containing Dunbuy, look out for guillemots and kittiwakes nesting on the ledges below.

Beyond Dunbuy, the path cuts across the Grey Mare headland, but it is worth walking out onto the headland itself for a fine view of the rugged coastline to the north. Continue pleasantly on a carpet of heather, ling, sea thrift and scabious, rounding a promontory into Robie's Haven, where there is another natural arch. The path skirts the edge of a narrow inlet before dropping down to a row of cottages. Walk along the front of the cottages and arrive almost immediately at the enormous collapsed cave

Dunbuy Arch

known as the Bullers of Buchan. Known as the 'Pot', this 200-ft deep amphitheatre of sheer cliff drops to the sea, which rushes in under a narrow roofed entrance. In 1773, the Bullers were visited by none other than Boswell and Dr Johnson (is there anywhere in Scotland they didn't get to?), who were awed by the 'dreadful elevation' of this 'monstrous cauldron'!

You can follow a precarious path round the Pot and walk out to a little grassy promontory, which is another excellent vantage point. Just north of the Bullers is North Haven, a fine cove worth a visit before making your way back to the main road only a short distance away. From here, it is only a mile's road walk back to your car.

CROVIE TO PENNAN

A fine and varied clifftop walk connecting two charming and picturesque villages, one the main location for the cult Scottish film *Local Hero*. The route takes in Troup Head, scene of the Scottish mainland's largest gannet colony. There is no official path and the route can be quite rough going in places.

Distance: 5 miles/8 km (linear)
Time: 3–4 hours
OS map: 29 or 30

THE VILLAGE OF CROVIE LIES JUST NORTH OF THE MORE substantial settlement of Gardenstown and in many ways is much more attractive than Pennan, famous for its *Local Hero* connection. Drive down the steep, narrow road to Crovie and park at the south end of the village, where there will doubtlessly be many other cars, as this is where the residents have to park. Note that there is a path from here to Gardenstown, only a quarter of a mile distant, and it is possible to begin the walk there rather than in Crovie.

Walk along the narrow promenade of Crovie, with its harmonious collection of delightful sea- and wind-battered stone cottages. This walkway is very narrow and cars are notable by their absence. At the end of the village, a sketchy path climbs up to a shoulder and abruptly ends. From here, the only option is to turn right and ascend steep gorse-covered slopes for several hundred feet to reach a grassy path. This may not be to everyone's taste, and a more gentle option is to return along the seafront to a gap in the houses where there is a red telephone box. From here, it is possible to ascend easier grassy slopes to reach the same point as mentioned before.

Follow the grassy path, which deteriorates somewhat as it takes a line by the left side of a fence. If the going becomes too rough then

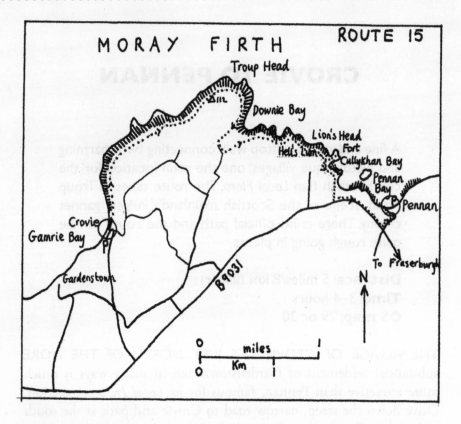

climb the fence and stay on the right. The route meanders its way along the clifftop, and the obvious promontory of Collie Head is a good point from which to view the line of cliffs leading to Troup Head. The triangulation point (112 m) is the highest point of the walk. From here, you should command a grand view of Troup Head with its immense cliffs, which support the Scottish mainland's largest gannet colony. This is a fairly popular spot with bird-watchers, and as you round the point you will no doubt meet other folk.

A track by the edge of a field high above Downie Bay leads to a parking area, and beyond here there is a gate leading into a field that can be crossed to reach the coastline once again. There are several little promontories that are well worth exploring before reaching the last one, known as Lion's Head. At the time of writing, some kindly soul had erected a wooden bench on this spot with the words 'Angel's Rest' engraved on it. If you have been lucky enough to be endowed with

Pennan

good weather then this seat provides a heavenly rest stop indeed. Before you lie Cullykhan Bay and Pennan Bay, with the little row of Pennan's white cottages strung out like a necklace round the bay.

Just down from here and before the next little promontory is the geological phenomenon known as Hell's Lum, which has two entrances: one below sea level, the other higher up. In rough seas, the sea enters the underground tunnel and spews out the higher opening. The fort marked on the map is Fort Fiddes, and although marked as sitting in the promontory above Cullykhan Bay there is little or nothing to indicate its physical presence. Beyond Cullykhan Bay, there is another small cove with a ruined building. From here, it is best to make your way up the main road and descend to Pennan village by the steep minor road.

If you are a fan of the 1983 film *Local Hero* then you will no doubt be aware that this was the location for it, and the Pennan Inn and red telephone box are both much-visited attractions. Note that the beach scenes of *Local Hero* were filmed on the west coast at the Sands of Morar (see Route 48).

Recommended pub: The Pennan Inn, Pennan

PORTKNOCKIE TO PORTSOY

This exhilarating long hike between two charming old fishing villages has everything the coastal connoisseur could wish for: dramatic cliffs, unique rock formations, long, sandy strands, quiet coves and an ancient ruined castle perched on a giddy promontory. This walk, which is part of the Moray Coastal Trail, is one to savour and enjoy.

Distance: 9 miles/14 km (linear)
Time: 4–6 hours
OS map: 29

THE RELATIVELY UNSPOILT FISHING VILLAGE OF PORTKNOCKIE, lying a short distance north-west of Cullen, provides the starting point for this marvellous walk, full of variation and character. A regular bus service links Portknockie with Portsoy, so two cars are not really needed.

In Portknockie, there is limited parking at the eastern end of the village for those visiting the remarkable Bow Fiddle Rock, an unusual coastal feature. This visitor attraction is only a few hundred yards from the parking spot and is signposted. It provides a fitting start to the walk. The Bow Fiddle Rock is a curious natural arch sculpted from steeply dipping quartzite and can be approached at low tide.

The grassy path on the clifftop above the Bow Fiddle Rock winds its way round the headland, from where you will gain a beautiful panoramic view of the golden sands of Cullen Bay, Cullen's stone cottages and the headland of Logie Head beyond. Further on, you have the option of descending a series of concrete steps eventually leading to the sands or, alternatively, remaining on the clifftop trail, which drops to the grassy area behind the beach. The walk across the sands of Cullen Bay at low tide is delightful. Near the end of the sands, pass a prominent quartzite rock stack and make your way up onto the promenade, passing the gable ends of houses facing the sea and the sadly disused railway viaduct. Cullen is a

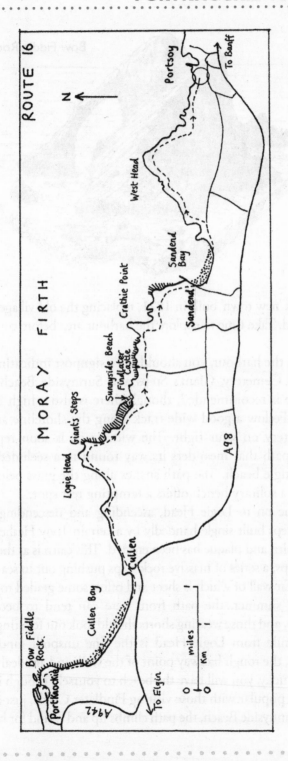

ROUTE 16

N

Portsoy

To Banff

West Head

Sandend
Bay

Sandend

Crathie Point

MORAY FIRTH

Sunnyside Beach

Findlater
Castle

Giant's Steps

Logie Head

A98

Cullen

Cullen Bay

Bow Fiddle
Rock.

Portknockie

To Elgin

A942

miles

Km

Bow Fiddle Rock

prosperous 'new town' built in 1821, replacing the old village, which was demolished. Take time to explore the harbour area before continuing the walk.

Beyond the harbour, you should see a signpost indicating the route to the Pet Cemetery, Giant's Steps and Sunnyside Beach. This low-level route is recommended, though there is also a high route above the cliffs. Follow a good wide track along the shoreline and pass the Pet Cemetery on your right. The wide track is soon replaced by a narrower path that meanders its way round to a secluded rocky bay with a shingle beach. The path snakes along the grass below the high cliffs, and a solitary bench offers a tempting rest spot.

Continue on to Logie Head, ascending and descending a series of concrete steps built single-handedly by a certain Tony Hetherington, for whom a cairn and plaque has been erected. This cairn is at the spot of the Giant's Steps, a series of massive rock steps pushing out to sea in a narrow ridge, the far wall of which is sheer and offers some graded rock climbs.

In high summer, the path from here can tend to become rather overgrown, and those wearing shorts should look out for stinging nettles! About a mile from Logie Head is the fine unspoilt sandy beach of Sunnyside, the rough halfway point of the walk and an ideal lunch stop. If you are lucky, you will have the beach to yourself, though it is tending to become popular with those visiting Findlater Castle, just east of here.

From Sunnyside Beach, the path climbs up and round for half a mile to reach the end of a track where there is a circular stone-walled cairn containing an information board about Findlater Castle. This crumbling edifice clings tenaciously to a grassy bluff about a hundred feet below and is reachable by a narrow, steep path. The ruins are surprisingly extensive and contain several roofed rooms with tantalising sea views. The castle dates from the thirteenth century but was rebuilt by Sir Walter Ogilvie around 1455 and was occupied by the Gordons during their uprising against Mary, Queen of Scots. It did return to the Ogilvies before they abandoned it for the more salubrious Cullen House.

The route beyond Findlater Castle winds its way through gorse bushes and keeps well away from the crumbling cliff edge. After a mile, you round Garron Point and enter Sandend Bay by climbing a stile and walking between two fences. Below, to the left, dozens of stone cottages are crammed together, forming narrow, characterful streets at right angles to the quaint seafront. This is the totally unspoilt village of Sandend. The path emerges on a well-manicured private drive leading down to the main street. From here, make your way down to the extensive silver sands, which can be crossed to reach the opposite side of the bay.

From here, ascend some wooden steps and continue on the path, which climbs steeply up to a grassy headland. A short distance further on, the path makes a sharp left-hand turn before a low gate. (Going straight on here leads to Redhythe Farm.) The path then follows a fence along the coast for a mile to West Head before turning south-east for the final mile

Findlater Castle

to Portsoy. Just beyond Redhythe Point, the path follows the edge of a field heading inland, joining a more substantial farm track at a gate. This leads to a parking area on the west side of Portsoy. Portsoy is a thriving fishing and holiday centre and claims the oldest harbour in the Moray Firth, dating to 1692, which is worth a visit if you have the time.

HOPEMAN TO LOSSIEMOUTH

This is a superb and beautifully varied walk along a section of the Moray Coast Trail. Points of interest include dinosaur footprints and an exciting optional descent by rope ladder to a cave containing ancient Pictish carvings. This route is great for children.

Distance: 6 miles/10 km (linear)
Time: 3–4 hours
OS map: 28

HOPEMAN IS A QUIET, UNSPOILT FISHING VILLAGE FOUNDED IN the early nineteenth century and provides the starting point of the walk. There is ample parking space at the seafront and signs indicate the route of the Moray Coast Trail.

The route leads along the edge of a sheltered bay behind some brightly painted beach huts and out onto a little headland before turning south-east to Clashach Cove. The cove has an idyllic sandy beach and some small caves – all worth exploring. If you are doing this walk in late spring or early summer then you will be accompanied by a grand display of yellow gorse bushes, and the trail winds its way through the prickly mass.

Beyond Clashach Cove, the path climbs up and heads slightly inland to the vicinity of a large quarry. Near here, you will pass a group of rock specimens containing scratch and claw marks made by dinosaurs 250 million years ago, when the whole area was once in the vicinity of the modern-day Sahara Desert. An information plaque gives more details. For the next mile or so, the route follows a wider track through the gorse with little or no view of the coast other than one or two gaps where it is possible to move to the cliff edge to enjoy a fine vista up and down the long line of red sandstone cliffs.

Eventually you will reach a junction with a grassy track where you

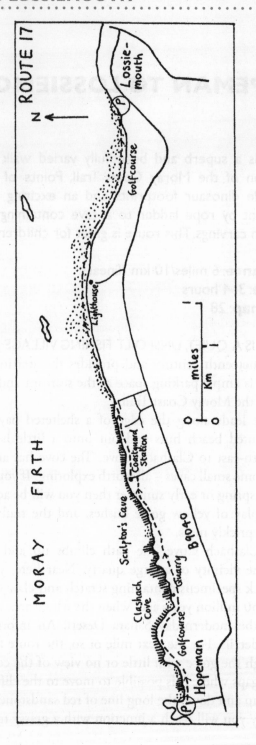

N

ROUTE 17

Lossie-
mouth

Golf course

Lighthouse

MORAY FIRTH

miles

Km

Coastguard
Station

Sculptor's Cave

B9040

Clashach
Cove

Quarry

Golf course

Hopeman

turn left downhill to an old coastguard lookout station. If you are interested in descending the rope ladder to the so-called Sculptor's Cave then the descent is very close to this point, but it is not signposted and is quite difficult to find. A description now follows. Continue along the path past the coastguard station for about 100 yards – you will pass an obvious angular rock with a claw mark on it. Shortly past this rock, a break in the gorse and heather leads down to a flattish heathery platform. Reach this platform and walk on a short distance to where there is a narrow fissure in the rocks about 4 ft wide. The rope ladder hangs on the vertical face of the nearer wall. This point can also be reached by another indistinct path that starts further along the main trail.

It should be stated at this point that the descent of the rope ladder (only six rungs) is not particularly easy, as it hangs flush with the vertical cliff-face, which is itself wet and greasy, and it is difficult to obtain purchase on the wooden rungs. Note also that it is harder ascending than descending!

Once at the bottom of the rope ladder, a double line of fixed rope can be used as a handrail for the final, much easier descent to the shore on gently sloping but still greasy rock. The cave itself lies about a quarter of a mile to the left (west) of this point, and you will need to be vigilant about the state of the tide and not get cut off!

Follow the coast round a small headland, staying close to the cliff edge. You will pass a large double-entranced vaulted roof cave that is sometimes mistaken for the Sculptor's Cave, but the real thing is still a short distance beyond at the far end of the next obvious cove. When you reach it, climb up to the shingle at the low double entrance, the right-hand one being partly boarded up for reasons unknown. A plaque at the left-hand entrance gives information about the cave, which is so called due to the Pictish carvings near the entrance, which date back to AD 500, though it is thought that the cave was in use thousands of years before this. The cave contained many ancient artefacts, which have long since been cleared out. Nearby Gordonstoun school is now responsible for the upkeep of the cave.

Return to the main coastal trail via the rope ladder and follow the winding path as it weaves its way high above the cliffs. Before reaching the west sands of Lossiemouth, you will notice a secluded shingle beach with a sea stack and cave at its far end. This beach can be reached from a fork in the path beyond the beach and, again, you should be aware of the tide, as reaching it involves rounding a rocky promontory on wet seaweed by a large vaulted cave.

Before the main sands, there is a fork in the path, the left one going down to the beach, which can be followed for 2.5 miles to Lossiemouth via the prominent cove sea lighthouse. On a fine sunny day at low tide, this is a fitting end to a fine walk. Alternatively, take the right fork and detour inland by the golf course and caravan park.

EATHIE TO ROSEMARKIE AND CHANONRY POINT

An adventurous walk and scramble from the old fishing station at Eathie to the attractive town of Rosemarkie, followed by an easy stroll out to Chanonry Point, famed for dolphin-spotting. Part of the route is tidal and this walk should only be attempted during the hours around low tide.

Distance: 9 miles/14 km (linear)
Time: 5–6 hours
OS map: 27

ALTHOUGH THE OS MAP INDICATES A PATH ALONG MOST OF this route, in reality this has long since disappeared, and much of the middle section involves rock scrambling or beach walking. You may also prefer to begin at Rosemarkie and walk north, from where an excellent grass path continues for a mile before ending at the cave section. The route has been described from north to south for the sake of continuity and because arriving at Rosemarkie permits an easier return to the starting point if you have access to only one car and wish to use a taxi to return to your car.

Between the firths of Beauly and Cromarty lies the peninsula known somewhat curiously as the Black Isle. Being firmly part of mainland Scotland and extensively covered with green fields and forest, it certainly is not an island or black, but nevertheless it possesses an insular quality. The stretch of coastline from Cromarty south-west to Rosemarkie contains the finest scenery anywhere on the peninsula. There are high cliffs, gnarled and ancient sea stacks, raised beaches, coves and a plethora of interesting wildlife.

Begin at GR 769636, where there is a small parking area at a track junction on the minor road connecting Rosemarkie and Cromarty.

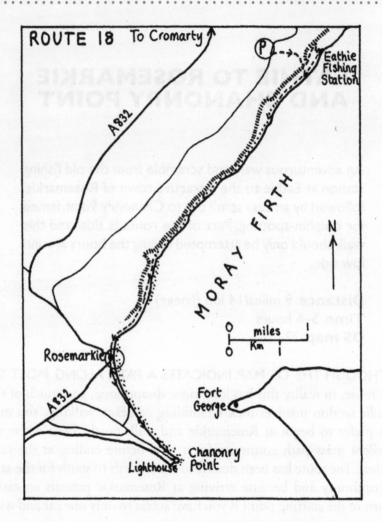

There is a signpost to Eathie Fishing Station and an information board about Hugh Miller, a local man who made his mark as an eminent geologist, writer and editor in the nineteenth century.

Follow the track eastwards by the edge of a wood and then steeply downhill in a series of zigzags through a dense Sitka spruce plantation. You will emerge on a grassy path by the shore between two buildings, the left being the old fishing station and the right a bothy used by the fishermen ('the salmon bothy'). The bothy is the most interesting building and inside there are several information boards about Hugh Miller, fishing and wildlife.

It is worth noting that what is now known about the Old Red Sandstone rock formations of the Black Isle derives from Miller's painstaking research. He made his first fossil discoveries on this very shore and discovered a huge variety of non-local rock types carried by glaciers from the glens of Ross-shire. The whole area is so geologically unusual that it is now an SSSI. During the walk, look out for a variety of bird-life, including eider and long-tailed ducks, fulmars, cormorants and oystercatchers, to name a few. In early summer, the range of wild flowers to be found is due to the ideal sunny aspect of this south-facing shore, as well as constant drainage from lime-rich weaknesses trickling down through the sandstone cliffs.

The bothy itself was used as a permanent residence for salmon fishermen between March and August each year long before the advent of the fish-farming techniques of more modern times. Notice the old iron boat winch outside the bothy.

The path goes along the edge of the spruce forest and is fairly well defined at first but gradually becomes more sketchy as it winds its way through pockets of gorse and hawthorn bushes. Reach a stony beach in less than half a mile, where the path becomes so overgrown that it is easier to keep to the shore. Pass a curious pillar of rock about 4 m high that teeters on a narrow neck of rock at its base and looks like it is too unstable to stay standing. This marks the beginning of the section where the cliffs rise upwards directly beyond the shore, and it is important that the tide is low enough to negotiate several parts where the cliff falls straight into the sea. Several caves are also passed, but none of them are deep and they certainly do not require a torch. You will also come across many sea stacks, some left stranded incongruously high on the raised beaches no longer touched by the sea. Some have cushions of grass and pink sea thrift on their tops, where herring gulls rear their chicks in relative safety.

Dolphins

On this two-mile section of coast, the 'path' is notable by its complete absence and you will be forced to take to the rocky shore, scrambling over jagged rocks on many occasions. The final sandy beach leading to Rosemarkie is blocked by a huge rock outcrop with a cave, and if the tide is high here it is not passable other than by climbing (not recommended).

Beyond here, there is an excellent grassy path for the last mile or so to Rosemarkie. Ironically, it isn't really needed as the beach provides fine walking. If you have heard bangs and booms throughout the walk, it is no doubt from the army base at Fort George, just a few miles across the water.

As you enter Rosemarkie, take the left fork in the path, going down some steps to a park area and the seafront. Chanonry Point is still another two miles of easy walking, initially on a minor road then by a fine sandy beach or, alternatively, the grassy track above. With any luck you will be rewarded by a fine wildlife spectacle usually attracting a good crowd of people. Here, the Moray Firth contracts into a narrow channel less than a mile across to the Fort George peninsula, where turbulent waters attract schools of bottle-nosed dolphins, their sleek bodies jumping and diving effortlessly in the heaving waters. This is the highlight of a magnificent walk.

Recommended pub: The Plough Inn, Rosemarkie

Dolphins

BRORA TO GOLSPIE

This walk follows an attractive and interesting stretch of coastline between two communities on the Sutherland coast. It is an easy walk on paths and shoreline with plenty of absorbing diversions, including a broch, a fine castle and, if you are lucky, seals.

Distance: 6 miles/10 km (linear)
Time: 2–4 hours
OS map: 17

THERE IS A FREQUENT BUS SERVICE BETWEEN BRORA AND Golspie and also a railway line with trains running at least three times per day. There should be little problem, therefore, returning to Brora from Golspie if you only have access to one car. The best option is probably to catch a morning bus or train to Brora from Golspie and then do the walk back to your car in Golspie. The walk can, of course, be done in the opposite direction, but the views are best walking south.

In Brora, turn east off the A9 down either Gower Street or Harbour Road, which lead eventually to the beach car park. Walk through the round car park towards an old flat-roofed building; this was an important listening station during the Second World War and was even used up to the time of the Falklands War, in the early 1980s. The path continues through sand dunes but has become rather eroded lately, and it may in any case be easier to walk along the extensive sands, especially at low tide. Keep an eye open for seals, which can often be seen sunning themselves on the rocks out to sea.

About a mile and a half out from Brora, pass a steep little section with a waterfall produced by the Sputie Burn. The path climbs steeply beyond the falls on wooden steps but may be overgrown with gorse bushes. Again, it is probably easier to stick to the shoreline. On a clear

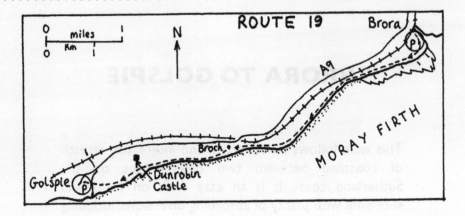

day you should spot Tarbat Ness lighthouse at Portmahomack and the sprawling mass of the Cairngorms.

Reach a flat grassy area where the path becomes more obvious and less prone to coastal erosion. As you turn a broad headland, the conspicuous landmark of Dunrobin Castle begins to dominate the skyline, as does the tall monument on the skyline above Golspie, a much-hated memorial erected in 1834 to commemorate the unpopular first Duke of Sutherland, who was responsible for some of the most brutal Clearances in the Highlands.

Another mile of pleasant walking brings you to the relatively well-preserved remains of a circular fortified dwelling known as the Carn Liath broch. These beehive-shaped stone structures are common throughout the northern highlands and islands and date back 3,000 years. They were defensive stone towers usually built near the sea. Carn Liath broch is a typical Sutherland broch built on a rocky knoll and survives to first-floor level.

Beyond the broch, the grassy path provides excellent walking, with Dunrobin Castle now dominating the view. After the path enters a wooded area, there is a fork, with the left option leading to a clearing. Take the left fork and follow it through the clearing, keeping left until you emerge on a track running past the extensive walled garden of the castle. From here, there is a grand view of the castle's facade, its ornamental towers giving the appearance of a French chateau rather than a Scottish castle.

Dunrobin's original square keep was built in 1275, but the present outward appearance was due to Sir Charles Barry, who made extensive changes and extensions between 1845 and 1850. Dunrobin is the

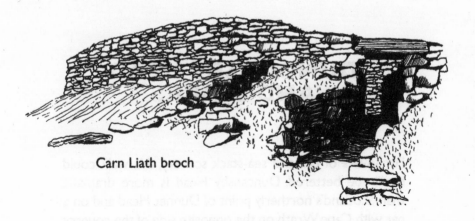

Carn Liath broch

ancestral home of the earls and dukes of Sutherland and today is open to the public during the summer months.

From Dunrobin Castle, another mile of pleasant walking on a grassy track and path lead to a gate and bridge over the Goslpie Burn, leading to a small parking area.

Recommended pub: The Ben Bhraggie Hotel, Golspie

Dunrobin Castle

Route 20

DUNCANSBY HEAD AND STACKS

For lovers of cliff and sea-stack scenery, this walk could hardly be bettered. Duncansby Head is more dramatic than Scotland's northerly point of Dunnet Head and on a par with Cape Wrath on the opposite side of the country. The immense, majestic Stacks of Duncansby are arguably the finest sea stacks off the Scottish mainland.

Distance: 3 miles/5 km (return)
Time: 1–2 hours
OS map: 12

DUNCANSBY HEAD IS THE NORTH-EASTERN EXTREMITY OF THE Scottish mainland, just a couple of miles from John o'Groats. The lighthouse on Duncansby Head commands fine views of Orkney and the Pentland Skerries and marks the entrance to the treacherous Pentland Firth, where tides rip at up to 12 mph. A short distance to the south are the huge sandstone needles of the Duncansby Stacks, rising proudly from the sea.

To reach Duncansby Head, take the minor road east from John o'Groats across open moor to reach the car park by the lighthouse. The walk down the coast to the stacks is signposted and can be boggy in places. Both stacks soon come into view, peeping out shyly from behind an intermediate headland. The path descends to the head of the Geo of Sclaites, a huge, deep gash in the cliffs, before crossing to the top of a shingle beach, where it is possible to descend. At the end of this beach, you should notice a natural hole in the rock called the Thirle Door. At low tide it is possible to walk through this natural arch to gain an unusual view of the stacks, but beware of the tide and do not allow yourself to become stranded beneath the cliffs.

Continue round the head of the shingle beach along the clifftop, at

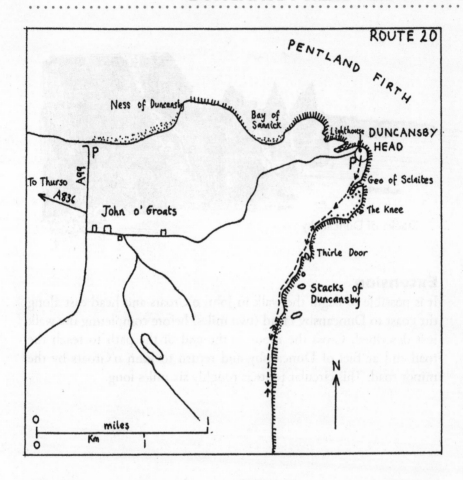

Route 20

PENTLAND FIRTH

Ness of Duncansby
Bay of Sannick
Lighthouse DUNCANSBY HEAD
Geo of Sclaites
The Knee
Thirle Door
Stacks of Duncansby
To Thurso A836
A99
P
John o' Groats
N
miles
Km

which point the stacks are seen to great advantage, but the view again improves as you reach the end of the path at GR 397714, where the natural arch, the lighthouse and the stack known as the Knee also come into the picture. As you gaze on this dramatic seascape, particularly on a wild day of churning sea and wave-lashed crags, it is easy to see that this is a dynamic coastline continually eroded by millions of years of pounding waves – forces that have produced the Duncansby Stacks.

Look out for the teeming bird-life in this walk, such as the bright-billed puffin, the ubiquitous guillemot in evening dress and also kittiwakes, razorbills and fulmars. At the right time of year, the grassy clifftop path should be a riot of colour, with yellow tormentil and pink sea thrift lining the route.

Return by the outward route.

Stacks of Duncansby

Extension

It is possible to begin the walk in John o'Groats and head east along the coast to Duncansby Head (two miles) before completing the walk just described. Cross the moor at the end of the path to reach the road-end at Biel of Duncansby and return to John o'Groats by the minor road. This circular route is roughly six miles long.

2

The West Coast 1:

SOLWAY FIRTH TO MULL

ROCKCLIFFE TO SANDYHILLS

This is undoubtedly one of the finest coastal walks in southern Scotland and has also been described as one of the best in Britain. Most of the walk is on a good path varying from earth to shingle and grass, and offers fine cliff scenery and imposing views across the Solway Firth to the Lake District.

Distance: 5 miles/8 km (linear)
Time: 3–4 hours
OS map: 84

THE DELIGHTFULLY PEACEFUL AND IDYLLIC VILLAGE OF Rockcliffe is one of Dumfries and Galloway's best-kept secrets and is the perfect starting point for a walk along the superb coastline. Reach Rockcliffe from Dumfries by either the A710 coastal road or the A711 Dalbeattie road.

At the top of the village, there is a large council car park with signs disallowing overnighting or cooking. Begin here and walk down towards the village, turning left at the coastal-path signpost to Castlehill. The first part of the route follows a quiet tarmac road past several well-maintained houses on the left with beautifully manicured gardens. Leave the road at a sign pointing right to a shingle path through shrubs and trees and out onto the rocky beach. The path continues along the beach and slightly inland, where you will spot an old gravestone set in the rocks. This is the final resting place of a sailor called Nelson who was shipwrecked near Castle Point, the next major point of interest on the walk.

Castle Point lies a short distance ahead and is in a commanding position atop a small grassy hillock with far-reaching views across the wide expanse of the Solway Firth. Unfortunately, the view is spoiled somewhat by the massive turbines of the offshore wind farm. Castle

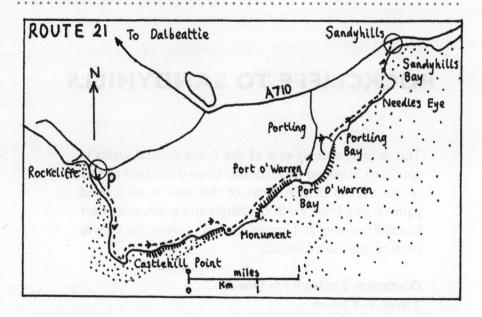

ROUTE 21 To Dalbeattie

Point (or Castlehill Point) was the site of an old Iron Age fort, although very little of the actual structure still remains. A topographic plaque shows landmarks, and on a clear day you should be able to pick out individual mountains of the Lake District.

From Castle Point, the path continues along the clifftop, where you should be able to spot a variety of nesting seabirds, such as cormorants, fulmars, razorbills and even peregrine falcons. The path is fairly undulating and can be quite overgrown with gorse in places, although parts have been burned. You will pass the remains of two old cottages before reaching a prominent cairn with a cross marking the location where the crew of a schooner climbed to safety in 1866. It should be noted that the path enters a field above this cairn that is sometimes occupied by cattle, and they can be quite inquisitive! The gorse around this section is also rampant.

Beyond here, the path climbs a steep grassy hill, and you will need to climb several stone dykes before dropping steeply down to the little village of Port o' Warren. The path reaches a minor road at this point via a stile at the left of a cottage. The route leaves the coast here and follows the road up to the left for several hundred metres before taking the minor road to the right signposted 'Portling'. A short distance along here, there is a footpath sign off to the left where the path

Memorial cairn

initially climbs up some wooden steps, but this is not immediately obvious.

A short distance along the coast from here lies the Torrs viewpoint, from which the path again descends steeply. Just past a kissing gate, you should gain a good view of the natural arch known as the Needle's Eye by looking back along the coast. Descend gradually through trees to a quiet little cove with a wooden seat where you can relax and gaze out to the mudflats of the Solway, stretching for miles.

To reach Sandyhills Bay, take the right fork after the footbridge and keep to the right of the campsite. Several paths lead up to the main road from here. A circular walk can be completed by simply following the road back to Rockcliffe (only three miles). Alternatively, catch a bus or have prearranged transport available.

BALCARY TO RASCARREL

This is a delightfully satisfying circular route on good paths and tracks, with much variation possible. It is a very popular walk, as it has some tremendous views and situations. It is ideal for older children.

Distance: 5 miles/8 km (circular)
Time: 3–4 hours
OS map: 84

THE WALK BEGINS AT BALCARY BAY, WHICH LIES TWO MILES from the small village of Auchencairn on the A711 road. It should be noted that there are two options available to shorten the walk if so wished, and these are mentioned further on in this description. Cars can be parked past the Balcary Bay Hotel, just before the point where the road makes a sharp left turn. You will see the coastal-path sign at this turn.

Follow the path for a few hundred yards and enter a large field through a kissing gate. Keep to the left edge of the field on shorter grass until you reach a Land Rover track and a second kissing gate. Go through this and enter a pleasant wooded section on a narrow path. You will pass a secluded private dwelling-house, formerly the lifeboat station, and there is also a bench from which it is possible to gaze out to Auchencairn Bay and Hestan Island. This island is tidal and is also known as 'the Green Island of the Solway'. It is steeped in mystery and legend and features in S.R. Crockett's novel *The Raiders*.

Beyond the wooded section, the path meanders its way over open heath and moor to reach Balcary Point. At various times of the year, it should be easy to spot many wild flowers, such as primroses, heath spotted orchids, sea thrift and birdsfoot trefoil. Balcary Point is a wonderful spot to rest and drink in the views and fresh sea air.

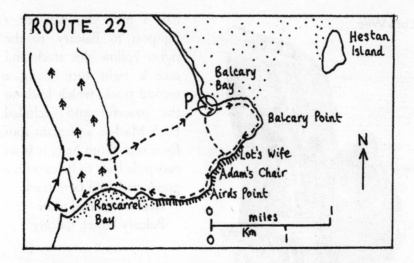

ROUTE 22

Hestan Island

Balcary Bay

Balcary Point

P

Lot's Wife
Adam's Chair
Airds Point

N

Rascarrel Bay

miles

Km

Beyond the point, the path gradually ascends and clings precariously to the top of the cliffs. Care should be taken, especially with children. You will soon reach a wooden bench giving a grand bird's-eye view of the sea stack known as Lot's Wife. By now, the raucous cries of guillemots, kittiwakes and cormorants will be heard, especially in the early summer months as they jostle for the best breeding sites.

Beyond here, there is a slightly overgrown gorse section, and at a metal kissing gate it is possible to turn right and return to Balcary in only half a mile if so wished. This is the first shorter option.

The coastal path continues on above the cliffs and passes another rest-tempting seat dedicated to a certain Irdie Kirk (1925–2005). This whole coastline was awash with smugglers in the 1700s, when there was a good trade in tea, lace and whisky between Scotland and the Isle of Man, where tax laws were more relaxed.

From the seat, follow the path as it gradually descends to a stony beach and eventually to some holiday chalets just before a forest plantation. At this point, a second option to shorten the walk is to follow a path right, behind the chalets and to the right of the plantation. In less than half a mile reach Loch Mackie, where you turn right and follow the path back to Balcary.

The longer option follows the track through the forest and round to the car park. Walk up to the main road from here and turn right. In

Lot's Wife

half a mile you will see a signpost to Balcary, to the right. Follow this track and take a right turn along a second track, which leads to the peaceful and secluded Loch Mackie, a pleasant spot for a rest. From here, it is an easy mile back to Balcary on a grassy path and farm track.

Recommended pub:
Balcary Hotel, Balcary

ISLE OF WHITHORN TO PORT CASTLE BAY

This is a beautifully varied walk on good paths, beginning at the picturesque little fishing village of Isle of Whithorn and finishing at St Ninian's Cave in Port Castle Bay. The walk is linear, but a return option is also described.

Distance: 6 miles/10 km (linear)
Time: 3–4 hours
OS map: 83

ORIGINALLY THE PORT FOR THE INLAND TOWN OF WHITHORN, the village of Isle of Whithorn is now a busy but unspoiled sailing resort, and its colourful terrace of stone houses surrounds an idyllic sheltered harbour. A causeway links the village to the grassy mound of what was once a true island, and on it sits the thirteenth-century St Ninian's Chapel, an ideal starting point for the walk. In fact, St Ninian himself is reputed to have regularly tramped to his place of refuge at St Ninian's Cave from here, and you will be following in his hallowed footsteps!

As you drive into Isle of Whithorn, there is parking on the left. After first visiting the chapel, return to the village and look out for a sign saying 'Burrow Head Footpath' just beyond some cottages on the seaward side of the road. A narrow gravel path leads from the right of these cottages out onto an open field and passes through several kissing gates. From here, there is a fine retrospective view of the picturesque harbour and surrounding houses.

The route soon develops into a fine grassy clifftop path, which was established by Solway Heritage in the 1990s but was a popular route even before then. The feature known as 'Devil's Bridge' on the OS map is not at all obvious from the path and could be one of several rock formations. At Burrow Head, the path swings from south-west to

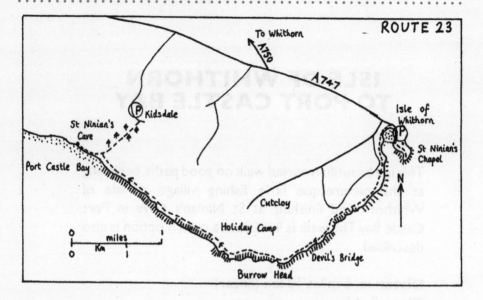

west and appears to become increasingly wild until you spot the hand of civilisation at Burrowhead Holiday Village, a motley collection of mobile homes and holiday chalets. During the war it was an artillery camp, and you will no doubt spot an assortment of concrete bunkers and other eyesores.

Beyond the holiday camp, the character of the walk again resumes its wild feel and you should spot a signpost saying 'St Ninian's Cave – 2 Miles'. Follow the path along the tops of the cliffs until it descends steeply in a zigzag to the shingle of Port Castle Bay. The cave is situated at the far end of the bay, and on a summer's day there will probably be no lack of people about, having walked down from the parking area at Kidsdale.

St Ninian's Cave gives the impression of being a much larger affair than it actually is and is something of an anticlimax. It is certainly not deep and is more like a cleft in the rock than an actual cave – don't bother with a torch! Yet it is an important place of pilgrimage, however humble, and has been visited by both kings and paupers. St Ninian himself was the first Christian missionary to Scotland, preceding St Columba by 150 years, and used this as a sacred place of retreat and quiet prayer.

If you are finishing the walk at this point, you will need to have a car or bike parked at the car park at Kidsdale, which can be reached by

Port Castle Bay

returning along the beach for several hundred yards and following the signpost marking the path going up through the wooded defile to the minor road.

If returning to Isle of Whithorn on foot, the quickest option is to retrace your steps to Burrowhead Holiday Village and then take the minor road past Cutcloy, which leads in less than two miles to Isle of Whithorn.

Recommended pub: The Steam Packet Hotel, Isle of Whithorn

Route 24

THE MULL OF GALLOWAY

This is a short but bracing clifftop walk around the rugged and dramatic headland that forms the southernmost tip of Scotland and is only suitable for children if they are well supervised.

Distance: 2 miles/3 km (circular)
Time: 1–2 hours
OS map: 82

THE 'LAND'S END OF SCOTLAND' IS A WORTHY SOUTHERN extreme and the focus of a fine short walk beginning and ending at the Mull of Galloway lighthouse. A glance at the map shows the mull to be 'squeezed out' by the bays of West and East Tarbet into what is almost a separate island.

There is an ample car park just above the tea room. Go through the gate into the lighthouse grounds and follow a grassy path that heads towards the lighthouse. A secondary path forks off to the left that can be followed to its termination at Lagvag Point, but great care should be taken on the steep grass slope. Retrace your steps and take the path to the lighthouse, where there is an interesting exhibition in a converted cottage. Another optional grassy path descends in a few hundred yards to a good viewpoint: it has been said that you can see seven kingdoms from the headland: Scotland, Ireland, England, Wales, the Isle of Man, Strathclyde and Heaven!

Return to the lighthouse, where you can pay an optional visit to the foghorn. Otherwise, walk to the right of the lighthouse buildings and return to the car park. From here, go through the gate in the fence on the south side and aim for the cliff edge, following it down to the tea room, where you may wish to indulge in some refreshment before continuing the walk. The cliff scenery west of the tea room is the highlight of the walk and, again, you should go through the gate near the tea room and follow the cliff edge to gain a real appreciation of this dramatic landscape.

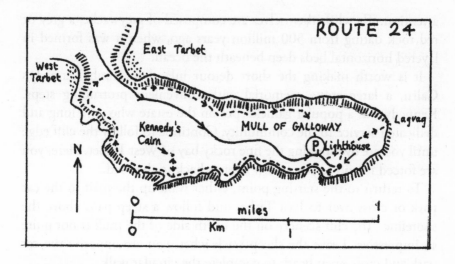

As you head west, some fine retrospective views of the cliffs and lighthouse open up. In the spring and summer months, the narrow cliff ledges are crowded with squawking herring gulls, black gulls, razorbills, guillemots and fulmars. The springy turf of the clifftops is a blaze of colour in late spring and early summer, with sea thrift, yellow vetch and the tiny star-like flowers known as spring squill all vying for

The Mull of Galloway

attention. The cliffs themselves are composed of greywacke, a grey or red rock dating from 500 million years ago, when it was formed in layered horizontal beds deep beneath the ocean.

It is worth making the short detour inland to climb Kennedy's Cairn, a large stone memorial with convenient protruding steps. Kennedy was a popular gamekeeper on the estate who gave long and dedicated service to the community. Continue to follow the cliff edge until you are overlooking the fine rocky bay of West Tarbet. Here, you are forced inland as you follow a fence back to the road.

To return to the starting point, either walk up the road to the car park or cross over to East Tarbet and follow a steep path above the shoreline. The cliff scenery on the north side of the mull is not quite so impressive. Leave the sheep track when you are opposite the car park and cross open heath to complete the circular walk.

PORTPATRICK TO BLACK HEAD

The coastal path from Portpatrick to Black Head forms the first small section of the 212-mile coast-to-coast route known as the Southern Upland Way. It is a beautifully scenic walk along clifftops and visits some delightful coves and shingle beaches. The route is ideal for children provided they stay clear of cliff edges.

Distance: 2.5 miles/4 km (linear)
Time: 1–2 hours
OS map: 82

PORTPATRICK WAS ONCE THE SCOTTISH END OF THE SHORT sea crossing from Northern Ireland but transferred to Stranraer in 1862. Portpatrick retains a quaint but bustling fishing port atmosphere with its picturesque sheltered harbour and is a magnet for summer tourists. It provides a fitting start to the walk and, indeed, to the more demanding Southern Upland Way.

Cars can be parked at the north end of the harbour, where there is a Southern Upland Way information board. This marks the beginning of the walk. Begin by climbing a long flight of concrete steps, the first few with markings of geological timescales. At the top, there is a fine view of Portpatrick and also of the Scottish Baronial-style Portpatrick Hotel in a splendid position overlooking the town.

Follow the well-marked trail left of the British Telecom Radio Station until it turns right, away from the cliff edge, to join a gravel drive alongside Dunskey golf course. The route soon leaves this drive to continue as a grassy path above the cliffs before descending to the two secluded coves known as Port Mora and Port Kale. Cross both these on sand and shingle beaches. At the second cove, there is a wooden footbridge and an old coastal interpretation centre – now sadly closed.

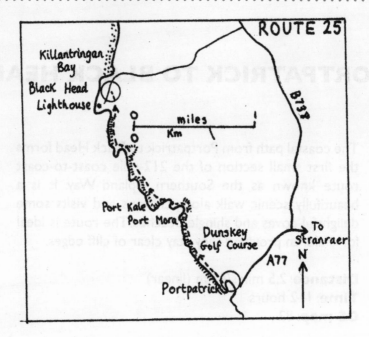

At the end of the beach, the path disappears round the back of a huge rock and then climbs steeply up the cliff face on steps with a hand-assisted chain rail. At the top of the cliff, climb a stile and continue along a delightful section of springy turf for a mile until the prominent Killantringan Lighthouse comes into view. The path joins a gravel track near the lighthouse, which should be followed until you are able to gain a view of beautiful Killantringan Bay lying to the north. This marks the end of this short walk.

If transport back to Portpatrick has not been arranged, the best option is simply to return by the same route. Another option is to follow the minor road east past Killantringan for a mile to the B738 (following the Southern Upland Way) and then turn right back to Portpatrick in another 2.5 miles.

Recommended pub: Crown Hotel, Portpatrick

CULZEAN BAY TO MAIDENHEAD BAY

A splendid and varied coastal walk connecting two fine sandy beaches and offering glorious views to Arran and the volcanic stump of Ailsa Craig. The highlight is the imposing grandeur of Culzean Castle with its associated parkland of trees, gardens and secluded coves. The route should not be attempted in a high spring tide.

Distance: 4 miles/6 km (linear)
Time: 2–3 hours
OS map: 70

THE BULK OF THIS WALK FOLLOWS THE RECENTLY ESTABLISHED Ayrshire Coastal Path (see Appendix) and, as such, is reasonably well signposted. The route is described from north to south, because ending at the village of Maidens provides easier opportunities for securing a lift back to the start at Croy. If this is not a concern, then doing the route from south to north may be preferable, as any prevailing wind should be at your back.

Begin at Croy shore near the caravan park, where there is ample parking. This is situated south of the Electric Brae, just off the A719 coastal road south of Ayr. Walk immediately down to the beach and turn left. If the tide is partly out, the walking is easy on firm sand; otherwise, the going can be considerably harder. The first section of the walk is an ideal leg-stretcher giving a fine view out to the Isle of Arran and to Ailsa Craig off to the left. You will pass two cottages on the seafront and then a third building consisting of two terraced cottages just before a small rocky headland. This point is just over a mile from the start and marks the start of a short path that makes its way under the trees and round the headland to the next small cove. The headland is a superb vantage point from which to view

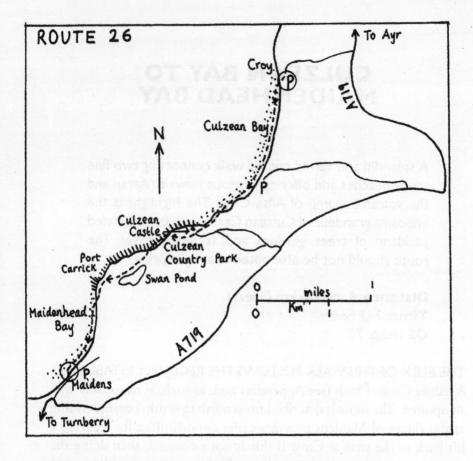

Culzean Castle, perched high on the rugged cliff beyond the small cove.

The building ahead with the round brick tower is the gas house. It is reached by a stone ramp leading up from the shore and marks the beginning of the middle section of the walk, through Culzean Country Park. The gas house was built in the 1840s, when the castle itself (built in 1790 by Robert Adam) started to be supplied with coal gas – even before Princes Street in Edinburgh was supplied! The gas house and the gas keeper's cottage are both open to the public and offer a fascinating diversion.

From the gas house, a wide path zigzags up to the castle itself, or, alternatively, ascend the wooden steps. Once at the castle, a number of options are available. You may wish to spend some time exploring the castle grounds on the numerous paths or you may want to see the interior of the castle. To continue the coastal walk, follow the Ayrshire Coastal Path signs, though these become scarce in the castle grounds. There will almost certainly be plenty of folk about, as year on year the castle notches up the largest number of visitors of any National Trust property in Scotland.

To reach the clifftop path beyond the castle, enter the stone arch leading into the beautiful garden at the castle front and continue on the path to the right of the lawn. At the end of the garden, follow the sign saying 'Cliff Walk'. This goes across an open grassed area to some old cannons. To the right, a flight of wooden steps leads down to the boathouse beach and the Dolphin House, which is now an outdoor centre. It is possible to turn right here and clamber round the cliffs to Segganwell Gorge, a cleft cut deeply from the softer sandstone east of the castle. There are also entrances to a network of interconnected caves, but great care must be taken with tides, as it is easy to become cut off. The above option is not part of the described route.

Follow the shoreline left past Dolphin House and the curious round stone building on the beach. Scramble over a rocky section to reach a

Culzean Castle

set of wooden steps and ramps that bridge a boggy area. This leads back up to the main cliff path. Take the second fork to the right, which leads around the north shore of the Swan Pond, a placid lily pad-covered expanse of fresh water nestling among the trees.

At the western end of the Swan Pond, the obvious path going off to the right leads down some wooden steps to an idyllic little sandy beach known as Port Carrick, a grand spot for a rest. A second set of wooden steps leads back up to the clifftop walk, although it is possible to clamber round the cliffs from here to reach Maidenhead Bay. The upper clifftop walk leads through the trees and descends gradually by wooden steps to the welcoming expanse of Maidenhead Bay. A pleasant half-mile walk along the sands leads to the village of Maidens and the end of a marvellous walk.

Recommended pub: Dunure Inn, Dunure

SEAFIELD TO THE HEADS OF AYR

This walk forms a small part of the recently established 100-mile Ayrshire Coastal Path. It is a marvellous beach walk that should be undertaken at low tide and is often busy in the months of high summer. It is ideal for children.

Distance: 9 miles/14 km (circular)
Time: 4–5 hours
OS map: 70

ALTHOUGH THE WALK TO BE DESCRIBED IS CIRCULAR, THERE IS a reasonably good bus service between Dunure and Ayr and this could be used to shorten the walk.

Extensive free parking is available all along the seafront promenade in the part of Ayr known as Seafield, lying south of the main centre. Follow the promenade south along the coast, which is also the NCN 7 cycle route (marked with green dots on the OS map). Alternatively, wander down to the expansive sands. The prominent silhouette of Greenan Castle and the distant cliffs of the Heads of Ayr should both be visible far ahead.

Cross the River Doon by a new pedestrian footbridge, then walk down to the shore and follow the sands, with the hugely impressive clifftop ruin of Greenan Castle now dominating the scene. Off to the right, the mountainous profile of the Isle of Arran provides a suitable backdrop to the scene. It is possible to reach the castle via a path just beyond the castle itself, but it is easier to inspect on the return route.

Beyond the castle, pass around a small headland and continue along a fine stretch of beach with an extensive holiday caravan and chalet park on the left. The imposing cliffs of the Heads of Ayr lie just ahead. Pass under the towering, vegetated cliffs on slabs of calciferous

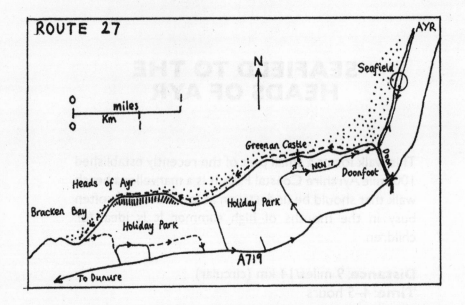

ROUTE 27

sandstone interspersed with sand and gravel patches. At the head itself, two obvious narrow buttresses give the impression of offering potentially good climbing and scrambling. However, the cliffs are composed of soft, loose and unstable lava rock. They have been the scene of several rock falls and climbing is not recommended.

Beyond the Heads of Ayr lies another fine, picturesque bay known as Bracken Bay, which is the turning point of the walk. At the end of the bay by a small ruined building, a path doubles back up the hill, just before a waterfall on the next band of cliffs. Walk up this gravel path where it widens to a track at the top of the hill. Go through a gate and under a railway embankment and turn left to reach a caravan park. There are two options at this point. For those who are walking back to Seafield, continue through the caravan park and exit via a gate at the far end. Carry straight on over an old gate along the route of the old railway embankment before climbing a fence to reach a rough track leading up to the main road. If you are returning to Seafield by bus or car then turn right at the caravan park to reach the main road.

Once established on the main road, follow it east past the entrance to the Craig Tara Holiday Park, a vast metropolis of static caravans on the site of what used to be a popular Butlin's holiday camp, which survived for a while as a theme park before becoming the present

Greenan Castle, Ayr

holiday park in the 1990s.

About a mile past the park entrance, turn left down a pleasantly secluded tree-lined lane that is part of the NCN 7 cycle route. Turn sharp right at the bottom and after several hundred yards take the optional little path leading out to Greenan Castle. The castle's entrance has been bricked up for safety reasons. The castle is a Kennedy tower house dating from the early 1600s – this whole coastline was a Kennedy clan stronghold for many centuries.

Return to the cycle path and follow it down into a housing estate, where it leads back to the pedestrian bridge at Doonfoot and the promenade back to Seafield.

Route 28

ARRAN: THE COCK OF ARRAN

Quite simply, this is the classic coastal walk of Arran and one of only a few sections of the Arran Coastal Way that is entirely removed from the main coastal road. The route described begins at Lochranza and returns by the hill track from Laggan but could easily be extended to include the section from Laggan to Sannox. This route is suitable for older children.

Distance: 8 miles/13 km (circular)
Time: 4–5 hours
OS map: 69

LOCHRANZA SITS AT THE NORTHERN TIP OF ARRAN AND IS possibly the most picturesque of the island's villages, nestling in the secluded, sheltered inlet of Loch Ranza and dominated by a fine ruined castle surrounded by brooding hills. The village also lays claim to the island's only whisky distillery, which opened in the mid-1990s. If you are arriving on Arran using the lesser-known Claonaig–Lochranza car ferry then you haven't far to travel to start this glorious walk.

The walk begins at the minor road near St Bride's kirk, about half a mile north-west of the distillery. You will see a sign for a collection of footpaths and for the Whins Craft Workshop. Follow the minor road down to a T-junction, where again you should spot various footpath signs, the one to the left saying 'Fairy Dell' and 'Ossian's Cave', which is the outward route. The right-hand route is the path you will return by and is signposted 'Cock of Arran' and 'Laggan'. Turn left and continue along a tarmac lane past some cottages until you reach the head of the loch and a track leading off to the right. At this point, there is a choice of two routes, both roughly the same distance and both ending at the Fairy Dell, further along the coast.

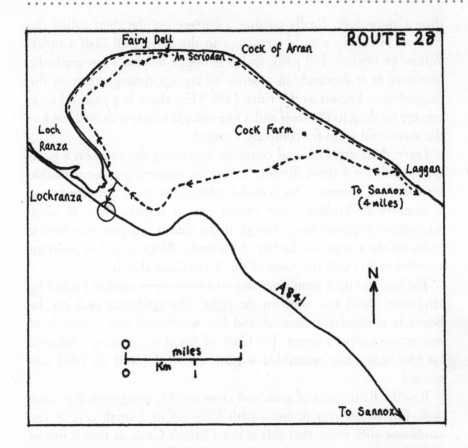

The first route adheres strictly to the coastline and is fairly obvious, while the second takes the track leading to the right and follows a higher parallel route above the coastline. For quality of views, the second option is recommended – and also gives you the chance of visiting the Whins Craft Workshop. On the other hand, if you opt for the lower route you will reach the location known as Hutton's Unconformity. This is where the famous eighteenth-century geologist Dr James Hutton was inspired by Arran's complex geology to dream up his 'Theory of the Earth', which asserted that the earth was millions of times older than previously believed. Take your pick of the two routes! The second option is now briefly described.

The right-hand track makes a sharp turn left through an avenue of trees and continues up the hill, passing the Whins cottage on the left higher up. After passing more cottages on the right, take a left fork then a right fork, finally passing a cottage on the right called the Knowe. Here you should see a sign to the Fairy Dell (half a mile). Follow an obvious hill path, which is boggy in places but gradually improves as it descends in a series of zigzags through trees to the magical spot known as the Fairy Dell. Here there is a peaceful little cottage nestling in the trees and a fine shingle beach with nothing but the waves and wind for company – enjoy!

Leave the Fairy Dell and continue east along the coast on a good grassy path for a short distance before encountering an unavoidable boulder field known as An Scriodan (the Gaelic word *sgriodan* means a quantity of broken stone spread over a slope). There is some scrambling required here, though if the tide is out you may find it easier on the shingle to the left of the rocks. Blobs of yellow paint on assorted rocks mark the route of the Arran Coastal Way.

The boulder field soon gives way to a more open section backed by sandstone bluffs and cliffs on the right. The sandstone rock on the beach is particularly unusual and has weathered into a wealth of interesting sculpted forms. The Cock of Arran is a massive sandstone boulder that once resembled a giant cockerel, until its head was severed.

Reach a flatter area of grass and cross an old, overgrown dry-stone wall. Just before this point, a path leads up to a small cave in the sandstone cliff. Note that this is not Ossian's Cave, as that is out of sight further on and much higher up the hill. Cross a second, more obvious dry-stone wall and pass a small headland with stunted trees. A third wall is crossed and a boulder path leads on to a wide grassy bay backed by a copse of broad-leaved trees where there is a small cairn.

Shortly beyond the cairn, pass a series of ruined buildings curiously known as Duchess Anne's Salt Pan, the site of an early eighteenth-century salt-production industry. Helped by the discovery of local coal, seawater was evaporated to leave especially pure and greatly valued Arran salt. Look out also for an old millstone to the left of the path.

The cottage at Laggan remains stubbornly out of view until the very last moment, suddenly appearing after passing through a gap in a low crest. The white cottage has boarded up but painted windows and is used intermittently. Note that it is privately owned and is not a bothy! If you see any sign of vandalism, please report this to the police back

Laggan Cottage, Arran

in Lochranza. Laggan Cottage was once part of the farmstead centred on Cock Farm about a mile west, and the dry-stone walls are also part of the farmstead.

Laggan is the point at which the return walk is made to Lochranza via a superb hill path that begins at the immediate right of the cottage. There is a small sign saying 'Escape to Lochranza'. The path is initially muddy but soon develops into a fine grass path snaking its way uphill through the bracken and heather. It makes a rising traverse westwards to reach the flat col west of Creag Ghlas Laggan before descending gradually to a more substantial track in Glen Chalmadale. The views all along this part of the route are glorious in good weather. Finally, reach the T-junction met on the outward route and turn left to reach the start point.

Extension
The full coastal walk from Lochranza to Sannox is nine miles long: that is, it continues from Laggan Cottage for another four miles. This route would entail the need for a second car or the use of public transport – or a very long road walk back to Lochranza!

Recommended pub: The Drift Inn, Lamlash

Route 29

ARRAN: BLACKWATERFOOT TO KING'S CAVE

This is a beautiful coastal walk on the west side of Arran with several options available for shorter or longer routes. King's Cave can also be accessed from a car park two miles north of Blackwaterfoot on the A841 road. An ideal walk for children, the route is part of the Arran Coastal Way (see Appendix).

Distance: 4 miles/6 km (return)
Time: 2–3 hours
OS map: 69

BLACKWATERFOOT IS THE MAIN SETTLEMENT ON ARRAN'S west side and provides the focus of this excellent walk. Park at the car park next to the golf clubhouse and shop, where there is a sign marked 'King's Cave: 2 miles'.

Walk directly down to the beach and follow the sands north-west out to Drumadoon Point, less than a mile from the start. Here, the route changes direction and begins to head north. The sand also gives way to shingle and boulders. By now, you should have a fine view of the western columnar cliffs and separate stack of the hill known as the Doon. At the far end of the golf course, there is a sign warning of the dangers of getting too close to play and another telling walkers to follow the path round the base of the Doon. Probably the best option is to go through the gate at the end of the golf course and walk along the seaward side of the Doon to gain a closer appreciation of the cliffs. This involves some clambering over large boulders but is not unduly difficult. If this is not to your taste, take the path that goes round the eastern side – this is the return route.

Once beyond the Doon, it is only a mile to King's Cave along a clear path through grass and bracken. Just before the cave, the path

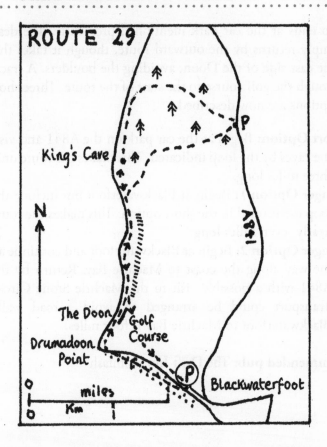

ROUTE 29

King's Cave

N

A841

The Doon

Golf Course

Drumadoon Point

miles

Km

Blackwaterfoot

climbs slightly and you should spot a signpost saying 'Return route to car park', which is the one two miles north of Blackwaterfoot. King's Cave is actually one of a group of caves on a sandstone cliff on a raised beach. It is easy to spot, as it is the only one with an iron gate at the entrance, which at one time was locked in an effort to prevent damage to the Christian and pre-Christian carvings inside the cave. The king of the cave's name is Robert the Bruce (King of Scots), who is alleged to have hidden in the cave during his escape from the English and to have seen the famous spider that spurred him on to great deeds there. Believe this if you will! The cave is also associated with Ossian's legendary Irish hero Fingal. All the caves here were created only 6,000 years ago, when the sea level was higher than it is now.

Continue further along the beach for several hundred yards to discover more caves. At a rocky outcrop you will see a path leading uphill through a gap in the rocks, which leads to a metal gate. This path also ends at the car park mentioned previously. The described route simply returns by the outward route, though it takes the path round the east side of the Doon, avoiding the boulders. A track then leads through the golf course to the start of the route. Three shorter or longer options are now described.

> **Short Option:** Begin at the car park on the A841 and visit the caves by the loop indicated. This makes the route only three miles long.
>
> **Longer Option 1:** Begin at Blackwaterfoot but include the loop mentioned in the short option. This makes the route nearly seven miles long.
>
> **Longer Option 2:** Begin at Blackwaterfoot and continue all the way along the coast to Machrie Bay. Return by the A841 with a possible visit to the Machrie Stone Circle. Transport could be arranged to avoid a road walk. Blackwaterfoot to Machrie Bay is four miles.

Recommended pub: The Drift Inn, Lamlash

HOLY ISLAND CIRCUIT

Arran's little offshore neighbour of Holy Island provides the setting for one of the finest small-island walks in Scotland. The route climbs to the highest point of Mullach Mor and returns along the sheltered west coast.

Distance: 4 miles/6 km (circular)
Time: 3–4 hours
OS map: 69

HOLY ISLAND IS A HAVEN OF PEACE AND SOLITUDE, SO NEAR and yet so far from the hustle and bustle of Lamlash, less than two miles away. The island is only two miles long but rises abruptly to over 1,000 ft in height and is very prominent from much of Arran's eastern side. The name derives from the fact that a sixth-century Christian saint, St Molaise, lived in a hermit's cave near a holy spring. The 'holy' tradition has continued, and the island was bought in 1992 by the Rokpa Trust, a Buddhist group that has successfully transformed the island into, as the trust describes it, 'an environmental and spiritual sanctuary dedicated to world peace and health'. A visit to Holy Island is a unique and memorable experience.

From a practical point of view, it should be noted that a full coastal circuit of the island is not an option, as the east side is reserved for rare breeds of wild animals and so public access is prohibited. The walk to be described is the recommended circuit and includes a climb to the highest point, an absolute must for all walkers.

Holy Island is reached by passenger ferry from the pier at Lamlash, with the first sailing usually at 10 a.m. and the last return trip around 5 p.m. It is not usually necessary to book, but contact the Holy Island Office on 01770 601100 if in doubt. It should also be stressed that

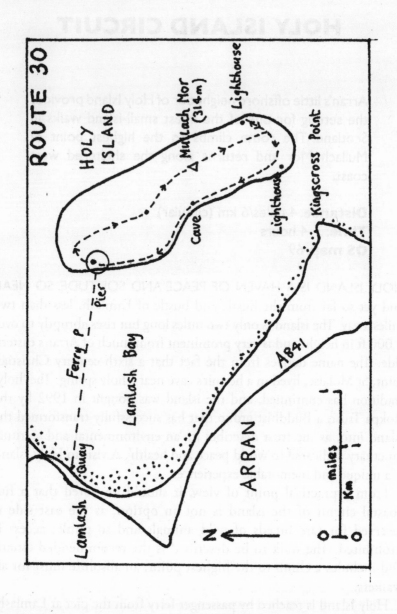

Holy Island

pets are not allowed on the island, and smoking, alcohol, drugs and music systems are not permitted.

Once on the island, you will probably be met by a representative from the Centre for World Peace and Health, the large white building ahead, who will offer a brief outline of the island and direct you to the start of your walk.

Begin by going left from the pier and through a gap between two Tibetan flags into a large field. Walk uphill through the field with the fence on your left. Cross a stile at the top of the field and enter an area of recently replanted forest of mainly birch and rowan trees. The trust has planted an amazing 35,000 mature trees on the north side of the island, and the path zigzags its way up through here onto the heathery north-west shoulder of Mullach Beag. Cross another stile and continue up the sometimes-muddy path to the smaller summit of Mullach Beag, where there is a large cairn. The view from here across the sparkling water of Lamlash Bay and further to the right to the jagged profile of Goatfell and Cir Mhor is truly amazing.

At this point in the walk, you may well come across some of the island's resident Soay sheep, which wander freely over the hill. Beyond Mullach Beag, there is a slight drop to a col then a steep little ascent with a little mild scrambling to reach the high point of Mullach Mor, crowned by a triangulation pillar. This is a marvellous vantage point and an excellent excuse for a long and leisurely lunch stop.

Continue south from the summit along the path and carefully

descend a fairly steep craggy ridge until the path levels out again on a broad heathery shoulder. There are fine views looking southward to the prominent volcanic plug of Ailsa Craig. Look out for a section of path passing between a roped-off area with danger signs warning of deep crevasses. These narrow fissures in the rock are on either side of the path and should be given a wide berth.

As you descend, the lighthouse and associated buildings come into view across to the right. The buildings are home to a Buddhist retreat for women engaged in long-term solitary meditation and should not be approached. The little wooden chalet nestling in a hollow to the right is the home of Lama Yeshe Losal Rinpoche, the executive director of the Holy Isle Project.

Reach a junction with the main coastal path and turn left, where in a few hundred yards you will reach a lighthouse at Pillar Rock Point. Access is barred beyond this point. Return to the junction and continue along the path that leads round to the west side of the island past the second lighthouse and retreat buildings. The path following the coast from here is on pleasant short grass with bracken on each side. The views are beautiful and there is plenty of interest along the route, including traditional Buddhist rock paintings and the cave of St Molaise, situated near the Holy Spring. The pier and centre are just over a mile and a half from the lighthouse.

If you still have some time before the ferry departure, it is worth continuing round the north end of the island until you reach the 'No Access' sign.

Recommended pub: The Drift Inn, Lamlash

DAVAAR ISLAND CIRCUIT

This is an interesting and unusual walk across to and around one of the few relatively large tidal islands off Scotland's mainland coast. Much of the route involves boulder hopping and scrambling, and there are some unique caves, the largest containing the celebrated Crucifixion painting. The route is suitable for accompanied older children.

Distance: 3 miles/5 km (circular)
Time: 2–3 hours
OS map: 68

DAVAAR ISLAND IS A PROMINENT LANDMARK LYING AT THE entrance to Campbeltown Loch on the west coast of the Kintyre peninsula. It rises to a height of 115 m, and its south-eastern edge presents a bold line of red microgranite cliffs containing a series of caves. It can only be reached on foot via a doglegged spit of shingle beach roughly three hours either side of low tide, giving a maximum six-hour window in which to complete the walk. Before attempting the walk, it is advisable to contact the tourist information centre at Campbeltown Harbour for up-to-date tide times.

To reach the start of the walk, take the minor road from Campbeltown along the southern shore of Campbeltown Loch to a large lay-by just over two miles from Campbeltown itself. Here, there are various signs warning you to be aware of the tide situation. Even when the tide is fully out, there are often large areas of (albeit fairly shallow) water that sometimes need to be crossed. Generally, it is better to stay further left as you cross the Doirlinn, as it is known in Gaelic. During the walk over to Davaar, keep an eye out for waders and eider ducks. In just over half a mile, reach the island.

Head off to the right on a grassy path to begin an anti-clockwise

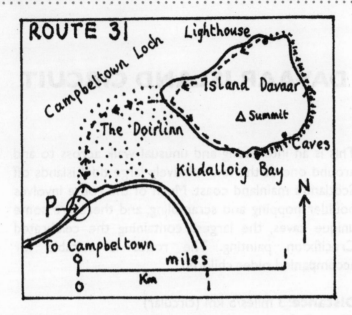

ROUTE 31

Campbeltown Loch · Lighthouse · Island Davaar · The Doirlinn · △ Summit · Caves · Kildalloig Bay · P · To Campbeltown · N · miles · Km

circuit of Davaar. The path ends at the start of the cliffs, and you will then have to navigate a beach of shingle and water-rounded boulders. The series of caves begins almost immediately, but some are little more than large hollows in the cliff. The one with the Crucifixion painting has a double entrance on a wide grassy platform and directly faces Ailsa Craig.

The Crucifixion painting is high up and is fully life-size, using irregularities in the rock to create a three-dimensional effect. Painted by local artist Alexander MacKinnon in 1887, it has since been retouched by the artist himself in 1902 and in 1934 and by other local artists relatively recently. Apparently MacKinnon had to strap his paintbrush to his walking stick in order to reach high enough. A lead shelf has recently been inserted above the painting to prevent running water ruining it.

The story goes that the painting was discovered by a yachtsman who had entered the cave for a rest, whereupon he duly lit a match to light his pipe. The flickering match lit up the painting and the yachtsman was flabbergasted at his pious discovery! Believe this if you will.

Leaving the caves, the going becomes increasingly rough and some scrambling over seaweed-covered rocks is unavoidable. If this is not your forte, simply return by the outward route. Eventually you will

Davaar Island

spot the lighthouse high above the cliff at the end of a rock-strewn bay.
The lighthouse is unusual in that it was created brick by brick on the
mainland before being transported across to Davaar. As you turn to
the headland where the lighthouse stands, the cliffs soon give way to
more gentle boulder-laden slopes, and it is possible to climb up from
the shoreline to reach a wide track. This leads back to the point at
which you landed on the island in only half a mile.

As a final part of the walk, it is worth climbing up one of the many
grassy paths leading up to the highest point, which is fairly flat and
crowned by a triangulation pillar. The views are out of proportion to
the modest height, and in clear conditions you should easily spot Ailsa
Craig, Arran and much of the Kintyre coastline. Don't linger too long
on the summit, though – the tide may be coming in!

Route 32

ISLAY: THE MULL OF OA

The wild and rugged southern peninsula of Islay, known as the Oa (pronounced 'O'), has a superb, fractured coastline with many cliffs and caves formerly associated with smuggling and illicit whisky distilling. This short but classic walk visits the famous clifftop American Monument and the spectacular Dun Athad, an Iron Age hill fort perched on a stack over 100 m high and connected to the mainland by a narrow grassy neck. A longer alternative route is described in the text. Look out for wild goats and choughs, also known as 'fire crows' for their bright-red legs and beak.

Distance: 5 miles/8 km (circular)
Time: 3–4 hours
OS map: 60

FOR THE FIT AND ADVENTUROUS WALKER, A COMPLETE FIFTEEN-mile circuit of the Oa is a stunning but challenging expedition, with an added three-mile road walk if only one car is available. It should be noted, however, that the path and track running parallel to the coast from Kilnaughton Bay on the south-eastern part of the Oa is at best sketchy and at worst a mudbath in many places and is not recommended. The most scenic sections of the peninsula are the area described here and Rubha Mor, near Kintra, covered in the Route 33 description.

From Port Ellen, take the road left at the end of the beach signposted 'Mull of Oa'. After a mile, take another road left for about five miles until you reach a fork with a sign saying 'American Monument' to the left. Follow this road for half a mile over a cattle grid and you will reach a large gravel parking area. There is an information board in the car park describing a shorter two-mile walk, but this does not include the dramatic Dun Athad.

THE WEST COAST I

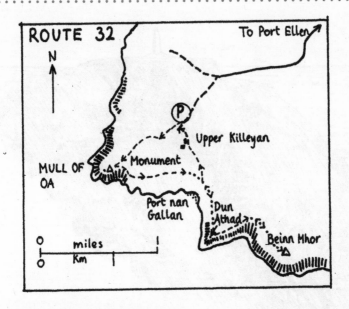

On a clear day, the huge monument at the Mull of Oa is plainly visible, and this can be reached easily from the car park by following a new ash and gravel path through several kissing gates before crossing several boggy areas on a succession of boardwalks. The monument itself is a massive stone tower standing on a grassy knoll overlooking the surging Atlantic, where in 1918 six hundred and fifty American servicemen were lost in two tragic naval disasters: the *Tuscania* was torpedoed in February and the *Otranto* was wrecked in a severe gale in October. Many of the bodies were washed up at the foot of the cliffs where the monument now stands.

To appreciate the dramatic cliff scenery, it is worth walking down the grassy promontory just beyond the monument, where there is an excellent vantage point of the enormous quartzite cliffs and the bay of Port nan Gallan. On a clear day, you may make out the Antrim coastline of Northern Ireland, which is no further away than the Scottish mainland.

From here, a good grassy track marked by wooden posts follows the clifftop south-eastwards, where excellent views can be enjoyed looking back to the monument. After passing through the second kissing gate, leave the path and branch off down easy grassy slopes, heading for the vicinity of Port nan Gallan. Cross a stream and climb up to another path that goes inland from here. The going underfoot is quite rough

The Mull of Oa, Islay

and heathery but improves further on. Go through a gate and head directly across heather and sphagnum moss to the prominent slopes of Dun Athad. As you gain height the walking becomes easier, and you will eventually descend slightly to reach a narrow grassy neck. A short, steep climb on grass and rock takes you up to the dun itself, a superbly situated ruin on an almost impregnable 108-m-high stack. It would be hard to find a more suitable defensive position. The airy summit of the stack is surprisingly extensive, with sheer drops on all sides, and is an ideal spot for a rest and from which to admire the surroundings.

From the dun, the walk continues round Port an Eas to climb up to the high point of the day at Beinn Mhor (202 m), where there is a fine view of the Oa coastline. Those who wish to return to the start from here should retrace their steps to the high ground above Port nan Gallan, where a path leads to the farm at Upper Killeyan and the car park.

Extension

For those who wish to complete a longer circuit, it is possible to continue along the coast to the ruined farm of Stremnishmore, then take a muddy track running parallel to the coast before turning inland after a mile. After another mile, turn off left along a track through the farmyard at Risabus leading to the single-track road. A three-mile road walk then leads back to the starting point.

Recommended pub: The Whitehart Hotel, Port Ellen

Route 33

ISLAY: KINTRA CIRCUIT

This short but spectacular circular walk on the northern part of the Oa peninsula is full of historical, geological and topographical interest, featuring deserted villages, an ancient chapel, a dramatic sea stack and a natural arch, together with varied wildlife. The route can become boggy in places and should not be attempted after a prolonged wet spell.

Distance: 5 miles/8 km (circular)
Time: 3–4 hours
OS map: 60

THE WALK BEGINS AT THE CAMPSITE AT KINTRA, WHICH occupies a wonderful position on the southern end of the marvellous six-mile-long golden sand edging Laggan Bay. This is arguably the finest, and certainly the longest, sandy beach on Islay and is an ideal location for a long summer's evening beach stroll.

Kintra can be reached from Port Ellen by taking the minor road signposted 'Mull of Oa' and then the right fork after a mile, which leads to Kintra in 2.5 miles. Cars can be parked at the small parking area through the metal gate but not in the farmyard, and there are several notices to this effect. This walk has become more popular in recent years and there is now an information plaque describing the walk and including associated history and points of interest.

From the campsite, follow the farm track round to the left, passing a bungalow on the left and going through a gate. The track climbs gradually after crossing a stream, and fine views begin to open up northwards over Laggan Bay. After a mile, reach an old, ruined croft and an obvious hairpin bend in the track. There may be cattle around this area, and you should give them a wide berth if there are calves about.

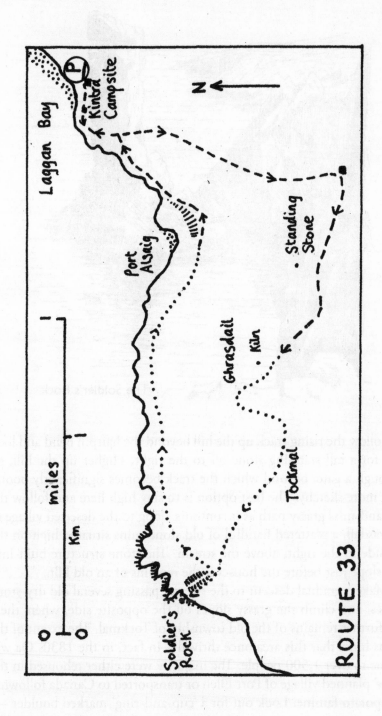

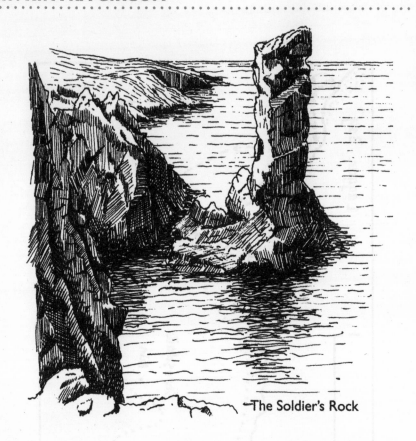

—The Soldier's Rock

Follow the rising track up the hill beyond the hairpin bend and look out for a tall standing stone off to the right. Higher up the hill, go through a gate, beyond which the track becomes significantly poorer and more sketchy. The best option is to stay high here and follow the hit-and-miss grassy path as it contours along to the deserted village of Ghrasdail, a scattered handful of old stone ruins situated high on the hillside to the right, above the stream. The stone structure built into the slope just before the houses is the remains of an old kiln.

Make a gradual descent to the stream, passing several old dry-stone dykes, and climb the grassy slopes on the opposite side, where there are further remains of the old township of Tockmal. The extent of the ruins hints that this area once thrived – in fact, in the 1830s Oa was home to over 1,500 people. The majority were either rehoused in the 'new' planned village of Port Ellen or transported to Canada following the potato famine. Look out for a 'cup-and-ring' marked boulder – a remnant of prehistoric times. Just beyond a small tributary to the main burn is the ruin of an old chapel and a walled graveyard.

Leave this wild and lonely spot and continue to follow the burn towards the sea as it gradually leaves this marshy area, developing into a series of small falls and forming an increasingly steep and deep gorge. Keep to the left of the stream, following the edge of a now spectacular gorge where the water tumbles down to dark rocks far below.

Suddenly you reach the coastline at the edge of imposing cliffs and one of the finest spots on Islay's Atlantic edge. The most obvious feature is the fine sea stack known as the Soldier's Rock, so named because of its upright appearance and quartz-veined intrusions resembling a soldier's belt. Continue out to an obvious grassy promontory where you cross over a natural arch and are able to gaze down at the churning sea through a hole in the rock. Take great care around here, especially if children are about! From this grassy perch, there is a dramatic view of the Soldier's Rock and a dizzying drop down sheer cliffs to the deep pool of Slochd Maol Doiridh. The steep gorge formed by the stream is now so narrow that it is little more than a deep fissure in the rock, and it is tempting to step over. It is safer, however, to return upstream and cross at an easier point.

To return to Kintra, simply follow the coastline eastwards along numerous sheep tracks, generally staying high above the cliffs. About a mile further on, cross a vegetated gorge on a high path before reaching a pocket of natural birch thicket just before Port Alsaig. Do not attempt to outflank this higher up the hillside, as there is a reasonable (but muddy) sheep track going through the wooded area.

Emerge from the birch wood at a large man-made reservoir surrounded by a stone wall that overlooks the fine sheltered bay of Port Alsaig. Further on, pick up a farm track leading directly to the main track used on the outward journey.

Recommended pub: The Whitehart Hotel, Port Ellen

Route 34

ISLAY: SALIGO BAY TO SANAIGMORE BAY

This highly indented and fascinating stretch of coastline on the Rhinns peninsula of Islay provides a grand and relatively unfrequented walk including some of the island's finest coastal features and viewpoints. The complete walk from 'bay to bay' is not long but involves much ascent and descent in the second half. It would be useful to leave a second car or a bike at Sanaigmore. Return by road walking would entail a further 4.5 miles, but shorter options are described in the text. As well as seabirds, look out for golden eagles, merlins, kestrels, hen harriers and peregrine falcons.

Distance: 6 miles/10 km (linear)
Time: 4–5 hours
OS map: 60

LONELY SALIGO BAY CAN BE REACHED BY FOLLOWING THE A847 from Bridgend and then the B8018 before turning left at a telephone box for a final two miles to a small parking area at a gate, just before a stone bridge. There may be a sign on the gate warning of dangerous undercurrents in Saligo Bay. From this gate, a vehicle track extends northwards for a mile and a half to Smaull Farm, which would provide a suitable return route for those not attempting the full walk to Sanaigmore.

Go through the gate and almost immediately turn left on a grassy path past some Second World War ruins to the fine sandy beach at Saligo. This is a smaller version of Machir Bay two miles to the south, and Saligo's glorious white sands are constantly buffeted by Atlantic rollers, but swimming is not advised due to exceptionally strong undercurrents.

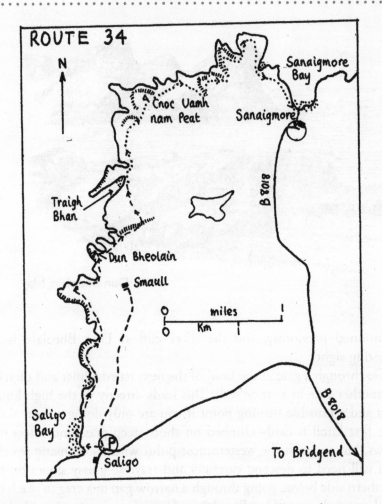

ROUTE 34

N

Sanaigmore Bay

Cnoc Vamh nam Peat

Sanaigmore

B 8018

Traigh Bhan

Dun Bheolain

Smaull

miles
Km

Saligo Bay

P
Saligo

To Bridgend

B 8018

Follow the sands northwards and on over short, sheep-cropped grass to a second, smaller beach. In the distance you will notice three prominent high knolls, the leftmost one plunging sheer into the sea. This is the start of the area of hilly ground around Dun Bheolain and is a 'must' to reach even if you are only contemplating a short stroll! From the second beach the walking is excellent, with several paths to choose through the close-cropped *machair*. Pass Port Ban and go through a gate before eventually reaching an area of low rocky outcrops at Rubha Lamanais. There is much room for exploration around this spot, but it can be bypassed by heading right if so wished. The far side of this little promontory gives a superb view of the high knolls

Dun Bheolain, Islay

mentioned previously, and the sheer cliff at Dun Bheolain is an arresting sight.

Go through a gate at the head of the next narrow inlet and then on to another gate in a stone wall. This leads directly to the high-knolls area and a possible turning point if you are only doing a short walk. The first knoll is easily climbed on short steep grass and offers fine views, but to reach the westernmost point with its dramatic sea cliff you will need to descend carefully and traverse grassy slopes on the northern side before going through a narrow gap in a crag to reach the final grassy slopes of Dun Bheolain, a fantastic vantage point. Nothing remains of a fortification here, but its almost impregnable position is not in doubt.

For those wishing to complete only a small circular walk, this is an ideal point to return via the farm track from Smaull, only half a mile distant. Alternatively, you may prefer to retrace your steps back along the coast.

To continue northwards, return along the north side of the knolls and climb a prominent small hill via an obvious grassy ramp on its seaward side. Follow the top of an inland escarpment until you reach a break in the cliffs. Descend and cross a grassy shoulder to reach Traigh Bhan ('white beach'), an idyllic little beach backed by low grassy mounds. On one of the mounds is a small monument to the *Exmouth* Sea Tragedy of 28 April 1847, when two hundred and forty-one Irish emigrants died en route from Derry to Quebec at the time of the great famine. One hundred and eight bodies, mostly women and children, were recovered and buried at this spot. A more substantial monument stands at Sanaigmore.

Between Traigh Bhan and Sanaigmore lies a complex area of cliffs, bluffs and coves dominated by the high point of the route at Cnoc Uamh nam Fear ('hill of the man of the cave'). This can be reached from Traigh Bhan by rounding a small inlet and making a gradual rising traverse above the coastal crags on tussocky grass and heather. The top, at 128 m, with its trig point is another magnificent viewpoint from where the sandy beach at Sanaigmore is now visible, only 1.5 miles to the east.

The route continues north-east following a meandering line along the top of low cliffs. Little remains of an old settlement and fort on a small cliff-bound knoll a short distance further on. The final high point of Ton Mhor looks down on a tiny sandy cove, and from here it is just a short stroll to the end point of the walk at Sanaigmore Bay, another beautifully remote and wild beach. From here, a track leads up to the road end and car park, where there is a large monument to the *Exmouth* tragedy and, in the summer season, a tea and craft shop.

Recommended pub: Bridgend Hotel, Bridgend

Route 35

ISLAY: McARTHUR'S HEAD

This walk from Claggain Bay to McArthur's Head on the east coast of Islay follows an old track for much of the route. Having said this, the track has not been maintained and becomes very boggy after heavy rain. The coastline lacks the drama of parts of the west coast, but the route itself has a quiet charm and serenity with fine views across the Sound of Islay to neighbouring Jura and the Paps. There is an opportunity for those with a second car to continue along an inland hill track from Proaig to reach Storakaig, near Ballygrant.

Distance: 9 miles/14 km (return)
Time: 4–6 hours
OS map: 60

FROM PORT ELLEN, FOLLOW THE A846 TO LAGAVULIN AND TURN off on a minor road just before Ardbeg. Follow this road for over six miles past Kildalton to the north end of Claggain Bay, where there is a parking area on the right at the end of the public road.

Go through the gate and walk along the partially tarmacked track to Ardtalla Farm and self-catering cottage. Go through the yard and a gate before crossing a field and a stream. Bear left to go through another gate and follow the rather muddy track as it meanders gradually uphill to cross the shoulder of Maol Ardtalla. The path eventually begins to descend through an area of scrubby bushes and low trees, becoming waterlogged in several places. From here, there is a fine view northwards of a wide bay backed by high hills and the little cottage of Proaig over a mile distant.

Cross a stream and take the right fork beyond, the path rising for a short distance before gradually descending to the coastline, where the path improves significantly. This wide bay is a wonderful place to

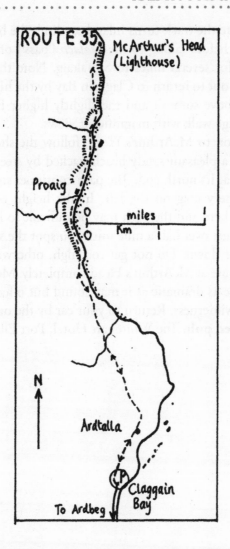

linger and soak up the wild atmosphere of this hidden corner of Islay.

To reach Proaig ('broad bay' in Old Norse), cross a river on some stepping-stones on the beach and walk up to the old cottage, now used as a bothy. Vikings settled in this bay centuries ago, and from the twelfth century the area became one of the most prosperous on Islay when successive farms were built and worked by families and clan chiefs of the Lords of the Isles. The house you see today was abandoned in the 1930s, but up until then the children who lived there walked to Ardtalla as well as several additional miles to the school at Ardmore on a daily basis.

Proaig is where the track turns inland to climb the broad east ridge of Glas Bheinn before taking to the *bealach* ('pass') on the right and continuing on for several miles to Storakaig. Note that experienced hillwalkers may opt to return to Claggain Bay by the high-level circuit including the above summit and the slightly higher Beinn Bheigier. This is a fine ridge walk with magnificent views.

To continue on to McArthur's Head, follow the shore path north until you reach a pleasant sandy beach backed by steep grassy slopes and small crags at its north end. The path continues steeply uphill on the stony, heathery crag on the left. In the height of summer, the bracken is high here and the path may be difficult to locate. Traverse the hillside for just over half a mile until you spot the white tip of the lighthouse lower down. Do not get too high, otherwise it is easy to miss the lighthouse at McArthur's Head completely. McArthur's Head itself is not quite as dramatic as it may sound but offers superb views across to Jura's wilderness. Return to your car by the outward route.

Recommended pub: The Whitehart Hotel, Port Ellen

ISLAY: RUBH' A' MHAIL

This fine, scenic circular walk is a sample of the spectacular northern coastline of Islay between Rubh' a' Mhail and Loch Gruinart. The complete walk from Bunnahabhain to Killinallan is a 16-mile coastal marathon suitable for adventurous and fit walkers who have arranged suitable transport. The walk described here is an ideal introduction to this wild and unfrequented coastline, and several other options are outlined in the text.

Distance: 10 miles/16 km (circular)
Time: 5–7 hours
OS map: 60

WALK ISLAY, THE ISLAY WALKING FESTIVAL HELD IN SPRING EACH year, includes the above-mentioned linear coastal walk from Bunnahabhain to Killinallan as one of its walking highlights, and for those with time, fitness and transport, the expedition is a classic route. It would also be possible to complete the whole route with two separate 'there-and-back' walks from Bunnahabhain and Killinallan respectively. A walk from Killinallan is described briefly at the end of the text. The route to be described begins near the distillery at Bunnahabhain and follows the coast for over six miles to Port a' Chotain before returning over Sgarbh Breac ('speckled cormorant'), a marvellous viewpoint. Longer circular options are also described.

From the A846 Port Askaig road, take the minor road signposted 'Bunnahabhain' and park in a small grassy parking area on the left just before the hairpin bend leading down to the distillery. Alternatively, park at the distillery visitors' car park. Follow the track left from the parking area for about 200 m before turning right past an old Second World War concrete building. Go through a gate and descend to cross

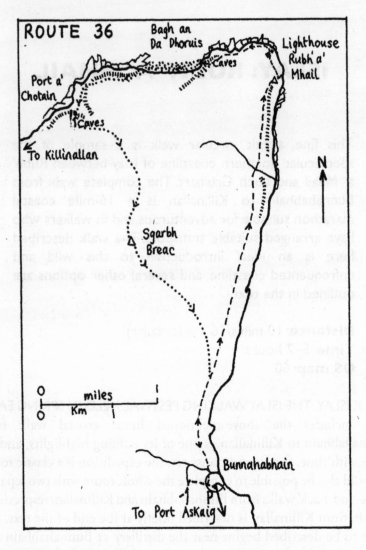

ROUTE 36

Bagh an Da Dhoruis

Lighthouse Rubh' a' Mhail

Caves

Port a' Chotain

Caves

To Killinallan

N

Sgarbh Breac

miles

Km

Bunnahabhain

To Port Askaig

the river by a footbridge. Note that this bridge is unmarked on the OS Landranger map. Climb steeply up the far side of the river on a gravel track to reach an unusually dry all-terrain-vehicle (ATV) track that winds its way north running parallel to the shore following a line of telegraph poles. A steady pace can be found along this wide grassy thoroughfare high above the shoreline, all the way to the deep gorge of Gleann Dubh some three miles on. The ATV track becomes a proper gravel track for the descent in and out of the gorge before becoming less distinct. Shortly before the trig point at Rubh' a' Mhail, it is easier to descend to the shoreline and follow a grassy track to an old stone storage hut and jetty just before the lighthouse.

Walk along a gravel track that doubles back before heading to the white-walled enclosed area containing the lighthouse and a private dwelling-house. This marks the beginning of a remarkable stretch of coastline leading for nine miles south-west to Gortantaoid Point. This wild and rugged Atlantic edge is characterised by raised beaches, caves, stacks, natural arches, curious rock formations and a peppering of idyllic sandy beaches: a veritable paradise for lovers of untamed, dramatic coastal scenery.

The first feature of interest is a fine little natural arch reached by following the lighthouse boundary wall down to the rocky shoreline. Go through the arch and continue along the coast, choosing your own route along this rocky thoroughfare, with numerous long inlets and geos causing you to make several detours inland. The quartzite rock has weathered into a sawtooth edge of amazing formations with several caves and it is difficult to establish any walking rhythm.

After little more than half a mile from the lighthouse, you should reach a fine grassy viewpoint looking out over Bagh an Da Dhoruis ('bay of the door'), a beautifully remote sandy beach almost completely enclosed by rocky cliffs and bluffs. This is a grand spot to admire the marvellous vista from the white sands out over rolling waves to the island of Colonsay, only four miles distant. A descent to the beach cannot be made until an obvious break in the cliffs a short distance further on, where a steep gravelly path leads down to the shoreline. At low tide, it is worth exploring the eastern end of the bay, where the surrounding cliffs have worn into a multi-entrance cave system at their base.

Follow the sands for half a mile west to an area of smaller crags and rocks where there are further caves and arches. Climb up to a flattish area of grass and follow the coast round to Port a' Chotain with its high, grassy raised beach. On the opposite side of this raised beach is another multi-entrance cave system, left high and dry after Islay rose up several hundred feet following the last Ice Age. The presence of stone walls around the entrances betrays the former use of the caves by humans at some time in the past.

The described route now heads inland and upwards over the prominent mass of Sgarbh Breac, but it would be perfectly possible to continue along the coast to the obvious conical peak of Mala Bholsa before returning to Bunnahabhain by way of Gleann na Caillich and Margadale. This option would add two to three hours to the above time.

Sgarbh Breac is best climbed from Coir' Odhar, where vague deer tracks lead up to Bealach Gaoth' Niar and the heathery north ridge leading to the 364-m summit, crowned by a trig point. On a clear day, the views from this airy perch are quite stunning, with the Paps of Jura arresting your gaze to the east. The descent south-eastwards from here is straightforward on mainly broad, easy-angled slopes leading directly downwards to the ATV track used on the outward journey. It is a little over an hour from the summit back to the car park at Bunnahabhain.

Brief note on the walk from Killinallan

Cars can be parked on the verge near the padlocked gate close to the farm of Killinallan. Follow the track for over two miles to Gortantaoid, where there is a detour inland to cross the river. Reach a vague path heading north across an undulating heather-covered area and cross the Doodilmore River, where the path ends. From here, the coastline continues north-east on a series of raised beaches where there are numerous coves, natural arches, inlets, stacks and skerries. It is about five miles from this point to Port a' Chotain, described in the main text. Worth reaching is a series of caves at Uamhannan Donna (only two miles from the path end), well above the tidal limit, some of which are over 30 m deep.

Recommended pub: Port Askaig Hotel, Port Askaig

JURA: BARNHILL AND CORRYVRECKAN

Any visit to Jura would be incomplete without a visit to Barnhill, where George Orwell wrote his book *Nineteen Eighty-four*. The famous whirlpool in the Gulf of Corryvreckan is also a magnet for walkers and explorers, and this walk combines both sights, with a possible extension to include some remarkable caves. Though most of this walk is on an excellent vehicle track, it is a return trip of exceptional length and only suitable for fit, seasoned walkers. Enquiries at the Jura Hotel may result in a possible lift to Barnhill by Land Rover.

Distance: 16 miles/26 km (return)
Time: 7–10 hours
OS map: 61

THE 'LONG ROAD' OF JURA EXTENDS FAR UP THE EAST COAST to just beyond the tiny settlement of Lealt. Cars can be driven about a mile north of Lealt Farm, where there is an old quarry on the right and a sign indicating the 'Road End'.

Walk northwards along the gravel Land Rover track that meanders its way parallel to the coast but a fair distance from it. The true wilderness of Jura is fully appreciated on the five-mile walk to Barnhill through barren moorland but with spectacular views across the Sound of Jura to the mainland.

The house at Barnhill comes into view a good half-mile before reaching it, tucked into a green hollow on the right of the track. George Orwell moved here in 1946, anxious to get six months' peace and quiet in order to write his next novel. He revelled in the remoteness of Barnhill and became extremely self-sufficient but didn't complete his book until 1948. After much thinking about the title, he finally

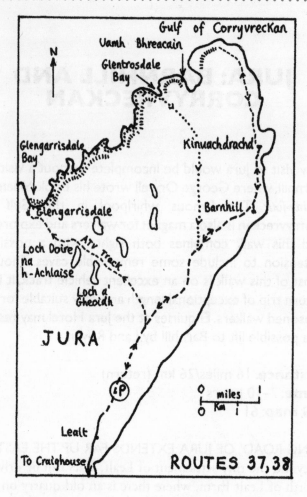

Gulf of Corryvreckan
Uamh Bhreacain
Glentrosdale Bay
N
Kinuachdrachd
Glengarrisdale Bay
Glengarrisdale
Barnhill
Loch Doire na h-Achlaise
ATV Track
Loch a' Gheoidh
JURA
P
miles
Km
Lealt
To Craighouse
ROUTES 37, 38

decided to reverse the last two digits of the completion year and the novel *Nineteen Eighty-four* was born.

Unfortunately, access to the inside is not possible, but Barnhill is sometimes offered on a short-let basis for holidays. North of Barnhill, the vehicle track continues for a mile, partly through deciduous woodland to the occupied farmhouse of Kinuachdrachd. Just before the farmhouse, a sign indicates an old track cum path that climbs uphill through bracken to a gate. Take this path and follow it northwards across open hillside parallel to the coast and with marvellous views across the Sound of Jura. As you ascend a small rise, there is a great view of the pudding-shaped Isle of Scarba, lying less than a mile away from the northern tip of Jura.

Barnhill, Jura

The path begins to contour round the eastern slopes of An Cruachan, and on a clear day the view north-east from here takes in a stunning array of islands, sea and mountains. The path gradually peters out at an area of crags and small hillocks where you can choose a spot to sit and observe the Corryvreckan Whirlpool. This stretch of turbulent water is the most dynamic tidal race in Britain, producing huge swirls of water, white breakers and deep eddies easily capable of overturning small boats. In fact, George Orwell himself was nearly drowned when he miscalculated the tide while on a boating trip to the west coast, his boat overturning in the whirlpool. Luckily, he and his party reached a small island and were picked up by a passing fishing boat.

From here, it is a long walk back the way you came, but an extension and an alternative part-return route are now briefly described. At the end of the path, it is possible to descend westwards to a large, flat area of raised beach where there are several caves. Walking round the bay of Bagh Gleann nam Muc takes you to Uamh Bhreacain, or Brecan's Cave. Brecan was a legendary figure said to have been buried in this cave after his ship fell foul of the whirlpool. Rounding the next headland takes you to Glentrosdale Bay, from where it is possible to head inland via Glen Trosdale and eventually back to the vehicle track by Gleann Dorch. This route is also described in the Glengarrisdale to Glentrosdale walk (Route 38), and ultra-fit walkers could combine these two walks into a single grand tour.

Recommended pub: The Jura Hotel, Craighouse

JURA: GLENGARRISDALE TO GLENTROSDALE

Jura's wild western coast has been described by celebrated photographer and mountaineer John Cleare as one of the last great wilderness walks in Scotland. Walking from Feolin Ferry in the south to Corryvreckan in the north along the west coast is a marvellous four- or five-day backpack with nothing but raised beaches, remote sandy coves, natural arches and scores of hidden caves: a real wilderness walker's paradise. This walk can only give a small sample of what this amazing coastline has to offer, but hopefully it will spur the dedicated explorer on to greater things. This is a long, challenging expedition that requires commitment, and some walkers may prefer to simply visit Glengarrisdale and return by the same way. For the very fit, this walk could be combined with the Corryvreckan walk (Route 37), which would essentially entail a grand circular tour of the northern part of Jura.

Distance: 15 miles/24 km (circular)
Time: 8–10 hours
OS map: 61

IT SHOULD BE NOTED THAT VERY FEW PATHS PENETRATE THE wild, barren moorland of Jura's interior and even reaching the west coast is an expedition in itself. The bulk of the 15-mile route therefore comprises rough moorland walking on all-terrain-vehicle tracks with four miles on the Barnhill vehicle track.

Cars should be parked in the same place as for Route 37; that is, in the old quarry at the end of Jura's only road (the 'Long Road') about a mile north of Lealt Farm. Walk north along the track for about a mile to a point where the track is at the top of a small rise. Ahead, a chain crosses the track and to your right is a small grassy hillock. This marks the point to leave the track by way of some flat stone slabs crossing the drainage ditch on the left. Beyond, an ATV track crosses the moorland, and although not a properly engineered track it is relatively simple to follow and takes the easiest line across the three miles to Glengarrisdale. It is not marked on the OS Landranger map.

For the first mile, the grassy track traverses open moor, crossing the Lealt Burn before gradually rising leftwards to give a distant view of the sea and the first of two hill lochans, Loch a' Gheoidh. The route passes high above the northern end of this lochan before descending steeply to the head of the second lochan, Loch Doire na h-Achlaise ('loch of the hollow' or 'grove'), a beautifully peaceful spot. In thick weather, these two lochans provide a useful navigational aid should you lose the ATV trail.

Climb up from the head of the lochan and pass to the left of an obvious crag. Just beyond here is a shallow gully with a cairn. Do not descend this gully; instead, keep right up a small, steep section before doubling back round a knoll. From here, the track descends gradually into the wide strath of Glen Garrisdale. At a large, flat, boggy area further on, the track makes a huge swing to the left before swinging back right below a rocky bluff. You are now in Glengarrisdale proper, and the tree by the river and white cottage with its red roof present a homely serenity in stark contrast to the wildness of the last three miles.

Cross the river on stepping-stones and wander up to the cottage, which is now a well-maintained bothy looked after by the Mountain Bothies Association. Although today Glengarrisdale possesses an idyllic, peaceful charm, it was the scene of a violent massacre in the summer of 1647, when a party of Campbells from Craignish sailed over to Jura and surprised a group of resident Macleans on a calm, sunny morning. A warning shouted by some Maclean women gathering shellfish on the beach was not heeded, and within minutes 18 unarmed men and boys were slaughtered in cold blood. The bodies were probably buried where they fell, and over a century ago a skull and juvenile skeleton were unearthed by a ploughman. The skull and two long bones were not reburied but placed on stones below a rock on the south-west side of the bay, which subsequently became known as 'Maclean's Skull Cave'. The cave marked on the OS map as 'Maclean's

'Skull Cave' is not in fact the original home of the skull but a long, low split rock several hundred yards west of this.

Looking across the bay from the bothy, you will notice the high, narrow entrance of the cave, which is easily reached by a path. The cave actually has two entrances, the other not visible from this spot. The sandy bay backed by the hilly Isle of Scarba is a grand place to linger and hopefully spot wildlife such as otters, seals and a variety of seabirds. During your coastal walk to Glentrosdale, you will almost certainly come across wild goats and deer. Jura is 90 per cent quartzite, the largest conglomeration of this rock in Scotland, and the rock formations to come are all composed of this hard, ancient metamorphic rock.

From the cave, continue along the coast on a vague path hugging the base of low cliffs. There is much ascent and descent required, with unavoidable rock scrambling in places and room for much exploration. Pass through a massive gap in some crags with white quartzite veins on the right-hand face. Eventually, after over a mile of superb coastal scenery, reach a tiny sandy cove at Bagh Uamh nan Giall. Round another headland on a raised beach to reach the bay of Bagh Uamh Mhor ('bay of the big cave'). Here, you will see the dark entrance to a huge cave on the opposite side of the bay.

Continue along a raised beach, crossing a couple of streams, to the massive entrance of the cave, which shows obvious signs of having been used for overnight shelter. As you round the next headland into Glentrosdale Bay, pass several other cave entrances stranded high and dry on raised beaches. This marks the end of the coastal section of the walk, unless you are combining the walk with Route 37, which takes you up to the Gulf of Corryvreckan.

The return route via Glen Trosdale is not difficult, as you are simply following the burn through a narrow grassy defile. Traces of ATV tracks can be found, becoming more distinct as you progress further up the glen. Pass some deciduous plantations on the right before a rather boggy section at the headwaters of the burn leads to Gleann Dorch and the final downhill section by another burn to the Barnhill track. You should reach the track in just over three miles at an old pony shelter. From here, turn right and reach the old quarry parking area in about 2.5 miles.

Recommended pub: The Jura Hotel, Craighouse

ISLE OF KERRERA CIRCUIT

The verdant, peaceful Isle of Kerrera may only be a few miles from the hustle and bustle of Oban, but its air of tranquillity and ease of access make it a true walkers' paradise. The route described is a circuit of the southern part of the island on good tracks and paths and would also be suitable for cycling.

Distance: 7 miles/11 km (circular)
Time: 4–6 hours
OS map: 49

KERRERA'S LUSH, GREEN PROFILE PROTECTS THE TOWN OF OBAN from the vagaries of the open sea. It is a small island, only about five miles long, but has a timeless old-world charm – as if a small slice of southern Ireland had drifted up to settle in Oban Bay. There are no hotels on the island, but there is a small bunkhouse, which is open all year round, and a tea garden at Lower Gylen. The tea garden makes an excellent rest stop for walkers but is only open from Wednesday to Sunday, Easter to October. Self-catering is available at Ardentrive Farm in the north of the island. Note that only bikes, not cars, may be taken onto the island.

A small passenger ferry operates from Gallanach, two miles south of Oban, and takes only five minutes, crossing every half an hour or so. An excellent visitor guide is issued free on the ferry. At the Kerrera slipway, go up the hill and turn left just below the Ferry House to begin a clockwise circuit. Almost immediately you are upon Horseshoe Bay, where, in 1249, King Alexander II died of a fever while attempting to reclaim the Hebrides from the rule of Norway.

Continue on to the Little Horseshoe Bay, which is the closest point to Carn Breugach, at 189 m the highest point on the island and well worth the detour, as it offers unparalleled views in all directions. It is

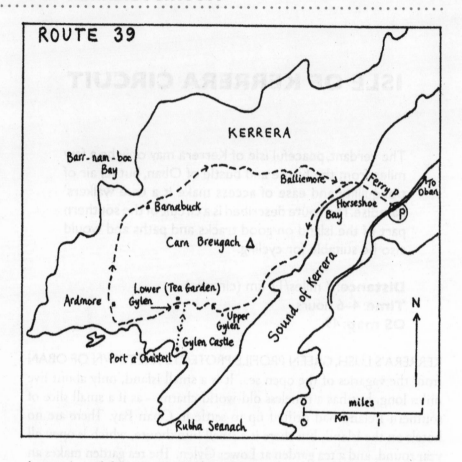

best accessed from Lower Gylen. Beyond here, the track heads inland to the farmhouse known as Upper Gylen. A track going off to the left before this should be ignored. Cross a high shoulder before descending to the whitewashed cottage and bunkhouse of Lower Gylen with its welcoming tea garden.

Just before Lower Gylen, a grassy path on the left leads through a gate and on down to an idyllic rocky bay hosting the dramatic and prominent Gylen Castle, perched right on the edge of a rocky headland. This is the highlight of the walk and should on no account be missed!

Built in 1582 by the MacDougalls of Dundlie, it was occupied for only 65 years because in 1647 it came under attack from General Leslie's Covenanters, leaving it uninhabitable. Ultimately, Gylen's downfall was said to be caused by a lack of water – ironic, given its location on the west

Gylen Castle

coast of Scotland! The castle's oriel window is surrounded by beautiful carvings and is one of the best surviving from this period.

On the opposite side of the bay west of Gylen Castle is another older fortification that is worth exploring, as are the sea cave, arch and raised beach.

After retracing your route to Lower Gylen and enjoying a few cups of tea, continue along the track to Ardmore, enjoying fine views south to the Garvellachs and the islands of Seil and Scarba. There is an imposing basalt pinnacle in the field in front of Ardmore House. Ignore any paths and tracks that fork off to the left; instead, pass in front of the house before ascending the hill on a rough track. As you climb higher, there is a superb panoramic view over to Mull and the surrounding islands, including Lismore.

Descend to another white cottage (Barnabuck House) and Barn-nam-Boc Bay. (Barr-nam-Bock means 'ridge of the roebucks'.) Interestingly, between 1760 and 1860 this bay was the terminus of the main Mull ferry and a busy port – hard to believe, considering the quiet backwater it has now become.

From Barnabuck, the track climbs steeply and winds its way inland, eventually reaching Balliemore and the starting point at the ferry slipway. This completes a most satisfying route.

Note that there is a northern circuit of the island, but it is not as interesting and only has a rough path for part of the route.

Route 40

MULL: THE CARSAIG ARCHES

The walk from the little hamlet of Carsaig along the coast to the Carsaig Arches is the most popular coastal walk on Mull – and for good reason. Not only are the Carsaig Arches one of the natural wonders of Mull, but the four-mile walk out to them passes below awesome cliffs populated by wild goats and golden eagles. A return along the top of the cliffs is the icing on the cake of a truly memorable outing. The clifftop return may not be suitable for young children.

Distance: 10 miles/16 km (circular)
Time: 6–8 hours
OS map: 48

THE TINY HAMLET OF CARSAIG, ON THE ROSS OF MULL, IS reached by car from the A849 via a minor road through Glen Leidle. At the end of the road there is very limited parking, so an early start is advisable!

The start of the walk is fairly indistinct, but from the pier a track runs west through the trees and continues round Carsaig Bay, crossing two burns and going over some planks at the muddiest parts. Beyond the bay, the vast cliffs of Sron nam Boc rear up to a height of almost 240 m and the path becomes hemmed in between cliff and sea. An hour's pleasant walking should bring you to the Nuns' Pass, a break in the cliffs above the so-called Nuns' Cave, where it is said that persecuted nuns took refuge after being driven out of Iona. The cave itself is not easy to spot, but look out for a strange Sphinx-like rock standing on the shore below the pass. A little back from this, hidden behind a low grass bank, is the cave. The entrance may be small, but once inside it is surprisingly roomy and old accounts say it can shelter some 300 people. The walls are scrawled with much modern graffiti, but with

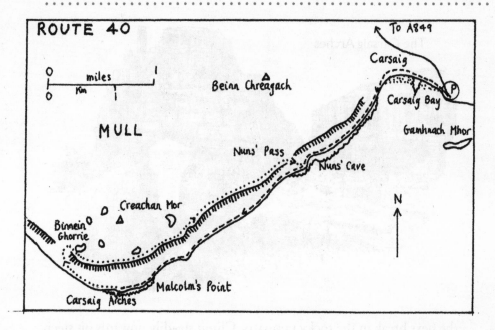

ROUTE 40

To A849

Carsaig

miles
Km

Carsaig Bay

MULL

Beinn Chreagach

Gamhnach Mhor

Nuns' Pass

Nuns' Cave

N

Creachan Mor

Binnein
Ghorrie

Malcolm's Point

Carsaig Arches

patience it is possible to discern carvings of Celtic crosses going back to possibly the sixth century. There are also several dates engraved there, the earliest being 1633, a carving of a sailing ship, and stonemasons' marks – rocks near the cave were used in parts of Iona Abbey.

Beyond the Nuns' Cave, the coastline becomes increasingly rugged, though the path is fairly distinct. Numerous opportunities present themselves to explore rock pools and observe wildlife.

Just beyond Malcolm's Point, the path appears to terminate suddenly on a rocky bluff above an inlet where the sea rolls in towards the first of the two Carsaig Arches. Backtrack a few paces and become established on a narrow path that climbs steeply up and over the grassy headland above. This path is quite distinct but very exposed in places, and great care should be taken. Beyond the first arch, the path goes down to the beach, where both arches can be admired. The first arch can be partially entered from this side. The second arch is taller with a small stack on its top and faces seawards.

A return route along the top of the cliffs is by far the most dramatic option, and this is described. However, you may wish to return by the outward route. To reach the top of the cliffs, continue along the shoreline for another half-mile until almost below Binnein Ghorrie,

The Carsaig Arches

the next break in the rocky ramparts. Climb steadily upwards on steep grass, keeping to the east side of the rock-choked gully for as long as possible. Near the top, cross the gully and climb up steeply on loose scree and dirt until you reach the lip of the gully and the clifftop. A short distance to the right of this gully is a prominent rocky outcrop perched right on the edge of the cliff – a truly marvellous vantage point and a grand spot for a well-earned rest. On a clear day, the view out to Islay, Jura and Colonsay is absolutely stunning.

The return along the top of the cliffs is airy and exhilarating. Keen Marilyn baggers will no doubt collect Creachan Mor and Beinn Chreagach. Descent via the Nuns' Pass is the quickest way down to the outward coastal path, but it is possible to continue right on round the eastern side of Beinn Chreagach and descend to the road above Feorlin Cottage. A mile of road walking leads back to the start point.

Recommended pub: The Mishnish, Tobermory, or The Glenforsa Hotel, Salen

MULL: THE ARDMEANACH PENINSULA

The full pedestrian circuit of this, the wildest and roughest of Mull's peninsulas, is a major expedition into remote and potentially hazardous terrain. The route along the southern shore to the most westerly point at the famous Fossil Tree, described here, is a less ambitious but more popular excursion, yet not without some exciting moments, such as the descent of a steel ladder down the cliffs. This is not a walk for those with a fear of heights!

Distance: 15 miles/24 km (return)
Time: 7–9 hours
OS map: 48

ARDMEANACH, GAELIC FOR 'MIDDLE PROMONTORY', IS THE APT name for this western peninsula separated from the Ross of Mull by Loch Scridain and from north Mull by Loch Na Keal. The high hills rising steeply to the west of Gleann Seilisdeir form a natural barrier that effectively cuts Ardmeanach off from the rest of Mull. The only road or track that penetrates into this wild landscape runs along the southern coast to the old township of Burg and forms part of the walk to be described. Beyond the Fossil Tree, so rough and rocky is the coastal terrain that it now bears the name of 'the Wilderness', a lure to the adventurous walker.

It should be noted at the outset that even reaching the Fossil Tree involves a laddered descent with several sections not passable at high tide. Beyond here for another five miles is wild, pathless terrain with several headlands again impassable at high tide unless an ascent to higher ground is made. Geologically, this is 'trap' country, where tertiary lavas have eroded into shallow steps, producing long lines of

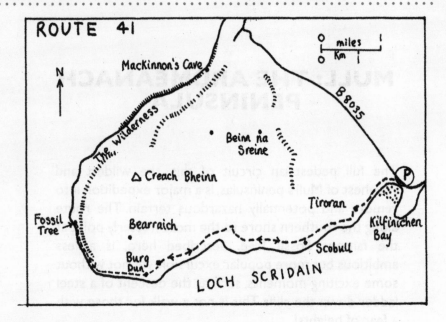

ROUTE 41

low cliffs and subsequent raised beaches: common features of Mull's landscape.

From the B8035 road at Kilfinichen Bay, take the turning signposted 'Tiroran House Hotel – 1 mile'. The road is tarmacked to the hotel only. Keep right at the hotel grounds and go through two gates, which should be closed at all times. The track winds round to the left past several cottages and outbuildings before turning right to end at the National Trust car park on the right of the track. This is only 1.5 miles from the B8035 and you may prefer to just leave your car at the small parking area at the road end.

Walk through a pleasant wooded section, taking a right fork a short distance further on. Climb steadily through trees to pass the old Scobull School, now used as a bothy. Beyond here stand four cairns on the left of the track, smaller versions of the original, more impressive memorials, which were sadly destroyed during forestry road building. Each cairn signifies a generation of MacGillivrays, the last family to have worked the land here. The cairns are a poignant reminder that this whole coastal strip from Tiroran to Burg (and beyond) once supported a population of over 300 souls. Some left voluntarily, but many were evicted in a ruthless manner during the notorious Clearances. Perhaps the most wicked incident was perpetrated by

MacArtair Dubh ('Black MacArthur'), who burned to the ground an old couple's house while they were working in his fields. The last remaining member of the MacGillivray clan was Chrissie, born in 1898, who lived to a ripe old age and is still fondly remembered by current locals. For a fascinating first-hand account of her life, it is worth getting hold of the book *Tea with Chrissie*.

Less than a mile past Scobull, the track begins to contour across open hillside where there is a fine view west along the coast and beyond, to the northern tip of Iona. At Tavool House, now an outdoor centre, fork left and continue onwards as the track winds it way round a steeply wooded section. Less than a mile beyond here, reach a fork in the track. Keep left, as signposted, to the Fossil Tree. The right fork leads to Burg Farm, which was Chrissie MacGillivray's last home. The left branch is a grass track running past the National Trust Burg bothy and onto a prominent grassy knoll on the left, which you will probably have spotted from several miles back. On the knoll stands an Iron Age fortification, Dhun Bhuirg, which originally guarded the entrance to Loch Scridain and is one of several fortifications along both sides of

The ladder near the Fossil Tree, Ardmeanach, Mull

the loch, each within signalling distance of the next. On the top of the dun is a memorial to Daisy Cheape, who was drowned on 15 August 1896 while attempting a boat trip around to Carsaig with her brothers and boatmen. She was twelve at the time and the only one to die when the boat capsized on a wild and windy day.

Below, and out of sight of Dhun Bhuirg, near the sheltered little sandy cove of Port na Croise, stand two large Neolithic cairns of beach pebbles dating back to around 4000 BC.

Beyond the dun, the path descends quite steeply to the beach and follows the shoreline for about half a mile before gradually climbing to meander its way along the top of a low line of cliffs. The narrow path soon becomes hemmed in by a second band of dark cliffs rising above to the right, producing a claustrophobic feel. On the rocky beach below are several curious rock formations of hexagonal basalt columns, some lying horizontally and radiating outwards like a fan.

In another half-mile, the path makes a steep descent towards the shore, and care should be taken here. You will then reach the top of a long, rusty (but sound!) ladder of more than 20 rungs. A long pole at the top acts as a necessary hand-hold to help you become established on the ladder itself. Climb down the cliff face on the ladder and then down a final muddy path to reach the boulder-strewn beach. From this point, it is less than half a mile to the Fossil Tree, which is just beyond the second of two long, narrow waterfalls cascading over the cliff. During an abnormally high tide you will not be able to reach the Fossil Tree, but even at low tide it is a slippery scramble over rocks to reach this interesting relic.

First impressions of the 'tree' may be slightly disappointing. The imprint of the 40-ft trunk is moulded into the vertical lava cliff just to the left of a small cave entrance, and to the right is a tree-like array of basalt columns. Some 50 million years ago, a whole forest of coniferous trees were enveloped in hot volcanic lava, and some, like this one, cooled the lava enough to force the surrounding basalt columns to bend horizontally. Much of the dark charcoal remains of the wood have been removed by fossil hunters since the tree's discovery in the early nineteenth century by Dr John MacCulloch, who first described the tree in his famous book *A Description of the Western Islands of Scotland*, published in 1819.

Return by the same way, unless you are both physically and mentally equipped to continue around the cliffs to reach the difficult and pathless terrain of the Wilderness. Note that the headland of Rubha na h-Uamha ('headland of the cave') lying just beyond the fossil tree is impassable even at medium tides and an ascent to higher ground may well be necessary to continue. The Wilderness contains many caves, some with signs of human habitation, and at Port Uamh Bride ('bay of Bridget's Cave') are the remains of a house and fank (a sheep enclosure). The only cave marked on the OS Landranger map is the famous MacKinnon's Cave on the northern part of the peninsula and is easily reached from Balmeanach on the opposite side of the peninsula.

For very fit hillwalkers, an alternative return route traverses the high arc of hills beginning at Bearraich (above Burg) and continuing to Creach Bheinn, Beinn na Sreine and Maol Mheadhonach with a descent to Tiroran. This is a magnificent round on a fine day.

Recommended pub: The Mishnish, Tobermory, or The Glenforsa Hotel, Salen

Route 42

MULL: THE TRESHNISH HEADLAND

A walk around the Treshnish headland gives the finest appreciation of coastal cliff scenery in north Mull, as well as the exploration of several caves and the best-preserved example of a Pictish dun in Mull. There are also a variety of shorter options described in the text. Two cars are not really necessary, as it is only a 2.5-mile road walk to reach the start. Some parts of this route may be impassable at very high tide.

Distance: 10 miles/16 km (circular)
Time: 6–8 hours
OS map: 47 or 48

THE TRESHNISH HEADLAND LIES BETWEEN LOCH TUATH IN THE south and Calgary Bay in the north, the B8073 Dervaig road going inland between the two. Cars can be parked in a small car park at a disused quarry a short distance south of the access track to Treshnish House, which marks the start of the walk.

Follow the track round a bend and past some trees on the right until you reach the farm at Treshnish. Here, a 'path' sign leads you sharp left past some steadings and farm buildings and along an old farm track to a couple of stone cottages at Haunn. Take the grassy path leading off to the right 100 m before the last cottage, which should be signposted. A well-engineered track cut into a ledge in the cliff descends gradually to a raised beach. Here, there are fine views of the Treshnish Isles, which look as if they are heaped one in front of the other. As you walk further round the coast, they gradually begin to appear as separate islands.

From this point, the walking is almost entirely on raised beaches and, as such, is very easy going on good grassy paths, sometimes

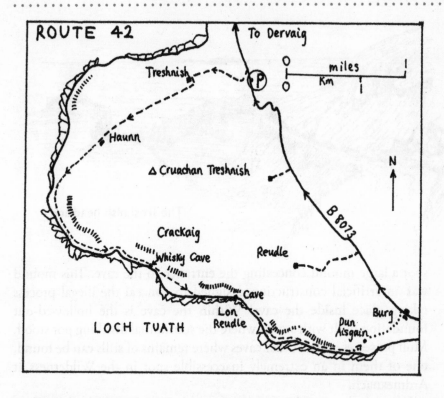

through deep bracken. Just ahead is an obvious flat grassy knoll that can be climbed by an easy scramble. At one time an old Iron Age fort stood on this spot, but it has long since crumbled away. Beyond the site of the fort there is easy access to the beach, and there is the option of either following a minor path below the cliffs along the shoreline or staying 30 m up on the raised beach.

Reach a dry-stone wall and another prominent grassy knoll. About half a mile beyond here is the Whisky Cave, where the best illicit still on Mull was located. The route down to the cave can be difficult to spot, but a good marker is when the top of the Dutchman's Cap is in line with the south Lunga cliffs. (The Dutchman's Cap is the southernmost of the Treshnish Isles and is so called, unsurprisingly, because of its resemblance to a Dutchman's cap. Lunga is the larger, middle island of the group, where landings can be made.) The grid reference of the Whisky Cave is 348462, and it can be found by descending a grassy gully where a faint path leads down to a shingle beach. Turn right at the beach and almost immediately you should

The Treshnish headland

spot a large mound concealing the entrance to the cave. This mound was an artificial construction designed to conceal the illegal process taking place inside the cave! Within the cave is the hollowed-out foundation built with stones where the substantial distilling pot stood. Mull possesses several other caves where remains of stills can be found, one of them in an extremely inaccessible spot in the Wilderness at Ardmeanach.

Leave the cave and return to the path, which soon leads on to a broad, flat grassy area after crossing a stream. For those wishing to complete a shorter outing, there is the option of heading inland at this point by following a zigzag path up through a break in the cliffs by a waterfall. This leads to the ruins of an old village at Crackaig and a second one at Glac Gugairaidh. The path eventually levels out and crosses a boggy area to reach the lonely house of Larach Mhor, where a track leads to the public road. It is less than a mile and a half from coast to road by this route. At very high tides the above route may be compulsory, as the next section of coastal walk entails boulder hopping at sea level.

From the level grassy area, the coastal walk continues below very steep bracken-covered slopes, following the rocky shoreline under a line of low cliffs. About half a mile along here is the largest of the Treshnish caves, with a massive, unmistakable entrance. Shortly beyond the cave, the cliffs peter out into Lon Reudle, a broad, rocky bay. This is the second point from which to complete a shorter outing, by following the Allt Reudle up to a restored house at Reudle and then via a good track back to the road.

To continue the coastal walk, climb up from the shoreline for about 50 m and follow the raised beach below a line of broken crags, much of it through bracken on good sheep tracks. After a mile, you will arrive at the wide bay containing Port Burg, and climbing up from here leads to the ruins of Dun Aisgain, the best-preserved example of a galleried Pictish dun on Mull. The dun is in the middle of a wide area of bracken at a height above sea level of around 60 m.

Finally, from the dun make your way directly up to the road via a variety of sheep paths, emerging at the cottages at Burg. From here, it is only a 2.5-mile road walk to reach your car.

Recommended pub: The Mishnish, Tobermory, or The Glenforsa Hotel, Salen

Route 43

MULL: ULVA CIRCUIT

A walk round the island of Ulva off the coast of Mull on a sunny spring day should be on every walker's priority list. This is an island with a difference: a quiet backwater a world apart from the hustle and bustle of contemporary life. Most of the walking is on good tracks and paths with handy signposting. There are no tarmac roads on Ulva.

Distance: 13 miles/21 km (circular)
Time: 6–8 hours
OS map: 47

THE MOST LIKELY DERIVATION OF THE NAME ULVA IS FROM the Old Norse name 'Wolf Isle', though the Gaelic *ullamh dha* ('ready for occupation') is also a possibility. Ulva is separated from Mull by a narrow channel only 150 m wide and is connected by bridge to the tidal island of Gometra, which is also worth a visit, perhaps on another occasion. Currently populated by only 16 people, the island is privately owned, but responsible walkers and sightseers are encouraged. Most people who visit the island do so in a single day, but limited accommodation is available in the form of a B&B. Camping is allowed with permission from the owners of the island (see www.ulva.mull.com). There is a licensed restaurant where the local oysters are something of a legend!

To reach Ulva, follow the Ulva Ferry road from Salen. There is a large purpose-built car park just above the point where the ferry leaves. The ferry works on a request system: to call the boat, just slide the wooden slat to reveal the red marker on the display board and the boat will come to meet you. The crossing takes five minutes. Currently there are crossings from 9 a.m. to 5 p.m. Monday to Friday and also on Sundays in summer, but there is no Saturday service at any time. If you wish to take more than eight hours on the walk then you will need

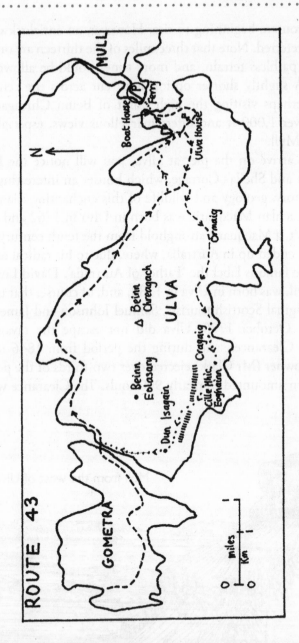

to consider accommodation on the island, though it may be possible to arrange a slightly later crossing.

The recommended circuit of the island is clockwise, as you will then return via the more substantial vehicle track on the north side when perhaps you are beginning to tire. However, an anticlockwise circuit may be preferred. Note that three miles of the thirteen are on relatively wild and pathless terrain, and more time should be allowed for this section. A slightly shorter option is to cut across the centre of the island, perhaps visiting the high point of Beinn Chreagach, which rises to over 1,000 ft and offers marvellous views, especially to Ben More on Mull.

As you arrive on the pier at Ulva, you will notice the Boathouse restaurant and Sheila's Cottage, which houses an interesting museum of the history, geology and wildlife of this enchanting island. Major-General Lachlan Macquarie was born in Ulva in 1762 and the island was, in fact, a Macquarie stronghold from the tenth century. Lachlan, of course, ended up in Australia, where, due to his radical reforms, he earned the famous label the 'Father of Australia'. David Livingstone's father, Neil, was born in Ulva in 1788, and, of course, that ubiquitous pair of original Scottish tourists, Samuel Johnson and James Boswell, visited in October 1783. Ulva did not escape the ravages of the Highland Clearances, and during the period from 1846 to 1851, a new landowner (Mr Clark) ejected over two-thirds of the population, which then amounted to nearly 900 souls. The Clearance was brutal:

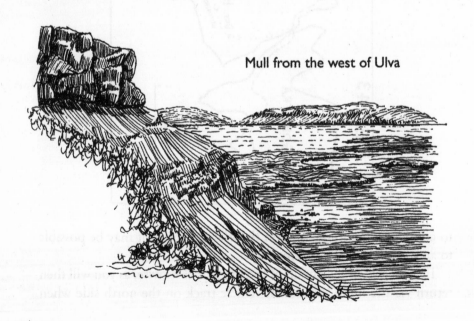

Mull from the west of Ulva

cottages were set alight with no prior warning and the residents had no time even to collect their meagre possessions. The Ulva Clearance has gone down in history as one of the most savage and cruel in all of the Highlands. As you walk round the island, the stark reminders of this ruthless eviction are ever present in the form of poignant ruined settlements.

From the Boathouse, follow the track off to the right round a sharp bend and continue for half a mile to a junction. Go left here and follow the track until you come to a building on the right. A sharp turn right here takes you uphill through a pleasant wooded area and out into open heath and bracken-covered slopes. Half a mile after leaving the wood, there is a signpost indicating a smaller footpath, which eventually leads down to the Clearance settlements of Ormaig and Cragaig. Follow this path delightfully on beautiful grassy sections through large swathes of bracken and numerous stone ruins. There is a grand view south-west across the scattered islets off the anchorage at Cragaig to the island of Little Colonsay. Look out for the little ruined water mill where the path crosses the stream in Glen Glass. Cragaig Bay is a beautiful and idyllic sheltered haven and an ideal spot for a rest and perhaps a bite to eat. This is the spot where the footpath ends at a private bothy and is an ideal location for spotting otters. Behind the bothy are a couple of standing stones worth a visit.

If you are planning on climbing to the island's highest point then this is probably the best place to start. Steep heather- and bracken-covered slopes rise up behind the bothy to the triangulation pillar on Beinn Chreagach at 313 m.

The described walk continues westward past the ruined chapel of Cille Mhic Eoghainn. Beyond here there are some lovely white sands at Traigh Bhan, but if time is pressing it is best to head away from the coastline to aim for an obvious gap in the line of basalt columns that appear to bar passage west. It is easier and safer to climb above this rock bastion before continuing west high above the coastline. From here, there are fine views of Ben More, on Mull. You may well spot one of the buzzards that frequent these cliffs, searching for suitable prey. Beyond the ruin of Dun Isagain, descend gradually on heather slopes, eventually turning northwards to follow the coastline to the vehicle track and bridge over to Gometra. The return route follows the vehicle track as it meanders round the northern slopes of Beinn

Eolasary and Beinn Chreagach, staying a good distance away from the northern sea loch, Loch Tuath. After four or so miles of pleasant walking, a footpath branches off to the left (GR 427396), which winds its way downhill to a track and an old church. Turning right here and taking the next left brings you back to the Boathouse and pier. Alternatively, ignore this footpath and stay on the main track, which leads back to the outward route. This option is marginally longer.

Recommended pub: The Mishnish, Tobermory, or The Glenforsa Hotel, Salen

IONA: THE NORTH CIRCUIT

This route could be combined with Route 45 to give what is effectively a rough coastal circuit of Iona. The walk to be described ascends the highest point of the island and visits some of the finest beaches. A linear 'there-and-back' option is also available for those with less time.

Distance: 6 miles/10 km (circular)
Time: 3–4 hours
OS map: 48

IONA'S BEAUTIFULLY INDENTED COASTLINE OF ANCIENT gnarled gneiss and fine white shell-sand beaches bathed in a pure west Highland light seemingly unique to this island make it a highly worthy destination for the coastal-walking connoisseur. The north circuit, including the ascent of Dun I, is a classic outing that should be reserved for sunny weather, when the sparkling colours show the true magic of Iona.

From the ferry jetty, walk directly up the road past some cottages and a shop and turn right past the ruins of a nunnery. This leads in less than half a mile to Iona Abbey, which you may wish to visit now or later. Continue onwards past some houses on the left, where there is a signpost for Dun I to the left of the road. Go through the gate and follow the path across a field to the craggy eastern slope of the hill. A path of sorts swings round to the left and meanders its way up to the 100-m summit of this remarkable little hill, where there is a large cairn and trig point.

The panoramic view from the top is out of all proportion to the meagre height and is arguably the finest view from any hill of comparable height in Scotland. The whole of Iona is spread out around you in verdant green, while Staffa, the Treshnish Isles and the wild

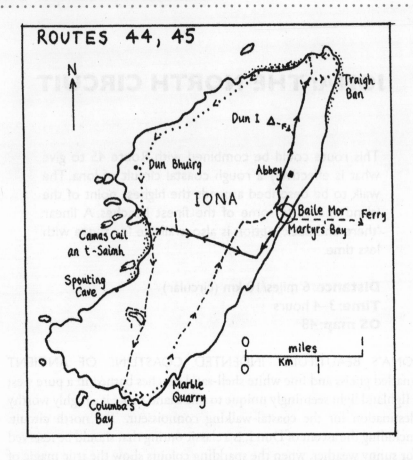

ROUTES 44, 45

N

Traigh Ban

Dun I △-Fₐ

Dun Bhuirg

Abbey

IONA

Baile Mor — Ferry

Camas Cuil
an t-Saimh

Martyrs Bay

Spouting
Cave

miles
Km

Marble
Quarry

Columba's
Bay

'Wilderness' coastline of the Ardmeanach peninsula on Mull all vie for attention. It will be hard to drag yourself from this sacred spot.

Return to the road and turn left until you reach its termination at a gate with a sign indicating the north shore. There is also a sign prohibiting camping. Go through the gate and follow the grassy path for a few hundred yards before branching off to the right across a field to reach the dunes backing the first of several marvellous beaches at Traigh Ban. Those who wish to end the walk here can simply return the same way.

Follow the white sands northwards around the rocky northern tip of Iona and then a grassy path across the *machair* to reach the wide, curving strand of Traigh an t-Suidhe on the north-western coast. To reach the sands, you will need to go through a fence preventing livestock reaching the beach. Walk delightfully along the sands and

Iona Abbey

round a small rocky headland to reach another small sandy beach (Traigh na Criche).

Beyond this point, the character of the walk changes from pleasant beach walking to more exploratory meanderings through an area of rocky knolls and grassy hollows. Welsh naturalist Thomas Pennant, who visited Iona in 1774, described the landscape as 'little rocky hills, with narrow verdant hollows between . . . numerous enough for every recluse to take his solitary walk, undisturbed by society'. This quotation reflects the area perfectly, and there is no set path through this unusual terrain. Simply pick a line parallel to the coast for just over a mile until you reach the obvious, much higher knoll of Dun Bhuirg at a height of 51 m. This can be climbed by an easy scramble and offers a stunning view southwards across the broad sandy bay and flat green *machair* of Iona's golf course.

Carefully descend Dun Bhuirg, leaving the hills and hollows behind, and follow the grand sweep of Camas Cuil an t-Saimh ('bay at the back of the ocean') either on the beach itself or on the grassy track at the edge of the golf course. This is a beautiful spot to simply relax and absorb the surroundings. Continue to follow the track as it turns left inland to the road that crosses back to the east coast in just under a mile. A sharp left turn then leads back to the ferry and jetty in half a mile, where a welcome point awaits you in the harbour bar near Martyrs' Bay, where 68 monks were brutally massacred in AD 806.

Recommended pub: Martyr's Bay Restaurant or Argyll Hotel, Iona

Route 45

IONA: THE SOUTH CIRCUIT

Although the northern part of Iona has the island's highest point, the southern half is generally more rugged, with a highly indented coastline and numerous inlets and caves. The walk to be described does not cover a complete coastal circuit but makes use of a well-used path to St Columba's Bay and returns by a lesser-known path on the east side. This route could be combined with the previous one to give a complete circuit of the island.

Distance: 6 miles/10 km (circular)
Time: 3–4 hours
OS map: 48

FROM THE JETTY, TURN LEFT PAST THE MARTYR'S BAY restaurant and follow the road for half a mile, where it makes a sharp turn to the right. Follow this road as it leads gradually uphill and then down to the golf course and flat green *machair* on the west side of the island. Shortly beyond the point where the road becomes a track, a smaller path heads off to the left, and this is the path to be taken. However, it is definitely worth continuing onwards to the fine, broad beach of Camas Cuil an t-Saimh before embarking on this path.

The path itself winds gradually uphill into a broad, stony gully before emerging suddenly at Loch Staoineig, the island's only freshwater lochan. From here, you may wish to make a diversion to search for the so-called Spouting Cave on the north side of the island. In rough seas, a plume of spray can be seen rising from a blowhole. Reaching the cave involves taking the path to the right before the lochan and leaving it again before it swings left. A direct line to the coast from here over a grassy hillock leads down to the cave. Further caves exist along the coast from here, but the terrain is extremely

St Columba's Bay, Iona

complex, with much ascent and descent required, and is not recommended.

From the lochan, continue on the main path as it heads southwards, crossing boggy sections on duckboards. This leads in half a mile to the idyllic, sheltered little bay of Port na Curaich ('port of the coracle') or St Columba's Bay, where it is said that St Columba landed from Ireland in his coracle in AD 563. The bay is a popular spot but also a peaceful and tranquil corner of Iona and a place to linger.

Most people who visit St Columba's Bay return by the same path, but the described route follows a lesser-known path on the east side and visits the old Iona marble quarry. To reach the quarry, climb the steep slopes to the left of the bay and descend into a hollow. Ascend a second ridge and follow a path downwards through bracken into a broad gully where there is an old ruin of a house. Follow the gully down towards the sea, where you will spot some of the old quarry machinery and rusty stanchions. The quarry was last worked about the time of the First World War.

Return to the ruin and pick up the path (unmarked on the OS map) that climbs out of the gully and meanders its way across the high moorland running parallel with Iona's east coast. In a mile, you should reach a gate leading to a grassy track between two fences, which, in turn, leads to the tarmac road crossing the island. Turn right and follow the road back to the jetty to complete a satisfying circular tour.

Recommended pub: Martyr's Bay Restaurant or Argyll Hotel, Iona

complex, with much ascent and descent required, and is not recommended.

From the lochan, continue on the main path as it heads southwards, crossing boggy sections on duckboards. This leads in half a mile to the idyllic, sheltered little bay of Port na Curaich ('port of the coracle') or St Columba's Bay, where it is said that St Columba landed from Ireland in his coracle in AD 563. The bay is a popular spot but also a peaceful and tranquil corner of Iona and a place to linger.

Most people who visit St Columba's Bay return by the same path, but the described route follows a lesser-known path on the east side and visits the old Iona marble quarry. To reach the quarry, climb the steep slope to the left of the bay and descend into a hollow. Ascend a second ridge and follow a path downwards through bracken into a broad gully where there is an old ruin of a house. Follow the gully down towards the sea, where you will spot some of the old quarry machinery and rusty stanchions. The quarry was last worked about the time of the First World War.

Return to the ruin and pick up the path (unmarked on the OS map) that climbs out of the gully and meanders its way across the high moorland running parallel with Iona's east coast. In a mile, you should reach a gate leading to a grassy track between two fences, which, in turn, leads to the surfaced road crossing the island. Turn right and follow the road back to the ferry to complete a satisfying circular route.

Recommended pub: Martyr's Bay Restaurant or Argyll Hotel, Iona

3

The West Coast 2 and North Coast:

ARDNAMURCHAN TO DUNNET HEAD

PORTUAIRK TO SANNA POINT

This is a beautiful walk close to Ardnamurchan Point, mainland Britain's most westerly point. The sandy beaches in Sanna Bay are arguably the most picturesque in Scotland, with sublime views out to Rum and Eigg. The route is flexible, with opportunities for extension if so wished.

Distance: 5 miles/8 km (return)
Time: 2–4 hours
OS map: 47

THE WALK BEGINS AT THE LITTLE HAMLET OF PORTUAIRK BUT can be extended by beginning near the caravan park one mile short of Ardnamurchan Point, where you will find a footpath sign to Portuairk. If you choose to begin in Portuairk but cannot find a parking spot down the hill, there is a large parking area at the top of the hill opposite the entrance to Borve House.

Turn right at the bottom of the hill and walk past three cottages, where you should see a sign to Sanna. Go through a little copse of trees to reach a small inlet where you cross a stream and follow the path upwards over a craggy spur. The path goes through a wooded area to reach a metal gate with a little stone cottage beyond. This is a magnificent viewpoint on a fine day, with the sandy beaches of Sanna Bay spread out below backed by the mountainous profile of Rum.

Go through the gate and follow the path down to a stream, which is easily crossed on big, rough boulders. Just beyond here, the path winds round to the right to avoid a craggy knoll and meanders its way up a shallow stony gully to reach a flat grassy area. This is another excellent viewpoint to Sanna Bay.

Walk down the path to a gate and descend directly to the sandy beach. The path continues to the right past an obvious flat-roofed

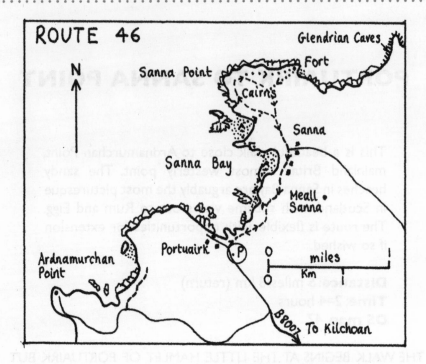

ROUTE 46

Glendrian Caves
Fort
Sanna Point
Cairns
Sanna
Sanna Bay
Meall
Sanna
Ardnamurchan
Point
Portuairk
.P
miles
Km
B8007
To Kilchoan

house: this is your return route. The sands are a delight to walk on, especially at low tide, and there are also paths through the dunes. Cross a small grassy headland and continue across another marvellous stretch of sandy beach. Either cross the Allt Sanna at its outflow or walk upstream for a few hundred metres to cross by a pedestrian footbridge just in front of a large two-storey cottage on the opposite side. The path goes round the back of the house, where, ahead, you will see several grassy knolls, each topped by a cairn. Looking south-west, you should notice Ardnamurchan Lighthouse.

Head for the highest cairn, from where there is a striking view looking back across Sanna Bay. It is worth continuing eastwards for just over half a mile to the ruined fort at Rubha an Duin Bhain, where there are extensive views beyond to the Rubha Carrach cliffs. As an optional extension for the fit and adventurous, it is possible to continue around the next rocky bay to explore the Glendrian Caves. This is rough and difficult going, however, and involves much rock scrambling on the beach. The caves are fairly shallow but are set amongst some curious rock formations.

Return to the footbridge, partly on a vague and often boggy path, and turn left along a grassy track away from the shore. This leads up to a large parking area, where you turn right at the junction to follow a good track past some white cottages.

An extremely worthwhile side excursion is to climb the conspicuous little hill behind Sanna Bay called Meall Sanna (184 m), which has extensive coarse gabbro crags and slabs, many at an easy angle, making for easy walking and scrambling. The view from the top of this fine wee hill is out of all proportion to its meagre height. Meall Sanna marks the western extremity of the Great Eucrite ring-dyke, a vast ring-shaped body of intrusive rock that formed from the repeated collapses of a 58-million-year-old volcano. Also known as the Ardnamurchan Ring, the feature is readily visible on OS map 47, where the ring of craggy hills is situated on a point roughly halfway between Achnaha and Glendrian.

The final leg back to Portuairk goes past the front of the flat-roofed house mentioned earlier to rejoin the outward route.

Recommended pub: Sonachan Hotel, Achosnich

Route 47

KENTRA BAY TO OCKLE

Although much of this walk is not coastal, it runs parallel to the coast and gives access to one of the most idyllic and sheltered beaches in Scotland. The route is a marvellous combination of secluded bays, forestry tracks and high, craggy moorland, with panoramic vistas of the surrounding islands and mountains. It is also entirely on excellent tracks and paths, which were originally an old drove-road used for taking cattle from the Small Isles to southerly markets.

Distance: 8 miles/13 km (linear)
Time: 4–5 hours
OS maps: 40 and 47

KENTRA BAY LIES A COUPLE OF MILES WEST OF ACHARACLE, ON the remote northern coast of the Ardnamurchan peninsula. From Salen, take the road to Acharacle before turning left on the B8044, then left again to the little hamlet of Arivegaig, where cars can be parked at the road-end, just before a bridge. There is a sign indicating the direction and distance to Ockle.

It should be noted that the walk is essentially one-way and therefore, ideally, a second car will be required at the end point in Ockle. Much of the route is suitable for cycling, so you may prefer to leave a bike at Ockle and cycle back by the outward route – much of which is downhill! However, cyclists should note that the return route by road is 26 miles long. There is an opportunity, discussed in the following route description, to turn the walk into a part-circular excursion by making a loop round the Acarsaid peninsula, but this involves a mile of very rough pathless walking.

At the start point, cross the bridge, where there is a warning sign about unexploded munitions. Follow the stony track as it winds its

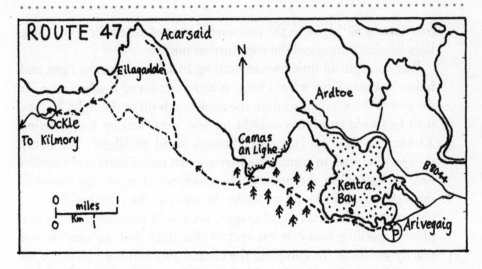

ROUTE 47

way round the gentle wooded shore of Kentra Bay for a little over a mile to the ford and bridge just before the large stone house at Gorteneorn. Cross the bridge and follow the track right before a metal gate, passing in front of the house. A short distance from here, the path leaves the shoreline and turns inland through a gate into an extensive plantation of Sitka spruce (the Gortenfern Estate forest). In recent years, the track has become very hemmed in by trees growing right at the edge of the track.

In a little over a mile into the forest, you should spot a sign to the right saying simply 'The Beach', which leads you down in a few hundred yards to an absolute hidden gem of a bay known as Camas an Lighe ('bay of the grave' or 'bed'). It is also known locally as the Singing Sands of Gortenfern and is one of those peaceful, romantic spots you will find hard to leave. The bay is a banner of beautiful white sands backed by low dunes, heather and trees and possesses a sheltered, remote character, far from the buzz of the outside world. You will be compelled to spend some time here, perhaps wandering on the extensive sands and looking out for otters, which frequent the bay.

Return to the main track and turn right, where you will soon cross a wooden bridge and leave the forest. The track then zigzags up the steep hill, the character of the walk gradually changing from trees and sheltered bays to wild, windswept moor and heath backed by vast mountain- and seascapes. At a fork in the path, go left, where there is a sign to Ockle. As you climb higher, there is a fine view looking back over Camas an Lighe to the prominent cone of Beinn Resipol, while Rois-Bheinn dominates the view further north.

Pass a delightful little lochan nestling in a hollow on the right and follow the grassy track for a long, straight section of nearly a mile. At the end of this straight section, the track bends off to the right, but the path to Ockle continues straight on and is marked by a sign saying 'Ockle, Up Brae to Left. No Through Road to Right'. For hardy walkers who wish to complete a part-circular route, there is the option here of staying on the main track, which wanders its way downhill through crags and knolls to rejoin the coast at the remote Clearance settlement of Acarsaid ('anchorage'), on a wild peninsula. There is a private dwelling-house at the end of this track and walkers are not exactly welcome! To complete the circuit, you will need to tackle an extremely rough mile of pathless terrain to reach the track end at Eilagadale, where there is another private house. From here, the Ockle track can be rejoined via an uphill track in only a quarter of a mile.

If walking directly to Ockle, simply follow the path 'Up Brae to Left' as it clings to the hillside above an obvious gorge on the right. Further on, the path deteriorates into a boggy trail but picks up again as it climbs gradually and makes a left turn round a craggy outcrop. The view north-west from here is very fine, with the Small Isles stealing the show. Eigg lies directly in front of the mountainous profile of Rum, while low-lying Muck is off to the left.

The path makes a loop round a small gorge formed by a stream before finally meeting the main grassy track connecting Ockle and Eilagadale. There is another signpost at this junction. The final mile and a half to Ockle is along an easy track contouring around the grassy hillside parallel to the coast, with glorious sea views to the Small Isles. Finally, pass a small lochan on your left before reaching the scattered settlement of Ockle and the end of the walk.

Recommended pub: Salen Hotel, Salen

THE SILVER SANDS AND MORAR

This walk has been chosen because of its glorious views out to the Small Isles and its linking together of a necklace of beautiful sandy beaches and coves. The breathtaking beach scenes of the cult film *Local Hero* were filmed here. The route is easier when the tide is far out, and there are many opportunities for exploring the countless little tidal islands and skerries.

Distance: 4 miles/6 km (linear)
Time: 2–3 hours
OS map: 40

THE OLD 'ROAD TO THE ISLES' FROM FORT WILLIAM TO MALLAIG has been vastly improved in recent years, and many of the older, winding sections of road have now been replaced by faster, more direct routes. One such older section is that linking Arisaig and Morar, a beautiful coastal route giving access to many of the beaches outlined in this walk.

The walk begins at the beach known as the Silver Sands and ends at the Morar Estuary in the north. Leave the main A830 trunk road at Arisaig and take the B8008 road leading to the beaches. After about three miles, pass a golf course and clubhouse on your right. There is a parking lay-by and toilet on the left just beyond the clubhouse. If the lay-by is full, there is another, more substantial parking area a short distance on at the north end of the bay. The bay in question is marked 'Lon Liath' on maps, *liath* meaning 'grey', but it is known locally as the Silver Sands. There may be a sign at the side of the road saying 'Traigh Beaches', which is actually the next beach north! The word *traigh* is Gaelic for 'beach', so this is a tautology.

As mentioned in the introduction to this route, the walk is much easier at low tide, as sand walking replaces rock scrambling, though some

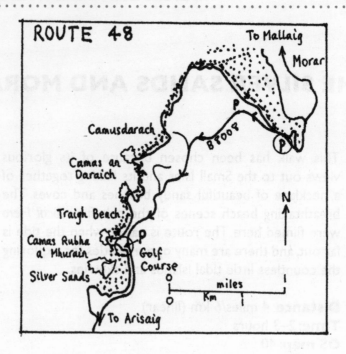

scrambling is unavoidable. Walk down onto the sands after first crossing the road bridge. The view west out to the Small Isles is immediately arresting and an iconic Scottish Highland landscape. The mountainous Isle of Rum and the lower profile of Eigg, with its distinctive Sgurr, are a magnificent backdrop to the sand, rocks and glittering sea.

At the end of the Silver Sands, cross a small grassy headland on a vague path leading round to Traigh Beach, another fine beach, which features a large white house (Traigh House). This act of walking round small headlands to fine sandy bays characterises the whole route, and if you are lucky you may find a whole beach to yourself – though don't bank on it at the height of summer!

Beyond Traigh is the idyllic little beach of Camas an Daraich, with a stone cottage overlooking the bay. Another headland is rounded to reach an old stone boathouse. A grassy path by a fence can be followed from here past another sandy cove. This leads naturally to a large bay with two obvious white houses at the opposite end. Cross a small stream and climb the rocks, following a grassy path to the next beach. This beach is backed by high dunes and is remote enough to probably have few or no people on it.

Eigg and Rum from
the Silver Sands

This point onwards until Morar Sands involves a very rough and rocky headland, and some less hardy walkers may wish to cut the route short here by heading up the road via the gap in the hills. There is a house beyond the dunes that is a useful landmark between the beach and the road.

To continue to Morar, cross a fence at the end of the beach and follow a very rough path round to some unavoidable rocky outcrops. You will pass two further tiny connected beaches and will finally reach the broad expanse of sands forming the Morar Estuary. Follow the coastline south-east, where it meets the road at a wooded area near a house. There is a good parking area just west of here, with a toilet, which would be an ideal spot for a pick-up point or at which to leave a second car. If transport has not been arranged, it is an easy 2.5-mile road walk back to the start.

EIGG: THE SOUTHERN COAST AND AN SGURR

This is a highly scenic and memorable walk including dramatic caves and an ascent of the distinctive wedge-shaped peak known as An Sgurr, which totally dominates the whole island. Visiting the caves and ascending An Sgurr can be completed as two separate expeditions if so wished.

Distance: 7 miles/11 km (circular)
Time: 5–7 hours
OS map: 39

EIGG HAS BEEN OCCUPIED SINCE PREHISTORY, AND SEVERAL ruinous forts are testament to this, namely on An Sgurr and Rubha na Crannaig at Kildonnan. St Donan, from Ireland, who was trained at Whithorn (see Route 23), founded a monastery on Eigg in the seventh century but was murdered together with most of his monks in AD 617. The island was part of the Norse empire and Viking graves were discovered in the nineteenth century. Eigg was to become the property of the Clanranald branch of the MacDonalds, Lords of the Isles, and was in all probability the site of the earliest recorded meeting of island chiefs.

In more modern times, the island has had a series of landlords, some good, some bad. In 1826, Hugh MacPherson, a professor at the University of Aberdeen, bought the island and by 1841 had boosted the population to 550; however, it declined to 300 only 40 years later. Robert Thompson, a wealthy shipbuilder, took over ownership in 1893 and made significant improvements. In the twentieth century, Eigg continued to be bought and sold by such worthies as the Runciman brothers, under whose ownership the island prospered. From the mid-1960s, however, the island's future looked decidedly

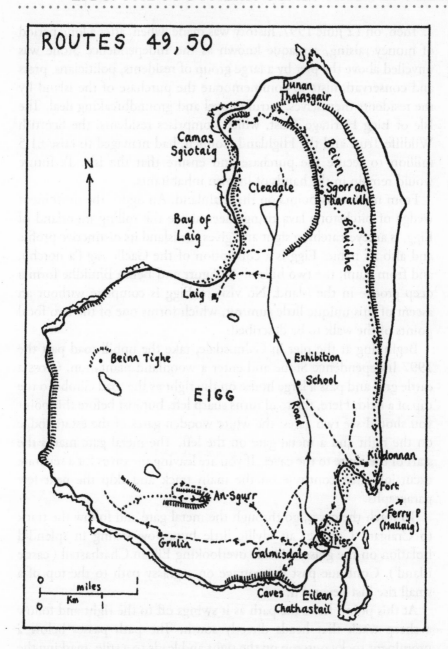

ROUTES 49, 50

N

Dunan
Thalasgair

Camas
Sgiotaig

Beinn

Cleadale

Sgorr an
Fharaidh

Bay of
Laig

Bhuidhe

Laig

Beinn Tighe

Exhibition

School

EIGG

Road

Killdonnan

Fort

An Sgurr

Ferry P
(Mallaig)

Grulin

Pier

Galmisdale

Caves

Eilean
Chathastail

miles

Km

shaky when a wave of new owners with some impractical ideas made
their mark. These included a Welsh farmer, Robert Evans; a Christian
charity; entrepreneur Keith Schellenberg; and a German artist known
as Maruma.

Then, on 12 June 1997, history was made, when, after a long period of money-raising, a plaque known as the Independence Stone was unveiled above the pier by a large group of residents, politicians, press and conservationists to commemorate the purchase of the island by the residents themselves: a truly novel and groundbreaking deal. The Isle of Eigg Heritage Trust, which comprises residents, the Scottish Wildlife Trust and the Highland Council, had managed to raise £1.5 million to secure the purchase and ensure that the island's future would remain in the hands of its own inhabitants.

From numerous points on the mainland, An Sgurr, the prominent wedge of pitchstone lava rising sheer above the rolling moorland of Eigg, is an eye-catching sight and gives the island its distinctive profile and also its name: Eigg is a corruption of the Gaelic *eag* ('a notch'), and from Rum, the two hills of An Sgurr and Beinn Bhuidhe form a deep groove in the island. No visit to Eigg is complete without an ascent of this unique little summit, which forms one of the two focal points of the walk to be described.

Beginning at the pier in Galmisdale, take the uphill road past the 1997 Independence Stone and enter a woodland plantation. Cross a cattle grid and pass a large house on the right as the road climbs to the top of a field. Here, the road turns sharp left, but just before this point you should see two gates: the white wooden gates of the estate lodge on the right and a metal gate on the left. The metal gate marks the start of the route to the caves. If you are leaving the caves for a separate excursion then continue on the main track and skip the next few paragraphs.

To reach the caves, go through the metal gate and follow the track to Craigard Cottage, an idyllic little bungalow sitting in splendid isolation on the grassy hillside overlooking Eilean Chathastail ('castle island'). Continue past the cottage on a grassy path to the top of a small rise just beyond it.

At this point, leave the path as it swings off to the right and follow a sheep track that heads directly south. The path passes below a prominent rocky outcrop on the right and leads to a stile, marking the beginning of a stepped zigzag descent of the cliffs. Near the base of the cliffs, a grassy path leads off to the right (west), leading in a few hundred yards to the first of two interesting caves. This is Cathedral Cave, a huge, deep, high-roofed cavern used for illegal religious

The Sgurr of Eigg

services after the Jacobite Rebellion in 1745, a time when Catholics were persecuted. Note that Cathedral Cave is tidal and cannot be visited at high tide (unless you plan on swimming!).

The second cave can be reached by returning along the grassy path to the burn and then descending an eastwards path to the beach. Continue for only a few yards and you should see a low entrance above a sloping grassy area. This is Massacre Cave, but it is not so easy to spot as Cathedral Cave. It is so called because almost 400 MacDonalds (all of the clan members resident on Eigg at that time) were hiding in the cave from the notorious MacLeods of Skye, who were hunting them down, bent on revenge for a pillaging-and-raping raid. Every one of the cave's inhabitants was suffocated from the smoke of brushwood, which was set alight at the entrance to the cave.

To begin the second part of the walk and the climb to An Sgurr, return to the main track beyond Craigard Cottage by the outward route. Follow the track as it winds its way up through the plantation to a gate heading into an open field. Go through the gate and follow the grassy track, where you will now have a magnificent view of the steep nose of An Sgurr rising proudly above Galmisdale House. An Sgurr is a remnant of an ancient lava-filled valley resulting from volcanic eruptions on Rum 50 million years ago. Fast cooling of the pitchstone lava produced the distinctive columnar formation, while glacial and post-glacial erosion have stripped the surrounding softer basalt to leave the hard ridge we see today.

Beyond Galmisdale House, take the track leading to the left, where you will spot some wind turbines off the path to the left. The track heads west initially, high above the shoreline, across heather moor, with fine views out to the islands of Muck, Coll, Tiree and Mull. The high Sgurr ridge is ever-present to the right, and it is worth looking out for golden eagles, which are regularly spotted soaring above the ridge. In spring and early summer, the plaintive cry of the cuckoo should be a constant companion, while kestrels, ravens and tiny wheatears should also be in evidence.

Just over a mile from Galmisdale House is the isolated whitewashed cottage of Grulin, formerly a bothy but now locked and privately owned. The main track ends here, but continue to follow the coastline on a vague footpath for around another half-mile. Remains of an old crofting township, which was cleared in 1853 to make way for sheep, are evident all along this path.

At the end of this path, or before if so wished, gradually begin to ascend the easy grassy slope to the right, avoiding any crags. An ascent of 100 m takes you to the complex, knobbly ridge of An Sgurr, dotted with several small lochans. Turn right and follow the skyline over rough ground, keeping to the crest of the ridge. There are some splendid opportunities for rock scrambling on unusual pitchstone formations, but these can be avoided if you like. Pick up a path on the crest and follow it to the triangulation pillar at the summit of this amazing little hill.

In clear weather, the view from here is absolutely breathtaking, with the rugged backdrop of the Rum Cuillin dominating the outlook to the north, while the surrounding panorama of smaller islands, together with Ardnamurchan and Skye, all contribute to the wild scene. It will be difficult to tear yourself away from this airy vantage point!

The return route to Galmisdale is the normal ascent route of the hill, which has a path. Reaching it involves backtracking along the ridge for about a quarter of a mile, then descending to the right by a small cairn. This is on a reasonably clear path, which then follows the base of the northern escarpment and the nose before crossing open moorland to Galmisdale House and the outward track.

Getting to Eigg

A CalMac passenger ferry (cars cannot be brought to the island) runs from Mallaig to Galmisdale most days, but crossing duration and times on the island vary according to the day of travel. For more information, contact:

Tel: 01687 462403

Web: www.calmac.co.uk

Email: enquiries@calmac.co.uk

Arisaig Marine run trips to Eigg from May to September on most days.

Tel: 01687 450224

Web: www.arisaig.co.uk

It should be noted that comfortably completing both Routes 49 and 50 will probably necessitate staying overnight on the island. Accommodation ranges from camping with limited facilities through to bothies, self-catering cottages, B&Bs and guest houses. There is a licensed tea room, restaurant and pub (An Laimhrig) at the pier in Galmisdale, which is the island's hub. An Laimhrig also houses the shop and post office, as well as a craft shop, toilets and showers. There is no hotel on the island. For further details on accommodation, see the island's website.

Web: www.isleofeigg.net

Route 50

EIGG: THE NORTHERN CIRCUIT

This is a varied and challenging excursion offering a wealth of coastal and hill delights, from wild, remote beaches to stunning clifftop walking. The view across to Rum from beautiful Bay of Laig is one of the truly classic seascapes in Scotland and just one of many superb vantage points on this impressive walk. Shorter options are possible.

Distance: 12 miles/19 km (circular)
Time: 6–8 hours
OS map: 39

THIS FINE WALK CROSSES OVER TO THE WEST SIDE OF EIGG AT the Bay of Laig and Cleadale, visiting the famous Singing Sands. Grand clifftop walking on the hill mass of Beinn Bhuidhe follows before the route crosses back to the east side of the island to descend to Kildonnan and finally returns along the coast to Galmisdale.

For those walkers who are pressed for time, it is possible to use the minibus or taxi services available at the pier. This would cut out the first 3.5 miles of road walking required to reach the Bay of Laig. To walk to this point, simply follow the only road as it winds its way round Galmisdale Bay before striking north across the low neck of the island. Pass the primary school on the right and the old post office, which now houses an interesting exhibition, much of it accomplished by the children of the school.

Descend the hill at Bealach Clithe, passing several crofts, and take the first track on the left, which leads in half a mile to the Bay of Laig. Laig is pronounced 'Laag' and derives from an Old Norse word meaning 'surf bay'. The view of Rum's mountainous profile beyond a blue sea and golden sands is simply spectacular, and on a sunny day this is a truly magical spot. If you are lucky, you may spot red-throated divers offshore, and otters can sometimes be found at the north end of the bay.

To walk north along the bay, cross the outflow of a stream and follow the sandy shore to the end of another track. This marks the beginning of a low line of cliffs leading in a mile to Camas Sgiotaig, or 'Singing Sands Bay'. Follow the rim of low sandstone cliffs, passing some remarkable rock formations formed from dolerite dykes. If the tide is low, it is possible to walk on this rocky pavement, though the going can be quite rough and slippery. As you approach the next bay, pick up a path by a fence along the top of the higher cliffs and follow it down to the bay. To the left are some interesting rock formations, consisting of a natural arch and a deep canyon, which can be explored. The Singing Sands of the bay are so called because if you scuff your heels along the dry sands they emit a singing sound, which is admittedly more of a bit of a squeak.

This point in the walk marks the start of the high-level return to Galmisdale via the tops of the terraced line of inland cliffs overlooking Cleadale. To complete a shorter walk, however, return to the clifftop via the same path you used to reach the bay and aim for the road-end at Cleadale (GR 476892) by crossing fields. The road can then be followed back to Galmisdale.

To continue with the main walk, climb onto an obvious grassy spur at the end of the bay and reach a grassy path that zigzags up to the prominent sharp nose of Dunan Thalasgair. This path is not marked on the 1:50,000 Landranger map. Near the top, cross a fence and climb the remaining steep slope to the airy vantage point. To the north, the cliffs drop down sheerly to rock-strewn grassy slopes, finishing at the wild north coast of Eigg. On a clear day, Skye is plainly visible in the distance, and Rum continues to dominate the view west. Follow the cliff edge south for several hundred yards to reach the triangulation point.

The highest point of this high, heathery moorland plateau is a mile south at Sgorr an Fharaidh (340 m), which can be reached by delightful clifftop walking along vague sheep tracks. Enjoy marvellous views westwards down to the scattered crofts of Cleadale and out to Rum's ever-present profile. From the high point, take a roughly south-easterly line across the moorland to reach the top of the eastern line of cliffs, which you should then follow southwards for around two miles to the scattered community of Kildonnan. A fence runs along the cliff edge, and as you approach Kildonnan the cliffs decrease in height and become gradually closer to the sea.

Just beyond Kildonnan House, there are some remains of an Iron Age fort sitting on a small grassy promontory overlooking Kildonnan Bay. A hollow surrounded by stones is all that remains of this ancient structure, which was once occupied by St Donan, who brought Christianity to Eigg. Turn north to follow the coastline in front of Kildonnan House. Near the head of the bay, a track can be followed northwards for about a quarter of a mile to a ruined church and graveyard.

Depending on the state of the tide, the bay (Poll nam Partan) can be crossed directly on sand and mudflats, but the best option is to gain a pleasant clifftop path on its west side. This path begins at the head of the bay where there is an old cornmill (now occupied). Go through a gate and join the path as it climbs up and along the top of the low cliff. Look out for eider ducks and sandpipers in the bay as well as common seals. Cross a stile and head gradually round to Galmisdale Bay, where you will need to cross a small stream before following a good track round by the old pier. This leads to the road and Galmisdale.

RUM: THE SOUTHERN CIRCUIT

This is one of the roughest, wildest, longest and most ambitious walks described in this book. Walking on the mountainous island of Rum is seldom anything other than rough or wet, often both together, and there should be no doubt that this is a route only for hardy, fit walkers with full mountain gear and focussed commitment. A shorter circuit is possible but involves more climbing.

Distance: 18 miles/29 km (circular)
Time: 9–12 hours
OS map: 39

RUM HAS BEEN OCCUPIED SINCE PREHISTORIC TIMES AND WAS in fact one of the earliest sites of human settlement in Scotland. The island later came under Viking rule, and most of the mountain names are of Norse origin. By the thirteenth century, Rum was back in Scottish hands and for a long while was owned by the Macleans of Coll.

In 1826, much of its population of around 400 people was persuaded to emigrate to Canada and the USA, leaving only about 40 inhabitants. The island was then used as a sheep farm, with the population stabilising to around 90 souls.

In the late 1800s, Rum was bought by Lancastrian MP John Bullough, whose wealthy and eccentric son George built the extravagant Kinloch Castle, a monument to the lavish Edwardian upper-class lifestyle of the time but which was out of place on Rum. George Bullough spared no expense on the castle, importing sandstone from Arran and paying the workmen extra to wear kilts. Live turtles and alligators were kept in heated tanks, and a minstrel's gallery, baronial hall, billiard room with air conditioning (for the cigar smoke)

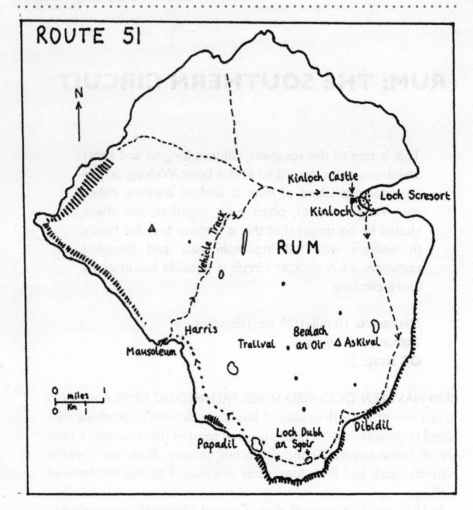

ROUTE 51

RUM

Kinloch Castle
Loch Scresort
Kinloch
Vehicle Track
Harris
Bealach
an Oir
Trallval
Askival
Mausoleum
Dibidil
Papadil
Loch Dubh
an Sgoir

N

miles
Km

and a Victorian jacuzzi bath were just some of the added extras contributing to the opulence. Today, the castle is open for tours and hostel accommodation is available (see the 'Getting to Rum' panel).

In 1957, Rum was bought by the Nature Conservancy Council and is now managed by Scottish Natural Heritage as a National Nature Reserve. The island is home to a large herd of red deer, and sea eagles have recently been reintroduced. The population is currently around 25 people. No cars are allowed onto the island.

Rum is the largest and most mountainous of the Small Isles of Eigg, Rum, Muck and Canna and has always possessed an air of mystery and uniqueness. Its classic range of mountains, known as the Rum Cuillin, are the main draw for hillwalkers and climbers, but its wild and dramatic coastline should also feature on any serious walker's list of priorities. The walk to be described is essentially a complete circuit of the Rum Cuillin and is an ideal challenge to be undertaken when the high tops are lost in thick mist – a common occurrence!

The walk encompasses roughly the southern half of Rum's complete coastline, and the obvious extension to include the northern half would involve a two-day expedition with full backpacking gear. It should be noted that there are two open bothies on the island, at Dibidil and Guirdil, but permission is required before using them (see the 'Getting to Rum' panel for further information on accommodation).

The walk begins at Kinloch, at the head of Loch Scresort, the ferry point and the centre of accommodation on the island. Head south along the main track from Kinloch Castle, and once past the reserve office look out for the signposted right turn that marks the route to Dibidil. This narrow stony path rises gradually to a height of 200 m on a broad, heathery shoulder with fine views of the jostling peaks of the mainland. Much new planting by Scottish Natural Heritage is taking place around this area and you should spot alder, rowan and silver birch as well as Scots pine.

Dibidil bothy, Rum

Go through a gate in the deer fence and cross the Allt Mor na h-Uamha ('big stream of the cave') burn below its waterfalls before contouring and descending slightly to cross the Allt na h-Uamha with its single waterfall. From here, the path contours round the rough hillside, well above the sea cliffs, but the going can become quite boggy at times. After heavy rain, the hillside becomes a seething mass of wild, white rivulets of streams and secondary streams, and the path can become a quagmire.

The path begins to descend beyond the Lochan Dubh and gradually approaches the coastline as it skirts around the shoulder of Beinn nan Stac. On a wild day, the booming and crashing of the waves onto the cliffs will assault the senses and there is a real feeling of entering an otherworldly wilderness. On a fine day, take some time to explore the coastline at closer quarters, as there are some fine little rocky promontories and sea stacks.

Beyond the sea cliffs, the path turns inland, descending to the foot of Glen Dibidil, where you should be able to spot the bothy nestling under the gaunt crags of Sgurr nan Gillean. Glen Dibidil, hemmed in on three sides by peaks and open to the churning Sound of Rum and the isles of Eigg and Muck on the south-east, has an elemental grandeur that has even been likened to Glen Coe.

Dibidil is a crucial point in the walk, as it is the only place where a relatively quick alternative route return can be made to Kinloch, via the Bealach an Oir and Bealach Bairc-mheall. However, if a decision is made to return from here then you may opt to just reverse the outward route. The climb up Glen Dibidil to the Bealach an Oir, at 450 m, follows a vague path and there is also a sketchy path contouring round the huge, boulder-strewn Atlantic Corrie.

To continue the coastal walk, regain the path a few hundred metres above the bothy and follow it around the southern flank of Sgurr nam Gillean, where it descends gradually to Loch Dubh an Sgoir. From here, the path becomes increasingly sketchy and boggy as it descends to Loch Papadil in another mile. Papadil ('valley of the hermit') is another lonely but attractive corner of Rum, where a lodge was once built by Sir George Bullough (who also built Kinloch Castle) but which was allowed to fall into ruin, as his wife hated it!

As the path approaches Loch Papadil, it makes a right turn to head for the now overgrown lodge, but it is easier to turn left round the

The Bullough Mausoleum, Rum

southern end of the loch to explore the unusual rock formations on the coast just beyond. From here to Harris Bay involves over three miles of wild, pathless coastal walking, and the route has a real exploratory feel. Reach the little rocky cove of Inbhir Ghil via a series of grassy hummocks. At this point, it is easier to climb the hillside for about 150 m and then contour round Ruinsival's southern flank. Keeping too low down involves unavoidable ascent and descent to negotiate gullies and rock outcrops.

After about 1.5 miles, the steep terrain gives way to flatter, more open grass as you approach the wide head of Glen Harris. In wet conditions, the Abhainn Rangail may well be in spate, and the best option for crossing might be to descend to its outflow into the sea, where it is much shallower. One other river must be crossed before you finally reach the somewhat incongruous Bullough family mausoleum standing on a raised beach, perhaps the oddest monument to be found on any Scottish island. Built in the style of a Greek temple, it occupies a lonely position in this equally lonely and remote part of Rum.

The coastal walking is now over, but it is still a long seven-mile trudge back to Kinloch, thankfully on a reasonable Land Rover track that meanders its way between the Rum Cuillin and the western hills before turning east down Glen Kinloch. This completes a long and memorable excursion.

Getting to Rum

CalMac run a passenger ferry from Mallaig on Monday, Wednesday, Friday and Saturday during summer and Monday, Tuesday and Thursday during winter. Note that cars cannot be taken onto the island.

    Tel: 01687 462403

    Web: www.calmac.co.uk

    Email: enquiries@calmac.co.uk

Bruce Watt Sea Cruises also run a ferry from Mallaig.

    Tel: 01687 462320

    Web: www.knoydart-ferry.co.uk

Seabridge Knoydart run another ferry service to the island from Mallaig.

    Tel: 01687 462916

    Web: www.knoydartferry.com

Hostel accommodation and meals are available at Kinloch Castle.

    Tel: 01687 462037

    Web: www.isleofrum.com/kinlochcastle-bu.html

ISLE OF CANNA CIRCUIT

The full 12-mile circumnavigation of the peaceful and idyllic Small Isles gem that is Canna is a whole day's hike taking in fine clifftop situations, a unique castle, ancient souterrains and an opportunity to observe at close quarters much bird-life. Canna is one of the best places in Scotland to see birds of prey, especially the white-tailed eagle, which nests on the remote cliffs in the north and west of the island. This is a tough but memorable walk for hardy walkers only.

Distance: 12 miles/19 km (circular)
Time: 8–10 hours
OS map: 39

The wind that comes from Canna
I feel it warm;
I like to be looking in your direction;
Short is the time until I'll be coming back to you.

From a Gaelic song collected by
D.C. MacPherson in the 1860s

CANNA, THE MOST WESTERLY OF THE SMALL ISLES, IS A STEEP-sided island made of distinctive terraced Tertiary basalt, which makes for ideal clifftop walking and easily provides the best coastal circuit of the Small Isles when compared with Rum, Eigg or Muck. It is linked by a bridge to the Isle of Sanday, which itself offers a pleasant circumnavigation.

Canna is rich in archaeological interest, and remains can be found from all periods of settled occupation in Scotland. Around 1,500 years ago, the island was a significant monastic site, and the remains of an

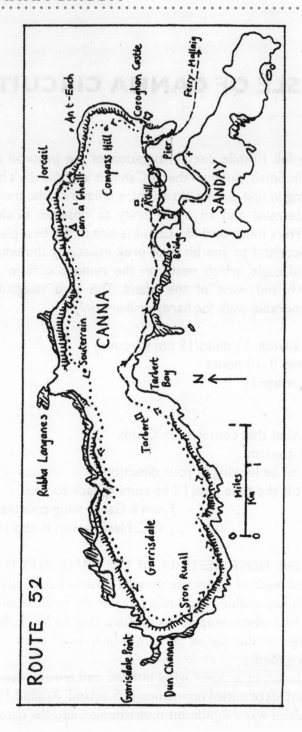

ROUTE 52

Labels on map:
- Ferry–Mallaig
- Coroghon Castle
- An t-Each
- Compass Hill
- Pier
- Ruail
- SANDAY
- Iorcail
- Carn a'Ghaill
- Bridge
- Souterrain
- CANNA
- Tarbert Bay
- Tarbert
- Rubha Langanes
- N
- Garrisdale
- Sron Ruail
- Garrisdale Point
- Dun Channa
- miles
- Km

Early Christian stone cross can be seen in the field behind the main farm buildings at A' Chill. The MacDonalds of Clanranald owned the island for many centuries, and there was a thriving population of over 400 until the Clearances of the nineteenth century depleted numbers drastically.

In 1938, the island was bought by Gaelic scholar John Lorne Campbell, who insisted he was not a laird but an owner-occupier farmer. His conscientious and pioneering work in the recording, collecting and analysis of Gaelic history, stories and songs has resulted in an unsurpassed archive of Gaelic material. In 1981, he gave Canna to the National Trust for Scotland, which continues to manage the island in the way he wished: as a modern, dynamic crofting community where the islanders play a major part in running their own affairs.

Canna is part of the European Union's network of Important Bird Areas, but recently the rapidly increasing rat population resulted in high levels of predation on eggs and small chicks, especially of birds such as the Manx shearwater. A subsequent rat-eradication scheme, in which over 4,000 bait stations were placed throughout the entire island, resulted in full eradication by 2007, but it is essential that rats do not return.

If you are resident on Canna for a few days, you may find it preferable to split the full circumnavigation into two or more days. The island has a natural narrow neck at Tarbert that forms an east–west break, and there is a good Land Rover track from A' Chill (your most likely base, because this is where most of the island's accommodation is located) to Tarbert.

The described route is an anticlockwise circuit, but a clockwise walk would be no less enjoyable. Walking east from A' Chill, the first main point of interest is An Coroghan, a grim ruined prison tower perched on top of an isolated sea stack where a Clanranald chief allegedly imprisoned his wife for the sin of adultery with her lover, a Skye MacLeod.

Sea eagle

North of here, grassy slopes lead up to

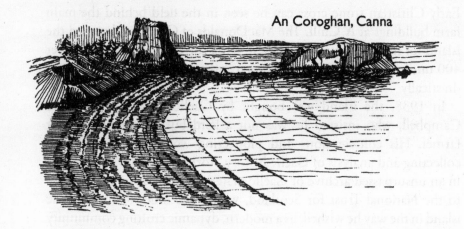

An Coroghan, Canna

Compass Hill, so called because of magnetic rock making a compass unreliable. From Compass Hill to the remote western end of the island at Dun Channa lie five miles of superb clifftop walking, wild and uncompromising and providing the ideal opportunity to spot sea eagles at close quarters. The going is fairly easy, on traces of sheep tracks, and an old dry-stone wall follows the edge of the cliff. Pass two inaccessible sea stacks, An t-Each and Iorcail, and pay an optional visit to the island's highest point of 210 m, at Carn a' Ghaill ('rocky hill of the storm'), where there is a triangulation pillar. Continue delightfully along the top of the cliffs until the descent to a grassy area south of the small promontory of Rubha Langanes. At this point, it is worth hunting out the souterrains, a pair of 2,000-year-old underground chambers located at GR 24440625, on a low rise at the edge of an enclosed field. It is a mystery as to what they were used for, but several ideas, such as storage, a place of safety or use for rituals, are all possibilities.

Evidence of Viking occupation can be seen at Rubha Langanes, where one of the finest examples of a ship burial was uncovered at the King of Norway's grave (GR 241065). West of here lies the high ground of Garrisdale, and excellent clifftop walking leads in 2.5 miles to the western extremity of Garrisdale Point and Dun Channa, the highlight of the walk in terms of quality cliff and wild coastal scenery. The ruined fort of Dun Channa lies south of Garrisdale Point and both can be reached by a steep descent at a break in the cliffs, but it should be remembered that there is still a long way to go to complete the coastal circuit. The triangulation point at Sron Ruail is a fine vantage point and offers grand views of the neighbouring islands of Rum and Skye.

The five-mile return stretch follows the clifftop for two miles before dropping gradually to the moor and the grassy area around Tarbert, where cattle often graze. From here, pick up a rough Land Rover track that winds its way pleasantly back to the starting point in just over a couple of miles.

Getting to Canna

Canna is accessible all year round by CalMac passenger ferry from Mallaig. It runs on Monday, Wednesday, Friday and Saturday in summer (late March to late October) and on Tuesday, Thursday and Saturday in winter (late October to late March).

> Tel: 01687 462403
> Web: www.calmac.co.uk
> Email: enquiries@calmac.co.uk

Accommodation on Canna is limited, but the National Trust, which owns the island, rents out a pleasant cottage (The Bothy). Contact NTS Customer Services for enquiries.

> Tel: 0844 493 2108
> Web: www.ntsholidays.com

Camping is allowed with permission. Contact the NTS warden for further information.

> Tel: 01687 462466

For general information on the island, contact the National Trust for Scotland, Balnain House, 40 Huntly Street, Inverness.

> Tel: 01463 232034

KINLOCH HOURN
TO BARRISDALE

Quite simply, this is one of the finest coastal walks in the Western Highlands. The route is one of only two footpaths leading into the wild and mountainous Knoydart peninsula. It hugs the southern shore of Loch Hourn, often described as the grandest of all the Scottish sea lochs and the nearest Scotland has to a genuine Norwegian fjord. Because the path runs along the foot of north-facing slopes, note that it is better to attempt this walk in the height of summer, as no sun shines on this coastline for five months of the winter.

Distance: 6 miles/10 km (linear) or 12 miles/19 km (return)
Time: 2–3 hours
OS map: 33

KNOYDART IS A RUGGED MOUNTAINOUS REGION BOUNDED on three sides by the sea and on the fourth by a complex jumble of wild mountains. It is only accessible either by boat from Mallaig to the tiny settlement of Inverie or via two long but scenic footpaths. For walkers and mountain climbers, it is a highly prized destination, and due to its remoteness, it often has the feel of being a separate island. Knoydart literally lies between heaven and hell, as its southern boundary of Loch Nevis translates as 'loch of heaven' and its northern boundary of Loch Hourn derives from the Gaelic *lutharn*, meaning 'hell'.

The road-head at Kinloch Hourn is the closest point to Knoydart reachable by car, but even getting here involves a formidable drive on a narrow, switchback, single-track road – be warned! For those walkers who wish to return to their car on the same day, the only option

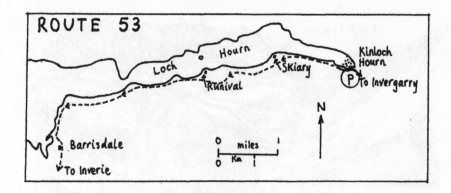

available is to reverse the route and walk back by the same path. This option involves a round trip of 12 miles. Many folk who walk this route are backpackers and are heading into the bothy at Barrisdale, which involves a six-mile-long route, or to the small hamlet of Inverie, which requires yet another ten miles of rough hiking over the high pass of Mam Barrisdale. The full sixteen-mile walk from Kinloch Hourn to Inverie is one of the finest long-distance treks in Scotland and is well worth considering if you have the time. Note that Inverie has accommodation, camping facilities and the Old Forge, the remotest pub in Britain!

There is a parking area some distance back from the road-end at Kinloch Hourn, and this marks the beginning of the walk. Immediately there is a feeling of being hemmed in by high mountains, and the 'loch of hell' inspired the author and naturalist Seton Gordon, in *Highways and Byways in the West Highlands* (1935), to describe it as 'a lake of the infernal regions. Above it rose vast hills, grim, ghostly and nebulous through banks of fog and soft stealing rain showers. Never in Scotland have I seen hills giving the impression of such vast size . . .' Despite these musings, however, the hills above Loch Hourn only reach Munro height beyond Barrisdale in the shape of the stunning Ladhar Bheinn, the most westerly mainland Munro and one of the grandest in Scotland.

Initially, the rocky path clings to the shoreline, and at one point the loch narrows to such an extent that it seems only a stone's throw to the north side. Gradually the loch widens again, leaving inner Loch Beag (a small, sheltered section of Loch Hourn), where the path turns westwards to a flat green area containing the house known as Skiary.

Loch Hourn

This has fairly recently been converted into a very fine guest house and is recommended, provided you are prepared to carry your belongings for 20 minutes along the coastal path! Skiary may be able to provide a boat, however. At this point, providing the weather is clear, there is a dramatic view of Ladhar Bheinn, its rocky ramparts thrusting skywards beyond a craggy bluff.

Beyond Skiary, the path climbs steadily to nearly 100 m above the loch before descending to cross some streams. Another climb follows to a small *bealach* where you pass remnants of native Scots pine trees, a refreshing and pastoral sight in this wild corner. A steep descent takes you down to the tiny settlement of Runival, nestling serenely on a lush green patch below the steep hillside. Skiary, Runival and Barrisdale were just a few of the long list of settlements cruelly cleared by Josephine MacDonnell in 1853 in what has been described as one of the most fearful and foul acts in the history of the Clearances. Her henchmen evicted 400 people using the most barbaric methods: their homes were burned, and the people themselves were herded and hounded like animals onto transport ships. Sixteen families refused to comply and sought refuge in the hills. The following lines, penned by an unknown evictee, capture the feeling perfectly:

No Cailleach's scream, no bodach's dream, can
overcome the fate,
To live the life, to know the strife, of destitutes of hate,
As I gaze o'er that lonely shore, my heart breaks and I
weep,
Those noble people, so proud, so simple, being cleared
away, for sheep.

As you pass these small settlements and ruined sheilings, the ghosts of past tenants seem to be all around you, and although you appear to be in the heart of an unpopulated wilderness, it is sobering to think that this land supported hundreds of people not that long ago.

After Runival, the path meanders pleasantly for a mile, staying close to the edge of the loch. Look out for otters, which are prevalent along the whole stretch of Loch Hourn. The loch narrows significantly again at Caolas Mor, where the path rounds a small headland. After crossing a couple of streams, it climbs up the hillside, well away from the loch edge, to arrive at a ruin near the beginning of a wider vehicle track.

Here, the character of the walk changes significantly. You are now in Barrisdale Bay, an oasis of flatness and tranquillity amid the rugged mountains, with mighty Ladhar Bheinn now dominating the view to the south-west. Continue south along the vehicle track for a mile to reach the end point of the walk at Barrisdale, the family home of the Knoydart MacDonnells.

Nearby is a small bothy with its own electric generator, a suitable place to shelter should normal Highland weather have returned. If returning to your car then this is the halfway point; if continuing to Inverie then you will still have a ten-mile tramp!

Recommended pub: The Tomdoun Hotel, Invergarry

Route 54

SKYE: BORERAIG AND SUISNISH

A hauntingly beautiful circular coastal walk dominated by the poignant Clearance settlements of Boreraig and Suisnish. This is a route with much potential for exploration and is one of the finest low-level walks on Skye.

Distance: 11 miles/18 km (circular)
Time: 6–8 hours
OS map: 32

THE START OF THE WALK IS AT THE OLD GRAVEYARD OF CILL Chriosd ('Christ's church'), just over two miles from Broadford along the Elgol road (B8083), where there is a small parking area.

Walk back along the road towards Broadford for a few hundred metres and turn right along a track, which ascends slightly to meet another track. Go right again, and follow this track as it gently ascends the lower slopes of Ben Suardal in a southerly direction. Part of this route follows the course of an old narrow-gauge railway that connected with Broadford and was used to transport marble from a former quarry, which can be seen a short distance ahead.

Continue to follow the path as it ascends into rougher moorland, reaching a high point near Loch Lonachan at the head of Glen Suardal. This is a beautifully remote and wild spot, and you should look out for red-throated divers, which sometimes visit the loch.

The path gradually begins to descend into a gorge following the right bank of the Allt na Pairte. Just above some waterfalls, you will pass an extensive area of trees nestling in a hollow, marking the Allt na Pairte cave on the opposite side of the stream. The adventurous walker may wish to cross the stream and explore the cave.

Follow the path as it meanders its way down steeper ground to eventually emerge on the coast at Boreraig. Immediately, you are

The Chain Walk (route 4)

Cellardyke Harbour, Anstruther (route 6)

North of Saligo Bay, Islay (route 34)

Sanna Bay, Ardnamurchan (route 46)

Isle of Rum from Eigg (route 50)

Cliff-top walking, south of Loch Eynort, Skye (route 57)

Rubha Hunish, Skye's northern tip (route 64)

The Postie's route, Coigach (route 71)

Looking north from Sandwood Bay (routes 75 and 76)

Boreray and the Stacks from Hirta, St Kilda (route 83) (photo by Ken Black)

Scarasta Beach from Chaipaval, Harris (route 84)

Bay of Skaill, Orkney mainland (route 91)

The Old Man of Hoy, Orkney (route 90)

Noup Head, Isle of Noss, Shetland (route 97)

The author at Hermaness, Unst, Shetland –
the most northerly point in the UK (route 100)

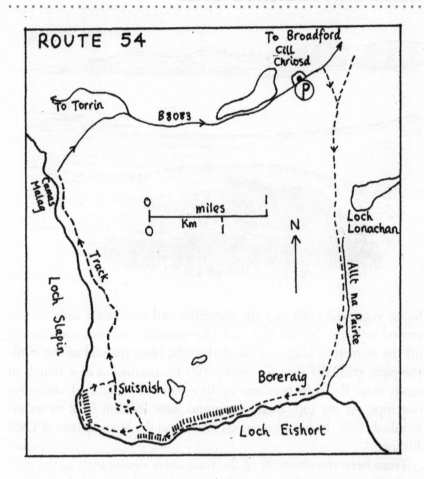

confronted by the sad remains of a once-thriving settlement. Crumbling, crooked lines of dry-stone dykes link dozens of long-since deserted houses, now reduced to ruins. Of all the Skye Clearances, those of Boreraig and nearby Suisnish are particularly remembered as being the most brutal and callous. In 1854, Lord MacDonald, the landowner, ordered the residents of Boreraig and Suisnish to be removed in order to provide grazing for sheep. As the innocent crofters would not leave voluntarily, they were ruthlessly driven out by a body of constables and their houses were torched. Wander through the peaceful green sheep-shorn meadow with its tell-tale runrig folds and black house ruins (a type of turf house once commonly found in the Highlands and islands).

As you leave Boreraig, the path is completely hemmed in between

A ruin at Boreraig

loose, vegetated cliffs and the shoreline and provides a mile of fine coastal walking. Several lacy, veil-like waterfalls bounce and cascade off the numerous ledges of the dark cliffs. Near the end of the cliffs, the path gradually rises for nearly 100 m, narrowing to a trench of sandy clay. The cliffs here rear up in a series of sculptured sandstone outcrops. At the top, there is a grand view looking back to water-streaked cliffs, the boulder-strewn beach and the blue expanse of Loch Eishort.

From here, the character of the walk alters significantly as the path gradually turns north, leaving the immediate vicinity of the coast to reach Suisnish. An excellent diversion can be made at this point by staying with the coast and continuing west to Rubha Suisnish. A rocky pavement leads below the cliffs, past Calaman Cave, to the twin rocky tops of Stac Suisnish. Note that this option is only available at low tide.

At Suisnish, pick up a track built by the Board of Agriculture in the early twentieth century when Suisnish had been briefly recrofted. This track meanders its way northwards high above Loch Slapin, where the views are dominated by the mighty ramparts of Blaven and the scree-covered red hills, forming a magnificent backdrop to a peaceful scene.

An alternative, more ancient and indistinct path runs north-east through the hills from Suisnish, reaching the road about half a mile south-west of the starting point, but is not marked on the OS Landranger map and is quite difficult to follow.

The track from Suisnish reaches the bay at Camas Malag in 2.5 miles, and a minor road can be followed to the B8083 just east of Torrin. From here, it is less than two miles to the start point of Cill Chriosd.

Recommended pub: The Broadford Hotel, Broadford

Route 55

SKYE: ELGOL TO LOCH CORUISK

For quality of scenery and situation, this route has no equal, and it is arguably one of the finest coastal walks in Scotland – if not Britain. It is a rough and varied walk offering incomparable views of the finest mountain range in Britain – the Cuillin ridge – but is only suitable for highly competent and confident walkers who have the scrambling skills necessary to negotiate the notorious Bad Step.

Distance: 7 miles/11 km (linear)
Time: 4–6 hours
OS map: 32

THE VIEW OF THE CUILLIN FROM THE LITTLE COASTAL HAMLET of Elgol has been described by some, including Alfred Wainwright, as the best view in Britain. On a spring day of sunshine with a dusting of snow on the sawtooth of the ridge and a sparkling-blue Loch Scavaig, it would be hard to disagree.

In the spring and summer months, regular boat trips depart from Elgol to Loch Coruisk, and with some pre-planning it would be possible to complete the walk without the necessity of a walking return trip. Alternatively, a boat trip could be taken early in the day and the route described accomplished in reverse, from Coruisk back to Elgol. Other return options are offered in the route description that follows.

At Elgol, take a track leading off to the right before the main road descends steeply to the jetty. This leads on to an easy grassy track that contours its way along the steep western slope of Ben Cleat. After a mile or so, the path descends to sea level at Cladach a' Ghlinne, meaning 'pretty stony beach'. It is pretty stony too! This is an ideal spot for a break.

Beyond the beach, the path climbs steeply and continues to contour

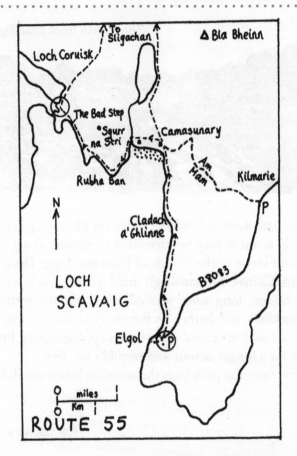

To Sligachan
△ Bla Bheinn
Loch Coruisk
The Bad Step
Sgurr na Stri
Camasunary
Am Mam
Kilmarie
Rubha Ban
P
Cladach a'Ghlinne
B8083
LOCH SCAVAIG
Elgol
P
N
miles
Km

ROUTE 55

along the steep, vegetated flank of Beinn Leacach. Here, the path has worn into a deep trench in places and you will soon become surrounded by a tangled mass of stunted trees and bushes, which obscure the awesome drops to the left. At one point, the path literally ends at a sheer drop, and at the time of writing this 'dead-end' had been marked by brightly coloured tape stretched across the path. Watch your step here, in case the tape is no longer present as a warning. Ascending to the right leads to the path's true continuation.

The next mile to Camasunary is delightful walking: the soaring south ridge of Bla Bheinn (or Blaven) to the right dominates the scene, while to the left of the bay the gabbro ramparts of Sgurr na Stri ('peak of strife') form an effective barrier between Camasunary and Loch Coruisk. Camasunary means 'bay of the white sheiling', but there are actually two white houses at the bay: one a private lodge and the other

The Cuillin from near Elgol

a bothy. The path runs behind the lodge on pleasant green *machair*, but if the tide is out it may be preferable to wander along the beach, enjoying grand views to the islands of Rum and Eigg. The crossing of the Abhainn Camas Fhionnairigh used to be made via a small suspension bridge, long since washed away, but the stumps of the support stanchions still betray its former position. At low tide, the river can be crossed at several points on stepping-stones, but at high tide prepare for a longer detour and possibly wet feet!

Beyond the river, the path hugs the coastline below the slabby slopes

Camasunary

Camasunary

of Sgurr na Stri and the going becomes increasingly rough on rock steps and bog. Once round the headland of Rubha Ban, you feel you are entering into a true wilderness. The stark and sombre peaks of the Cuillin totally dominate the scene. At the next headland, the path cuts directly through a gap away from the coastline. On reaching the coastline once again, the path climbs to cross huge boilerplate slabs before dropping down to the fabled Bad Step. Scramble over large blocks and then move round to the left to negotiate a corner before emerging on a sloping crack cum shelf. Carefully side step along this shelf until another one appears about halfway, going horizontally to easier ground. Do not be tempted to remain on the original shelf, as this leads to steep terrain.

Once beyond the Bad Step, Loch Coruisk is only about half a mile distant, but much clambering on rock is still required to reach it. The loch itself is the jewel set in the Cuillin crown: wild, untamed and atmospheric, and possibly more so when the Cuillin are shrouded in their usual mantle of cloud. Savour and enjoy what is undoubtedly one of the wildest spots in Great Britain.

If you are not returning to Elgol by boat, it is a long way back, but the route can be varied by following the Land Rover track from Camasunary up and over the hillside via the Am Mam. This leads in 2.5 miles to the B8083 Elgol road, with a final three-mile road walk to Elgol.

Recommended pub: The Broadford Hotel, Broadford

Route 56

SKYE: RUBH' AN DUNAIN

This is an easy and popular walk on a good track and path leading out to Rubh' an Dunain, the 'headland of the little fort', a veritable goldmine of historical ruins occupying a wild and lonely spot in the shadow of the Cuillin. The walk is ideal for children.

Distance: 8 miles/13 km (return)
Time: 4–5 hours
OS map: 32

THE WALK OUT TO THE LOW-LYING BUT EXPOSED promontory of Rubh' an Dunain from Glenbrittle campsite has often been regarded as a mere stroll, useful for whiling away a day off. Sitting as it does under the towering drama of the south Cuillin ridge, Rubh' an Dunain is upstaged somewhat, but leaving it for a wet day does not do justice to this fascinating corner of Skye, not least for the glorious view out to Rum and Eigg.

From the campsite at Glenbrittle, follow the path uphill from the toilet block to reach a wide farm track that heads south, following the coast well above the shoreline. It should be noted at this point that there is also a parallel path running close to the shoreline, but this fades out after about a mile. You may wish to return by this path to vary the route.

The track fords several streams, and one in particular, the Allt Coire Lagan, may be problematical to cross in spate conditions. In this case, descend slightly to a footbridge, which marks the end of the parallel shoreline path.

Continue along the track for a short distance until it diminishes to a narrow footpath at another stream crossing. This leads in another mile to the prominent little hillock of Creag Mhor, whose basalt crags provide sport for rock climbers when the Cuillin are out of bounds.

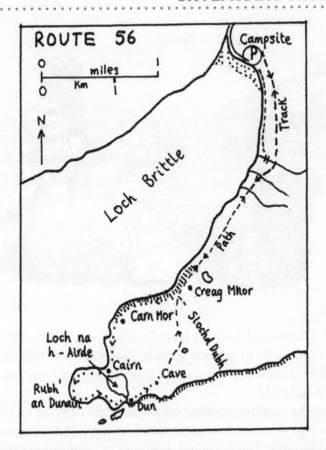

Just beyond Creag Mhor, the main path heads directly south, while a second path follows the natural sunken depression known as Slochd Dudh ('black pit'), which cuts across the headland and is marked by a dry-stone wall. Ignore both of these options and continue to follow the coast round the north flank of Carn Mor on a vague path. This leads naturally to Loch na h-Airde, which marks the start of the true headland and its associated history. Almost immediately you will spot the remains of a chambered cairn, the central chamber now being roofless but the entrance passageway still intact. When the chamber was excavated in the early 1930s, it yielded the remains of six people and some pottery dating back to the Beaker and Neolithic periods.

Continue along the coastline to reach the true headland, where there are magnificent views of the Small Isles and Soay, far to the left. Turn the headland to walk east past several rocky inlets and coves and

Rubh' an Dunain

reach the outflow of Loch na h-Airde, which was widened in the past by the MacAskills to provide suitable anchorage for their boats. The MacAskills dominated this area for generations, acting as coastguards for the MacLeods.

Across the outflow, standing on a beautifully exposed rocky spur, is an Iron Age dun, its landward wall 4 m high and its seaward side guarded by cliffs. This is a grand, wild spot to simply linger and absorb the magical surroundings.

Leave the Dun in a north-easterly direction, where on the hillside east of the loch is a low cave that yielded Beaker pottery and an Iron Age forge in 1932. A faint path leads up to the remains of Rhundunan House (the old MacAskill residence), close to a small lochan. Near this lochan, the main path leads north back to the junction at Creag Mhor. An alternative route from the dun to this same point is to continue along the coast to the southern extremity of Slochd Dubh and then follow the dry-stone wall. Return to Glenbrittle by the outward route.

Recommended pub: Carbost Inn, Carbost

SKYE: GLEN BRITTLE
TO LOCH EYNORT

This is a wild and essentially pathless clifftop walk offering unparalleled views of the Cuillin range and of Rum and Eigg. It is a grand introduction to serious coastal walking on the Isle of Skye and a satisfying circular route.

Distance: 11 miles/18 km (circular)
Time: 5–8 hours
OS map: 32

THIS FINE COASTAL WALK CONNECTS THE TWO SEA LOCHS OF Brittle and Eynort via some dramatic cliff scenery and returns to Glen Brittle by a combination of forestry tracks and an old drovers' track.

Begin at the parking area near the campsite in Glen Brittle and backtrack along the road for a few hundred metres to cross the rickety pedestrian suspension bridge over the River Brittle. Turn left to follow a vague path past a lone cottage before making a gradual rising traverse up initially tussocky, rough hillside, staying above the steeper slopes. Once established on the high moorland above Loch Brittle, enjoy a stupendous view of the craggy ramparts of the Cuillin across the loch, dwarfing the tiny coloured dots of the campsite.

Follow an obvious line of cliffs past two small lochans at An Crocan before gradually turning north-westwards, descending to cross a stream. Good sheep tracks lead along the top of another line of cliffs, which are followed for nearly a mile to a craggy high point known as Dunan Thearna Sgurr ('rocky sloping heap').

From here, an extensive inland detour is required in order to cross the yawning cliff-girt gap created by the Allt Mor ('big stream'). Do not attempt to cross this stream until you reach a point well beyond the waterfalls at the head of the cliffs. If the stream is in spate, you may

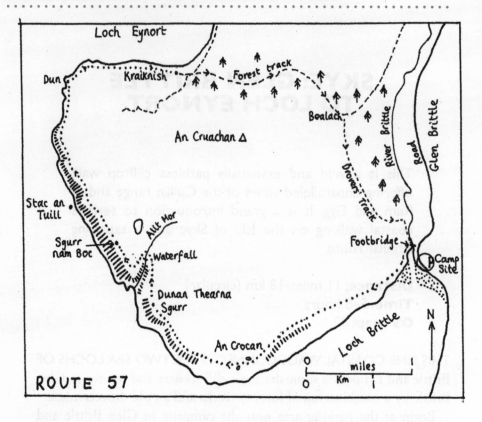

ROUTE 57

need an even longer detour. Once safely across, double back to the coastline via easier slopes often infested with scurrying rabbits and their burrows.

From this point, the walking becomes much easier on short, sheep-cropped turf, and the cliffs reach their high point at Sgurr nam Boc, at the dizzying height of 217 m above the churning ocean. The next half-mile or so forms the highlight of the walk and gives fine views of the impressive sea stack known as Stac an Tuill ('stack of the torrent'), with its sharp top and arched hole. Nearer the stack, move out onto a grand promontory where you can gain a superb grandstand view of the stack and the surrounding seascape crowned by the Small Islands of Rum and Eigg floating on the horizon. Bird-life is plentiful on the cliffs and stack, and the conspicuous black-and-white plumage of guillemots should be in evidence, as well as their raucous cries.

Beyond Stac an Tuill, the cliffs gradually drop in height, but interest is maintained by a series of craggy inlets and the walking continues to

The Cuillin from Glen Brittle

Cuillin from Glenbrittle.

be easy, with grand views of the cliffs north of Loch Eynort. Just before the turn east at the entrance to the sea loch, there is a well-preserved dun with a substantial part of its fortified stone wall remaining. Below this, you should spot the remains of a small settlement of black houses. Continue along the south shore of Loch Eynort along sheep tracks, which wind their way through steep bracken-covered slopes to the abandoned cottage of Kraiknish. This marks the end of the coastal section of the walk unless you intend to continue a further 2.5 miles on the forestry track to the road in Glen Eynort.

The return to Glen Brittle involves following the forestry track east just above the cottage for two miles to the Bealach Brittle. Leave the track a short distance beyond the *bealach* at the point where it curves round to head north. Contour south across boggy, heathery hillside and pick up an old drovers' path that follows a line above the forest. A final steep descent at the end of the plantation uses an eroded, trench-like path leading back to the bridge over the River Brittle and the point of departure.

Recommended pub: Carbost Inn, Carbost

Route 58

SKYE: LOCH EYNORT TO TALISKER

Next to the Duirinish coastal walk (Route 60), this is one of the finest clifftop walks on Skye. Much of the route is on wild, pathless terrain, but excellent sheep tracks can be followed on the clifftops. The route is essentially linear, but several options for completing a circular walk are described.

Distance: 9 miles/14 km (linear)
Time: 4–6 hours
OS map: 32

GLEN EYNORT AND TALISKER ARE BOTH REACHED FROM THE little coastal hamlet of Carbost on Loch Harport, where the Talisker distillery is situated. The peaceful little village of Eynort at the end of Glen Eynort provides the starting point of the walk, and limited parking is available at the end of the public road.

The first mile is a delightful, easy warm-up along a rough track past an old church and cemetery, followed by a path to the little peninsula of Faolinn. Beyond here, the going becomes increasingly difficult and it is best to remain on the shoreline, following a rocky promenade under the steep slopes of Biod na Fionaich. Shortly beyond this point, sea cliffs force a route upwards through steep, bracken-infested slopes to more level ground above some caves.

Easier ground and a small gorge lead to the broad green expanse of the hanging valley of Tusdale, with its waterfall and well-built dry-stone wall. Cross the Tusdale Burn and continue on a natural wide grassy terrace before climbing up to a second terraced area just before Glen Caladale. This whole area was once a thriving community but destined by the Clearances to become a scattering of ruins interspersed with old lazy-beds smothered by bracken. The only residents now are the ubiquitous sheep and rabbits.

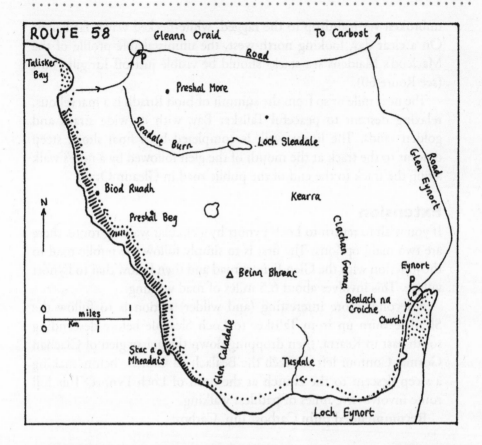

ROUTE 58 · Gleann Oraid · To Carbost · Road · Talisker Bay · Preshal More · Sleadale Burn · Loch Sleadale · Glen Eynort Road · N · Biod Ruadh · Kearra · Preshal Beg · miles · Km · Beinn Bhreac · Clachan Gorma · Eynort · Bealach na Croiche · Church · Stac a' Mheadais · Glen Caladale · Tusdale · Loch Eynort

Beyond Glen Caladale, the walking blossoms out into a full-blown clifftop extravaganza for an amazing four miles. This is coastal walking at its very best. Excellent sheep tracks on short grass make the going easy, and the only thing hindering steady progress will be the frequent stops to observe and photograph the stunning situations.

Pass the grass-topped sea stack of Stac a' Mheadais and continue along the cliff edge, crossing an immense gorge with waterfalls by following a fence on steep grass. The top of the cliff beyond this gorge forms an excellent viewpoint, and more than a mile ahead over a grassy strath is the highest point of the walk: Biod Ruadh, at a height of 285 m.

Descend into the wide grassy strath, following the line of the fence, and notice the striking basalt fluted columns of Preshal Beg, a hill off to the right. Climb easy grassy slopes to Biod Ruadh and enjoy the airy summit of this stupendous vantage point. In places, there is an unbroken vertical drop to the ragged, white-flecked waves far below. On a clear day, looking north-west, the unmistakable profile of the Macleod's Maidens sea stacks should be visible just off Idrigill Point (see Route 60).

The next mile or so from the summit of Biod Ruadh is a marvellous, relaxing descent to peaceful Talisker Bay, with its wide strath and golden sands. The linear walk is completed by a final short, steep descent to the track at the mouth of the glen followed by a mile's walk along the track to the end of the public road in Gleann Oraid.

Extension

If you wish to return to Loch Eynort by a circular walking route, there are two main options. The first is to simply follow the public road to the junction with the Glen Eynort road and then follow that to Eynort village. This involves about 6.5 miles of road walking.

A second, more interesting (and wilder) option is to follow the Sleadale Burn up from Talisker to Loch Sleadale before descending south-east to Kearra, then dropping down the grassy glen of Clachan Gorma. Contour left to reach the Bealach na Croiche before making a steep descent to the church at the head of Loch Eynort. This hill route involves five miles of pathless walking.

Recommended pub: Carbost Inn, Carbost

SKYE: TALISKER TO FISKAVAIG

As an ideal introduction to more serious clifftop coastal walking on Skye, this route could hardly be bettered. It is a satisfying and relatively short circular route mainly on rough sheep tracks with a handy return route on a good track. The coastal scenery and sea views are outstanding.

Distance: 7 miles/11 km (circular)
Time: 4–6 hours
OS map: 32

THE ROUTE BEGINS AT THE END OF THE PUBLIC ROAD NEAR Talisker Bay, where there is limited parking. Walk to the right, following a vehicle track past a cottage and farm, and go over a bridge. At the last cottage directly ahead, the track winds round to the left through a gate and up the side of the cottage garden, following the fence. At the first hairpin bend, leave the track (which is your return route) and gradually make a rising traverse of the hillside on various sheep tracks, taking you onto the summit slopes of Sron Mor.

Ahead, you should see a line of cliffs beginning above the sands of Talisker Bay. Head for the top of the cliffs on sheep tracks and pockets of boggy ground. Once on the cliff edge, the going becomes easy on excellent sheep-cropped short grass and the views open up considerably. There is a very fine view out to the headland of Rubha Cruinn ('round headland'), with the lacy ribbon of a waterfall cascading over the cliff providing dramatic foreground interest. Retrospectively, there is also a superb view across Talisker Bay to the terraced ramparts of the cliffs to the south (see Route 58) and Stac an Fhucadair ('the fuller's stack').

As you near the headland of Rubha Cruinn, the view out across Loch Bracadale begins to open out and the distinctive sea stacks known as Macleod's Maidens become visible (see Route 60). This is a

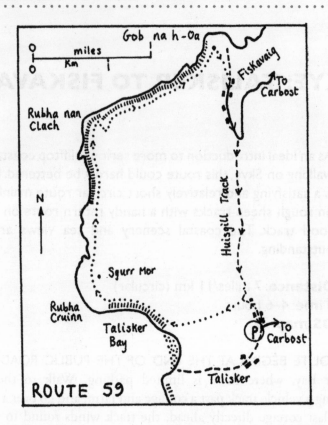

ROUTE 59

truly grand spot to rest and drink in the magnificent coastal scenery.

At Rubha Cruinn, the coastline turns northwards and the walking is less easy on tussocky grass and heather. Far below you will notice a wide grassy terrace, and just ahead you should stay to the right of a dry-stone wall before climbing up onto Sgurr Mor, keeping high. Beyond Sgurr Mor, there is a slightly awkward descent to a gorge, which should be crossed well back from the falls that plunge over the cliff to the sea. Less than a mile from Sgurr Mor, another line of obvious cliffs continues to the headland of Rubha nan Clach, where the coastline turns eastwards.

From this point, the route ahead is not always obvious, and several knolls and crags have to be negotiated, as well as a deep-cut gorge. You will need to head inland for several hundred metres before crossing the gorge at an obvious break with a path leading out on the far side. Continue onwards, following sheep tracks, crossing a fence by a stile and negotiating another small gorge. The little prominent knoll of

Talisker Bay

Gob na h-Oa ahead is the last high point of the walk. To reach it, climb a second stile further on, follow a fence before crossing it and ascend easy slopes to the flattish summit, which is a fine viewpoint. Another small knoll to the south of here contains the ruins of a broch, which can be visited on the return route. Otherwise, descend easily to a metal gate and track, which brings you to the tarmac road at Fiskavaig. Follow the road south for half a mile, and at the hairpin bend take the dirt track that continues straight on past a recently constructed barn. There is a Scottish Rights of Way signpost at the start of the track. This leads, in less than two miles, to your starting point.

Recommended pub: Carbost Inn, Carbost

Route 60

SKYE: MACLEOD'S MAIDENS AND SOUTH DUIRINISH

This is one of the finest, and most demanding, coastal walks in the UK. For the connoisseur of spectacular cliff, stack and arch scenery, the route is only matched by walks in Orkney and Shetland. The route as far as Macleod's Maidens would be suitable for children, but beyond, the walk becomes sensationally wild, exposed and uncompromising.

Distance: 14 miles/22 km (linear)
Time: 8–10 hours
OS map: 23

IT SHOULD BE STATED AT THE OUTSET THAT UNLESS YOU ARE only planning to visit Macleod's Maidens then the full walk to Ramasaig is a one-way trip and suitable transport will be needed at Ramasaig.

At the time of writing, at the start point of Orbost cars are no longer allowed beyond the farmyard near the entrance to Orbost House, but there appears to be no problem in leaving a car in the farmyard itself. Here, you should spot a sign indicating the route to Macleod's Maidens and Ramasaig. The route follows an often-muddy vehicle track down to the sheltered cove of Loch Bharcasaig, where there are several small cottages. Continue on the track as it winds its way round to the left over a bridge and into a forested area. Much of the forest has been recently clear-felled, and the track becomes a rough footpath after you cross a small stream. Go through a kissing gate and take the right fork in the path as it gradually climbs to a *bealach* west of Beinn na Moine. This whole area has been recently planted with Sitka spruce. Descend gradually to the bracken-covered amphitheatre high above Brandarsaig Bay, where the remains of old shielings are haunting reminders of a once-thriving Clearance settlement.

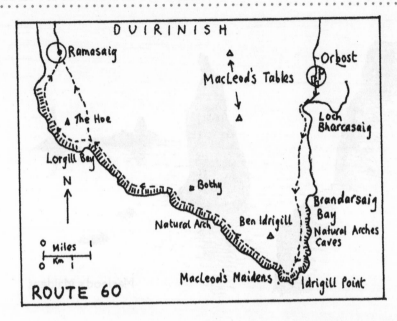

ROUTE 60

Beyond Brandarsaig Bay, the path ascends once again, passing through several more kissing gates and a sign saying 'Welcome to Rebel's Wood', which was planted in memory of Joe Strummer, co-founder of punk rock group the Clash, who died in 2002. His green credentials and maternal Skye connection resulted in this piece of woodland posterity.

After another small bay, the path enters an obvious defile west of the craggy escarpment of Ard Beag. A short diversion can be made here by climbing part way up Ard Beag and looking north to view a double natural arch. Return to the path, which passes through another kissing gate before crossing a boggy area between two knolls. The path beyond here becomes less obvious; if in doubt, aim to the right of two small hillocks on the horizon. This will bring you to the coastline in the vicinity of Macleod's Maidens.

An obvious wide, rocky platform 70 m above the restless sea is a dramatic vantage point for what is the highest sea stack on Skye, the Mother Stack, together with her 'children' looking out shyly from behind. Macleod's Maidens are traditionally thought to be the wife and daughters of a fourteenth-century Macleod chief who were shipwrecked and drowned on this spot. In 1959, the Mother Stack was first climbed by I.S. Clough and J. McLean.

Macleod's Maidens

The best view of the Maidens is gained by walking further on around the bay of Inbhir a' Gharraidh ('mouth of the dyke'), from where the Mother has an uncanny likeness to a statue of a seated Queen Victoria. This marks the turning point for those who only wish to visit Macleod's Maidens: return by the outward route.

For those hardy souls who are continuing all the way to Ramasaig, the day has hardly started! From the vicinity of the Maidens, the wild coastline stretches north-west as far as the eye can see in a twisting, contorted line of crumbling cliffs, skerries and sea stacks. A route description is almost superfluous, other than follow the cliff edge, but it should be heeded that although the path is marked on the map, it is often notable by its absence!

The descent to Glen Lorgasdal is delightful, where several stacks, a natural arch and a waterfall all add to the awesome scene. Beyond here, the next headland is a fine vantage point for a retrospective look at the Maidens. Descend to Glen Ollisdal, where a lonely bothy is situated about half a mile up the glen, one of only two Mountain Bothies Association bothies on Skye. This bothy would provide a convenient overnight shelter for anyone considering doing this route over two days.

Continue round the next headland to Glen Dibidal, crossing the river above the obvious gorge and waterfall. The section of coast between here and Lorgill Bay is one of the finest of the whole route and contains a myriad of natural arches, stacks and caves. Care and time should be taken to gain full appreciation of this truly wild corner of Skye. Further on, at the crossing of Scaladal Burn there are a couple of massive caves that are worth viewing, but great care will be needed to cross the burn, which is just above a waterfall.

Traverse the seaward slopes of Cnoc Fuar ('cold hillock') and descend steeply into the welcome shelter of Lorgill Bay. From here, there are two distinct options to choose from to reach the final destination of Ramasaig, both of roughly the same distance. True coastline devotees will climb the steep slopes opposite and continue round the cliff edge below the hill known as the Hoe. Other than sheep tracks, there is little trace of a path here, but the going is fairly straightforward.

The other option is to continue along the original path up Lorgill Glen to an old shepherds' bothy, where the river is crossed to reach a Land Rover track leading to Ramasaig in a mile and a half.

Recommended pub: The Stein Inn, Stein

Route 61

SKYE: WATERSTEIN HEAD AND NEIST POINT

This is a short but highly scenic walk to one of the highest sea cliffs on Skye and to the unusual little peninsula forming the most westerly point of the island. It is suitable for children provided they keep well back from cliff edges. Although the route takes in both the cliffs and the peninsula, either of these two could be omitted from the walk if time is short.

Distance: 6 miles/10 km (circular)
Time: 3–4 hours
OS map: 23

THE WESTERN EXTREMITY OF SKYE ON THE DUIRNISH peninsula is dominated by the strategic vantage point of Waterstein Head, which, at 296 m, is one of Skye's remarkable high points. The walk begins at the parking area for Neist Point (GR 133478). The prominent steep hill off to the left overlooking Moonen Bay is Waterstein Head and provides the first objective.

Begin by walking back along the road for just over a mile until you reach the north end of Loch Mor. Leave the road after the first steep climb away from the loch and head south to follow the top of an obvious escarpment. This soon develops into a delightful, easy climb on short grass and leads naturally to the triangulation pillar perched right on the edge of this airy viewpoint. To reach the edge of the cliff it is necessary to climb a fence, but getting to the edge is not compulsory!

The obvious feature of interest is Neist Point, jutting out into the ocean like the horny tail of some vast sea creature. To reach Neist Point, you must return to the road by the route of ascent; however, rather than following the road back to the car park, a more interesting

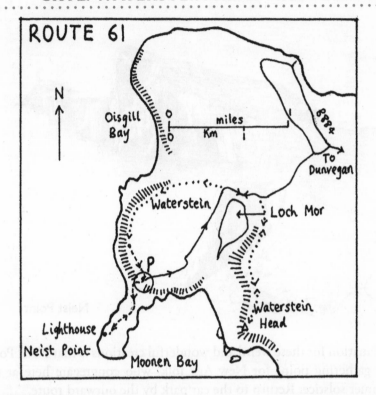

ROUTE 61

N

Oisgill Bay

miles
Km

To Dunvegan

Waterstein

Loch Mor

P

Waterstein Head

Lighthouse
Neist Point

Moonen Bay

coastal alternative involves leaving the road at the point where it turns sharply southwards and heading west across moor to reach the top of the cliffs at Oisgill Bay. Turn left and follow the line of the clifftop past a small lochan and on to the high point, crowned by an unsightly wartime concrete lookout building. Beyond here, there is a grand view of the northern cliffs of Neist Point, leading out to the lonely lighthouse at the tip.

From the lookout post, a path of sorts leads directly to the car park, marking the start of the walk out to the point. Well-constructed steps lead down a steep section to a tarmac path, which is followed to the lighthouse. At the end of the path is a mock graveyard, a set used in the film *Breaking the Waves*, which won the Grand Prix (the equivalent of a silver medal) at the 1996 Cannes Film Festival.

The final walk out to the true termination of the peninsula is on an unusual rocky platform littered with a 'forest' of man-made follies, ranging from simple stone towers to elaborate, labour-intensive structures reminiscent of Druid and Celtic mythology. The best

Neist Point

explanation for these weird and wonderful creations is that Neist Point is a gathering point for New Age folk, who congregate here at the summer solstice. Return to the car park by the outward route.

Recommended pub: The Stein Inn, Stein

SKYE: DUNVEGAN HEAD

This walk to the northernmost point of the Duirnish peninsula follows a continuous line of cliffs for over five miles and reaches a giddy high point at Biod an Athair ('sky cliff'), the highest sea cliff on Skye. It is essentially pathless, but excellent sheep tracks make the going easier.

Distance: 7 miles/11 km (linear), 11 miles/18 km (circular)
Time: 4–6 hours
OS map: 23

DUNVEGAN HEAD IS THE MOST NORTHERLY POINT OF THE peninsula lying between Loch Pooltiel and Loch Dunvegan. Its entire western aspect is an uninterrupted line of immense cliffs and forms the centrepiece of the walk to be described. From the northern extremity at Dunvegan Head, the route turns south to follow the eastern coastline, terminating at the public road-end at Galtrigill. Transport will be required here unless you wish to walk back to the start point by road (another four miles). A bike would be useful if deposited at Galtrigill before commencing the walk.

Begin at a point on the minor road that runs parallel to the head of Loch Pooltiel, just after the sharp bend right as the road turns inland (GR 171503). From an obvious ruin, assorted farm tracks and paths lead out to the short grass and heather of the clifftop. This marks the start of a glorious five-mile tramp along the top of the cliffs for which a route description is essentially superfluous. Good sheep tracks and, if you are lucky, a following wind help to produce almost effortless walking along this elevated highway.

The cliffs are initially less than 50 m in height, but as you near the high point they gradually increase to a dizzying 313 m (over 1,000 ft)

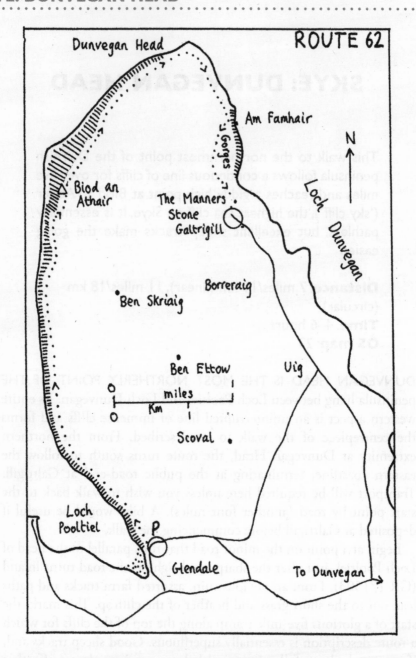

ROUTE 62

Dunvegan Head

Am Famhair

Gorges

N

Loch Dunvegan

Biod an Athair

The Manners Stone

Galtrigill

Borreraig

Ben Skriaig

Ben Ettow

Uig

miles

Km

Scoval

Loch Pooltiel

P

Glendale

To Dunvegan

at Biod an Athair. This is 3.5 miles from the start, and the summit is crowned by a triangulation pillar set slightly back from the cliff edge. A short distance before the trig point, the cliff edge dog-legs out and gives a superb vantage point for the dramatic, sheer rock face plunging

The highest sea cliffs in Skye, near Dunvegan Head

1,000 ft to the sea far below. The obvious summit several miles to the south is Waterstein Head (see Route 61). Beyond here, a gradual and increasingly heathery descent follows the continuing line of cliffs out to Dunvegan Head, now only 80 m above the sea. The moorland here is home to golden plovers, and their intermittent liquid whistles are the perfect accompaniment as you approach what feels like the end of the world, at Dunvegan Head. Look out for buzzards too and, if you are lucky, golden eagles.

From Dunvegan Head, head south, following the line of the eastern coast. The walking here is considerably tougher, being mainly through heather, tussocky grass and bracken, and there is no natural cliff line to follow. In less than a mile, reach the unusual natural arch named Am Famhair ('the giant'), a huge rock structure standing alone on the beach.

From Am Famhair, it is best to gradually ascend the hillside in a roughly south-westerly direction in order to avoid a couple of deep gorges that lie between here and the little settlement of Galtrigill. Just before the road-end is a famous stone known as the Manners Stone, a large, flat stone, which, according to tradition, gave you good manners if sat on! The stone is situated 100 m below a ruined cottage near a stile.

In Galtrigill itself there is a piping museum, and in Borreraig, a mile further south, there is a piping centre. Galtrigill marks the end of the linear walk unless you are planning to return to the start on foot, in which case you have an extra four miles of road walking ahead, or cycling if you have left a bike. The road route goes south to Uig, where a right turn takes you up over the hill and down to the start.

The really energetic may consider a wholly off-road route taking in the three high points of Ben Skriaig, Ben Ettow and Scoval, but this is probably too much like hard work!

Recommended pub: The Stein Inn, Stein

SKYE: WATERNISH POINT

A grand circuit of the relatively low-lying but remote and wild peninsula of Waternish, this route may lack the drama and grandeur of Duirinish and Dunvegan Head but possesses a quiet charm and serenity that provides a welcome contrast to its loftier neighbours.

Distance: 10 miles/16 km (circular)
Time: 6–8 hours
OS map: 23

THE ROUTE BEGINS AT THE SHARP BEND IN THE MINOR ROAD near Trumpan, four miles north of Stein. There is a fairly large car park, catering for visitors and walkers heading to Waternish Point. From here, a vehicle track heads northwards, deteriorating into a muddy path, especially after some wet weather – not uncommon on Skye! After about a mile, you will pass a cairn commemorating Roderick Macleod of Unish, killed in 1580 in a skirmish with the MacDonalds.

About half a mile further on, it is worth making a quarter of a mile detour to the right to visit the remains of Dun Borrafiach broch, one of the best preserved of such structures on Skye. Just under a mile beyond here, also on the right, is a more ruinous broch, Dun Gearymore. A short distance later, after crossing a stream, the path begins to wind right, eventually ending at the ruins of Unish House. It is advisable to leave the path at the bend and head directly to the coastline, where there is a small sea stack (An Camastac). Follow the top of the cliffs on easy close-cropped grass all the way to the lighthouse at Waternish Point.

It was here, on a wild and stormy night on 28 June 1746, where Flora MacDonald with her 'maidservant' Betty Burke appeared out of the gloom in a six-oared boat, having sailed from South Uist. The

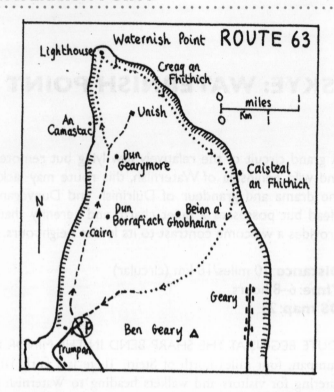

maidservant, dressed in a calico gown and petticoat, was, of course, Bonnie Prince Charlie in disguise. Their trip 'over the sea to Skye' was rudely extended when they were challenged by two MacLeod militia and they subsequently landed across Loch Snizort near Kilbride Point later that day.

The easiest return is by the outward route, but the continuation around this wild coastline should not be missed. At first, the going is relatively easy on excellent sheep-cropped short grass, but beyond Creag an Fhithich ('crag of the raven'), tussocky grass, heather and sphagnum moss gradually begin to slow the pace. Scenically, this 'raven's' coastline is rugged and has a wilder feel than the west coast.

Shortly after passing Caisteal an Fhithich, you should gradually turn inland and head for the lowest point on the skyline ridge halfway between Beinn a' Ghobhainn and Ben Geary. The saddle between these two hills can be quite boggy but will probably not deter determined summit baggers heading for Ben Geary (a Marilyn!). On the descent, pick up a grassy track that leads neatly back to the starting point.

Recommended pub: The Stein Inn, Stein

SKYE: RUBHA HUNISH

The northernmost tip of Skye is a vast grassy headland almost cut off from the rest of the island by 100-m-high cliffs. Its approach and circumnavigation provide a unique and unforgettable coastal walk with a curious 'lost world' atmosphere. The route is fairly short and suitable for older children.

Distance: 4.5 miles/7 km (return)
Time: 2–4 hours
OS map: 23

MOST CAR-BOUND TOURISTS WHO DRIVE ROUND THE A855 past Duntulm Castle Hotel in the north of Skye will hardly pay a second glance northwards to the true end of Skye at Rubha Hunish. It is only by walking the couple of miles north that the true nature of this remarkable peninsula reveals itself. Indeed the 'lost world' of Rubha Hunish is completely invisible from the road.

Begin in the vicinity of Duntulm Castle Hotel and take the path leading to Duntulm Castle, a rocky ruin perched precariously on a headland high above the sea. From here, follow the coastline northwards along the boulder-strewn shore of Tulm Bay, a popular spot for rock pipits flitting in darting displays.

Beyond the bay, climb the easy grassy slopes of Meall Deas ('south hill'). It is only when you reach the top of this hill that you will catch your first glimpse of remarkable Rubha Hunish. Instead of sea, a long green sward of grass pushes out for half a mile to the true northerly termination of Skye. Access to this final flourish of land seems barred by a curving bastion of sheer cliffs seemingly offering no chink in their armour. However, between here and the northerly top of Meall Tuath ('north hill') is a narrow defile, which is the key to finding the route down through the cliffs. A path snakes its way down from the end of

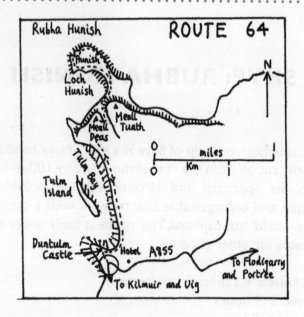

this defile through a weakness in the cliffs, finally fanning out in a chaotic jumble of scree and huge boulders. A further short grassy descent leads down to the broad sweep of grassy hummocks that comprise Hunish itself.

A clockwise circuit of the peninsula is a delightful excursion, with

Duntulm Castle

more of interest on the northern and eastern sides, where there are some fine sea stacks, including Bodha Hunish, an elegant 30-m-high blade of rock. Part of the cliff on this side is eroded and split, creating massive fissures, with one barely 20 ft wide, overhanging at the top and plunging 100 ft to murky depths.

Rubha Hunish is ideal for bird-lovers, as it is cut off from the rest of Skye and receives few visitors. As you head back along the eastern side of Hunish, the huge columnar basalt pillars of Meall Tuath dominate the view. Perched right on the edge of the cliffs is a tiny coastguard's hut, now used as a makeshift bothy.

Return by the cliff path and outward route.

Recommended pub: Duntulm Castle Hotel, Duntulm

Route 65

RAASAY: EAST COAST

The east coast of the island of Raasay is wild and relatively unfrequented but is famous for its haunting Clearance settlements of Hallaig and Screapadal. The full walk from North Fearns to the vicinity of Brochel Castle is a serious undertaking, as much of the path in the central section has been obliterated by rock and mudslides. This is a magnificent and memorable excursion.

Distance: 8 miles/13 km (linear)
Time: 4–6 hours
OS map: 24

The window is nailed and boarded
through which I saw the west
and my love is at the Burn of Hallaig
'Hallaig', Sorley MacLean

FOR THOSE HARDY WALKERS INTENDING TO COMPLETE THE whole route from North Fearns to Brochel, you will either require two cars or a kind driver to pick you up at Brochel. If a bike is deposited at Brochel first, it is still a 13-mile return journey to North Fearns. A long circular route is made possible by road walking from Brochel to the Dun Caan path start (GR 561406) and then following it to rejoin the coastal path at Hallaig. This option involves a total distance of 18 miles and was accomplished by the author, albeit with severely blistered feet!

A car can be parked at the scattered hamlet of North Fearns immediately before the last house on the left-hand side. From here, follow a fine grassy track northwards, an easy and pleasant start to the

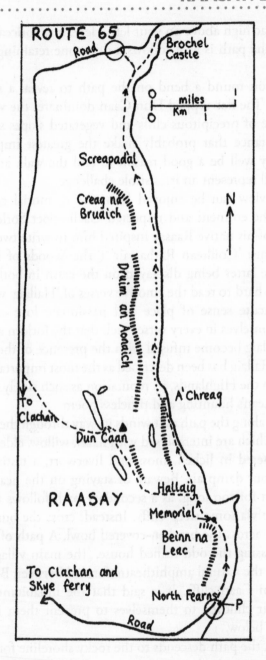

ROUTE 65

Brochel
Castle
Road

miles
Km

Screapadal

Creag na
Bruaich

N

Druim an Aonaich

A'Chreag

To
Clachan

Dun Caan

RAASAY

Hallaig

Memorial

Beinn na
Leac

To Clachan and
Skye ferry

North Fearns

P

Road

rigours that lie ahead. Enjoy spacious views east to the Applecross
Hills on the mainland and to the Crowlin Islands. As you leave a small
section of scrubby woodland, notice the towering, slab-like cliffs of

Beinn na Leac high above on your left. Here, it is noticeable how well engineered the path is as it follows a dry-stone retaining wall on the left.

Shortly, you round a bend on the path to reveal a striking vista northwards. The flat-topped Dun Caan dominates the view, but it is the long line of precipitous cliffs and vegetated slopes stretching far into the distance that probably make the greatest impression. For some, it may well be a good reason to end the walk at Hallaig; for others, it will represent an irresistible challenge.

The best view can be enjoyed from the memorial cairn built in honour of the eminent and respected Gaelic poet Sorley MacLean, whose love of his native Raasay inspired him to write two of his most famous poems: 'Coilltean Ratharsair' ('The Woods of Raasay') and 'Hallaig', the latter being displayed on the cairn in both Gaelic and English. It is hard to read the emotive verses of 'Hallaig' with dry eyes. MacLean's acute sense of place and passionate love of his people manifest themselves in every verse, such that the forlorn and poignant ruins of Hallaig become infused with the presence of their long-dead occupants. Hallaig has been described as the most important Clearance settlement in the Highlands, its reputation as such surely enhanced by Sorley MacLean's haunting and timeless poem.

Continue along the path as it winds its way through the birch woods of Hallaig, which are interspersed with hazel, willow, elder and rowan, many smothered in lichen, moss and liverwort, a testimony to the unpolluted but damp air. Beware of staying on the near side of the Hallaig Burn for too long, as a secondary path follows this down to the shoreline via some steep cliffs. Instead, cross the burn higher up and contour across the bracken-covered bowl. A path of sorts can be followed, passing the odd ruined house. The main village lies above this point in the natural amphitheatre formed between Beinn na Leac and the Dun Caan cliffs. It is said that the inhabitants of Hallaig tethered their children to themselves to prevent them falling down hidden cliffs below.

Gradually, the path descends to the rocky shoreline for around half a mile, where several other ruins are passed. At the rocky bluff known as A' Chreag, you are forced upwards on a narrow path that continues round the landward side of an obvious knoll. There is a ruined house in this sheltered spot, and if you are lucky you may spot a couple of

Hallaig memorial

otters. Just ahead, go through a gate and stay on the left side of a fence.

From this point, there is a fine view of the next section and the most challenging part of the walk. Essentially, the next two miles involve much clambering and ducking to avoid fallen trees and some descents to the immediate shoreline are unavoidable. It should also be noted that if the tide is very high then the route may be impassable, as some steep, vegetated cliffs reach down to the shoreline.

For the first half-mile, you will need to negotiate several mud- and rockslides before the path improves somewhat, only to be forced down to the shoreline near a stream. Beyond is an area of huge, house-sized boulders, some providing suitable shelter in the event of a downpour. The most difficult part of the route lies beyond this point, through hanging woodlands below Druim an Aonaich, where fallen trees and dense vegetation crowd out the path, and at one point you will again need to descend to the shore on slippery rocks below a small cliff.

Beyond here, the path thankfully improves, and you will gain a grand view of the massive, smooth crags of Creag na Bruaich far above on the left. At the final little headland before Screapadal, pass the enormous boulder on the shoreline known as Eaglais Breige ('false church'), so called because of its resemblance to a vaulted roof. As you approach Screapadal, cross a boggy section to reach a fine grassy path in the vicinity of a wooden hut. Above you on a series of terraces in the hillside are the forlorn ruins of the Clearance township of Screapadal. These ruins are more intact and concentrated than those at Hallaig and are definitely worth exploring if you have the time.

The final part of the walk goes through a recently felled forestry area, crossing a stream by a wooden bridge. At an obvious hairpin bend where the forest track turns left, another path goes off to the right to arrive at Brochel Castle in half a mile. Alternatively, stay on the main track and reach the road in a few hundred metres.

Recommended pub: Raasay Hotel, Raasay

WESTER ALLIGIN TO DIABAIG

A relatively short walk but with a distinctly wild and remote character round the rocky, stubby peninsula between Inveralligin and Lower Diabaig. The route is on a sometimes indistinct path throughout, with the option of a return route via the scenic Bealach na Gaoithe ('pass of the winds'). This walk could be combined with Route 67, from Diabaig to Redpoint, to make a longer, one-way excursion.

Distance: 4 miles/6 km (linear), 8 miles/13 km (circular)
Time: 2–3 hours (linear), 4–6 hours (circular)
OS map: 24

THE SINGLE-TRACK ROAD FROM TORRIDON TO LOWER Diabaig on the north side of Loch Torridon is the quintessential Highland drive: not to be hurried and, ideally, to be cycled or walked. Upper Loch Torridon has been widely praised as the most picturesque West Highland sea loch, and the view from Bealach na Gaoithe is indeed suitable proof of this assertion. At Wester Alligin (or Alligin Shuas), the road climbs inland over this high pass to avoid the complex, rocky terrain of small, crag-bound hills and forms the return route of this delightful walk.

Park in a small gravel parking area at the top of the road going down the steep hill to Wester Alligin. The path begins at the end of this road, which is just over half a mile from the parking area. The map shows another path leaving the road beyond the first house on the right joining the described path, but this is indistinct, underused and not recommended. Walk down the road round a big hairpin bend and continue along the track past a house on the right when you reach the end of the road. There is a sign here saying 'Camustrol – Footpath to

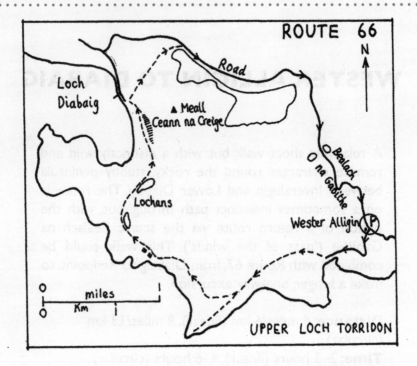

Diabaig', which directs you up the hill to the right through a stand of birch trees to cross a stream. Go through a gate and continue along the sometimes boggy trail as it winds its way upwards through heather and small, rocky outcrops, crossing a flatter area to the wide bay of Port an Lagaidh. Here, there is a marvellous view looking back to Upper Loch Torridon and the skyline of bold peaks beyond.

As the path goes round the bowl of Port an Lagaidh, look out for a right-hand fork that climbs steeply through the heather, going through a gap in the craggy spur ending at Rubha na h-Airde Glaise. This fork should be taken unless you wish to visit the point. For the next mile, the path runs parallel to the coast, dropping down to cross several streams and at one point passing an old ruined sheiling on the left. Around the next spur, there is an inhabited white cottage with a mature Scots pine tree nestling serenely on a flat green sward near Port Laire: a beautiful and idyllic hideaway only accessible by foot or boat.

The path runs along well behind the cottage and gradually climbs upwards to Lochan Dubh, a charming, peaceful little lochan huddling secretively in amongst towering crags. This is a grand spot to just sit and soak up the peace and tranquillity. The path crosses the outflow of

Port Laire

the lochan and climbs up to a second lochan. Beyond this point, the path makes a wide arc to the left through a gap in the crags where there is a fine view of Loch Diabaig and the little harbour and cottages of Lower Diabaig far below. The little peak of Meall Ceann na Creige on the right totally dominates the village of Diabaig, and its westerly profile comprises a series of bare, rocky, easy-angled buttresses consisting of Lewisian gneiss, which possess great scrambling potential.

The path descends quite steeply to weave its way round the base of these buttresses and can become indistinct in places. If in doubt, keep high above the shoreline until you reach a small clump of birch trees on a grassy platform. The path appears to go straight on here, but this leads to a sheer drop! Instead, go right and descend carefully into a broad gully. Go through a gate into a birch wood and descend a short slab where a length of rope has been secured to aid descent.

If you are ending the walk at Diabaig and have suitable transport arranged then continue onwards to the bothy-type building ahead, where you turn left to reach the road-end at Diabaig. Otherwise, turn right here and follow a path that climbs steadily through the woods to a ruined cottage, emerging from the trees at a fence. The path then ascends steep grassy slopes in a wide gully with craggy cliffs on the left, levelling off at the western end of Loch a' Mhullaich, where it meets the road. From here, it is a three-mile road walk back to the start point. As you pass Loch a' Mhullaich and climb up to Bealach na Gaoithe, a panorama of wild peaks opens up ahead of you. Just as you are wondering about the names of all the mountains on the skyline, a robust three-dimensional mountain plaque presents itself at a small parking area, which is a superlative viewpoint.

Recommended pub: Torridon Inn, near Torridon Hotel

DIABAIG TO REDPOINT

Although the long stretch of coastline between Diabaig and Redpoint lacks dramatic cliff and stack scenery, the wide, spacious views of open sea and craggy moor more than compensate. There is a well-engineered path for the first two and a half miles to the old youth hostel at Craig, but beyond here it deteriorates significantly. This is essentially a one-way walk and suitable transport will be required at Redpoint. This route could be combined with the previous route.

Distance: 8 miles/13 km (linear)
Time: 4–6 hours
OS map: 24

MURMURINGS OF THE CONSTRUCTION OF A ROAD connecting Diabaig with Redpoint have never translated into reality, and it is to be hoped that they never do as it would destroy the wild feel of this lovely stretch of coastline. The downside is that it is nearly a 40-mile drive from Torridon round to Redpoint (and nearly 50 miles from Diabaig!) via Kinlochewe and Loch Maree; leaving a bike at Redpoint is not, therefore, a viable option unless you are ultra-fit.

At Diabaig, turn right after driving down the steep hill and turn right again up a hill past a house to reach a small parking area near a large green shed. The last house sits at the end of the road just ahead, and you should spot a sign to the right of the house indicating the start of the trail.

Go through the gate and turn left, following the excellent path, which begins at an altitude of roughly 100 m above sea level, gradually increasing in height as it winds its way across the moorland and generally staying about half a mile away from the coast. This initial phase is excellent walking on a firm, well-drained footpath and sections

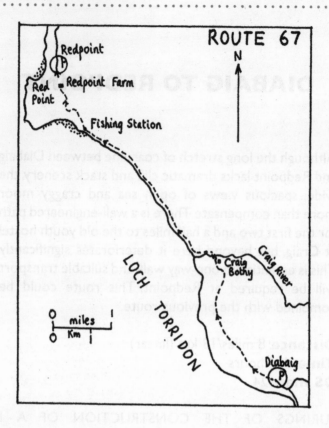

of broad sandstone slabs. If you are lucky, you will be accompanied by sylvan outpourings of song from skylarks high above and plaintive whistles from grey or golden plovers. Reach a prominent cairn on an extensive sandstone plinth after about half a mile. The path appears to turn further inland beyond here as it crosses a stream and descends, but it soon rises again, with fine views ahead to the southern sandy beach at Redpoint. Pass a small lochan on the right (Lochan Dubh) and gradually turn to the left, dropping down gentle slopes to the lonely cottage at Craig near a coppice of birch trees.

This remote two-up, two-down stone cottage was built in 1918 as part of Lloyd George's 'homes fit for heroes' policy, a sound though ultimately weak social ideal he championed following the First World War. For many years the cottage functioned as a youth hostel, and it is still marked with the standard red triangle on older OS maps. In April 2006, it was adopted by the Mountain Bothies Association, and compared to most of their bothies it is five-star accommodation!

As indicated earlier, the path onwards to Redpoint deteriorates significantly, and this is immediately noticeable as you descend boggy ground across some wooden planks to cross the Craig River on a wooden footbridge. The opposite side of the river is a sprawling birch wood with a scattering of rocks and boulders, making for difficult going. On crossing the bridge, turn left and follow the vague trail as it switchbacks its way up and down over slabs and into bogs, staying parallel to the river. This is probably the hardest section of the whole route.

Approaching the shoreline, the path turns northwards to follow the coast and stays much closer to the sea than the section to Craig. However, at times the path can be very hard to follow and after heavy rain can become a quagmire – be warned! Despite these negative comments, once you are established on this section a reasonably good rhythm can be gained and the three miles to the old fishing station at the south beach are soon accomplished. On a clear day, the view west out to north Skye and Rona is quite superb.

At the old fishing station, go over a stile and walk across the glorious golden sands before going up through the dunes to a wide area of *machair* to reach the path. After several kissing gates on open heath, reach Redpoint Farm and the vehicle trail beyond. This leads directly up to the road-head and parking area some distance beyond.

Recommended pub: Badachro Inn, Badachro

Route 68

RUBHA REIDH TO COVE

A wild and remote coastal walk amongst some remarkably dramatic and unspoiled scenery, the full walk from Rubha Reidh to Cove is a serious but rewarding and memorable excursion and is linear in nature. However, several shorter, circular options are also described.

Distance: 7 miles/11 km (linear)
Time: 4–5 hours
OS map: 19

OFTEN SPELLED RUA REIDH, THE NAME IS GAELIC FOR 'SMOOTH point' and not 'red point', as believed by some. The great geological fault line formed by Loch Maree and Loch Ewe continues from the small settlement of Midtown on the eastern side of the peninsula to end at the remote beach of Camas Mor, one of the highlights of this walk. The drive from Gairloch to Rubha Reidh Lighthouse is a classic West Highland single-track switchback of some fourteen miles, the last four of which are only just accessible by larger vehicles such as camper vans. Indeed, the last, short downhill section to the lighthouse via some hairpin bends is out of bounds to camper vans, so a parking space is provided higher up the road for these vehicles. At the lighthouse itself there is only limited parking, and you may need to park further up the road at one of the smaller parking bays near a quarry.

When the lighthouse was built in 1910 by David Stevenson, a cousin of Robert Louis Stevenson, there was no road access, the tarred road only having been constructed as late as 1962, the same year as the introduction of electricity, indoor toilets and hot water to the lighthouse buildings. These now function as tourist accommodation and there is also a small visitor centre with toilet facilities. Guided walks are also available.

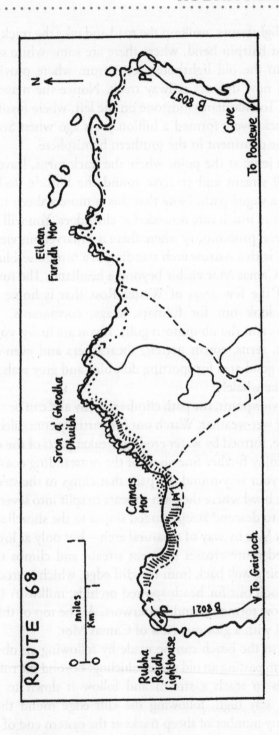

From the lighthouse, walk up the road and take the track leading off from the first hairpin bend, where there are some white stones. This track leads to the old lighthouse jetty, from where provisions were carried via a now defunct railway track. Notice the massive sloping platforms of Torridonian sandstone on the left, where fossilised ripple beds and cracks were formed a billion years ago when Scotland was part of a large continent in the southern hemisphere.

Above the jetty, at the point where the track turns, leave the track, cross a small stream and traverse round the hillside, following the coastline on a vague path. Note that this is more a sheep track than a proper path and much care is needed at cliff edges. You will soon reach an obvious level promontory where there is a marvellous view onwards to a sea stack with a narrow arch standing in a turquoise-blue sea, with the sands of Camas Mor visible beyond a headland. The route you are on is one of the few areas of Wester Ross that is home to nesting seabirds, so look out for fulmars, shags, cormorants, kittiwakes, oystercatchers and the ubiquitous gulls. If you are lucky, you may also spot gannets, terns, storm petrels, shearwaters and even sea eagles. This is also a good area for spotting dolphins and grey seals, with even the odd minke whale!

From this viewpoint, the path climbs steadily and can be notoriously slippery after wet weather. Watch out for partially concealed sinkholes in the hillside, formed by water eroding weaker parts of the underlying sandstone. Enjoy further fine vistas of the outstanding coastal scenery as you work your way round the path that clings to the steep hillside. Reach a wide bowl where the path appears to split into several options. It is possible to descend steep, eroded slopes to the shoreline here and reach Camus Mor by way of a natural arch – but only at low tide. The recommended route crosses the next stream and climbs the hillside beyond, keeping well back from the cliff edge, which is eroding badly. Underfoot, look out for heath spotted orchids, milkwort (small blue flowers), yellow tormentil and butterwort. At the top of this rise, you are presented with a glorious view of Camas Mor.

A descent to the beach can be made by following an obvious wide grassy platform passing an old ruined shieling. Beyond the ruin, descend steeper slopes to reach a stream and follow it down to the sands. Alternatively, stay high, following the cliff edge round the bay and descend by any number of sheep tracks at the eastern end of the beach.

Near Rubha Reidh

For walkers with modest aspirations, this may well be the turning point of the outing, and a return to the lighthouse can be made by either retracing your steps or perhaps attempting the low-level route by way of the natural arch mentioned earlier.

Those continuing onwards to Cove have a long distance still to cover, with much of the route on either extremely vague paths or none at all. The first mile beyond Camas Mor is quite difficult going across peat bogs and boggy ground with several small inlets to negotiate. Reach the point of Sron a' Gheodha Dhuibh, and some distance beyond, cross a narrow river. Beyond here, you will need to ascend a small hillock to avoid crags and steep-sided inlets, from where you gain a fine view of the next wide bay of green sward, sand and rounded boulders. The walking improves significantly from here and it is a pleasant descent to the bay.

This is essentially the last point at which a different return can be made to Rubha Reidh via a good path cum track that leaves this bay and heads inland in a south-westerly direction, passing several lochans to reach the main path running from Midtown to Camas Mor along the Loch Maree fault line. Parts of this return track, particularly the beginning, are firm and stony, but others are very soft and boggy. At the junction with the Camas Mor track, you can either turn right and rejoin the outward route or climb the hillside ahead, enjoying panoramic views north and west to the Coigach peaks before tramping across to the Maol Breac transmitter and returning by way of the minor access road.

Those continuing to Cove should follow the beach to its termination and then climb slightly to a raised beach. This leads easily to another craggy headland with a huge detached block at its northern extremity. The attractive green island of Eilean Furadh Mor lies a short distance to the north-west. Leave the headland and gradually turn southwards to a picturesque bay where there is a plaque describing the sinking of the USS *William H. Welch*, which was grounded on rocks off Eilean Furadh Mor on 26 February 1944. Only a dozen of 74 crew members survived, and the plaque commemorates the local services and crofters who battled their way from Cove in appalling conditions to help the survivors.

The last mile and a half or so to the road-end beyond Cove is generally drier underfoot with several sections of wide, rocky pavements and a more obvious path. As you approach the road-end, note the Second World War lookout station sitting high on a prominent crag above the road. A fairly recent large gravel parking area here reflects the popularity of this scenic spot.

Recommended pub: The Old Inn, Gairloch

MELLON UDRIGLE AND THE RUBHA MOR CIRCUIT

This is a grand, long and beautifully scenic circular walk around one of the finest peninsulas in the Western Highlands. The spacious views and rugged, remote coastline around Greenstone Point are a particular highlight, while the bay at Mellon Udrigle is simply one of the most magical sandy beaches in Scotland. Although unmarked on the map, a reasonable path exists for much of the way, hinting at the route's popularity.

Distance: 12 miles/19 km (circular)
Time: 6–8 hours
OS map: 19

THE RUBHA MOR PENINSULA SITS BETWEEN LOCH EWE AND Gruinard Bay and, like Rubha Reidh (see Route 68), has a minor road on either side. The walk starts at Mellon Udrigle on the western minor road beginning at the little settlement of Laide, near the A832. There is ample parking space for day visitors to the popular beach at Mellon Udrigle.

Due to the usual prevailing south-westerly wind, the route is described in a clockwise fashion, which results in the short four- to five-mile inland section of the walk being completed first. An excellent vehicle track cuts right across the peninsula, making for fast walking.

From the parking area, walk back along the road for just over a mile until you see a gate and a track going off to the right. This is just beyond Loch na Beiste ('loch of the beast'). The reference to 'beast' may well refer to Highland cattle, which roam around here, and at the time of writing there is a warning sign to this effect on the gate. Cattle wander about the area from April to October, and although generally

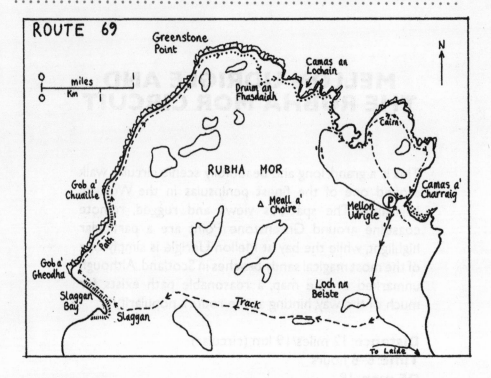

docile creatures they can become mildly aggressive if calves are about. Giving them a wide berth is probably the best policy!

Go through the gate and follow the track for three miles to lonely Slaggan Bay. This part of the walk is not without interest, and you pass a couple of freshwater lochs nestling in the folds of verdant, partly wooded hills. Look out for mergansers and even black-throated divers. The old ruined farmhouse of Slaggan has been reduced to just two gable ends, and here you go through a gate to join a smaller path leading to the edge of steep scarp slopes dropping down to the wide sandy expanse of Slaggan Bay, an ideal spot for a short breather before the real coastal walking begins.

From Slaggan Bay, a fairly distinct path follows the edge of the steep slope on beautiful springy turf and crowberry, making for delightful walking. At the point of Gob a' Gheodha (*gob* is a bird's beak and *gheodha* is a narrow creek between steep rocks), notice the extensive sloping slabs of Torridonian sandstone, similar to those at Rubha Reidh (see Route 68). As you turn at this point and head north-west, you will notice further fine sandstone formations before passing a tiny, idyllic lochan on the right. Go round a wide rocky bay, still on a well-defined path, to reach Gob a' Chuaille (*chuaille* is a stake), a rocky platform connected to the main cliff by a short, narrow crest. This is negotiable with care and is a fine vantage point.

Continue northwards on easy ground and cross the outflow of Loch na Doire Duinne, one of several large lochans, some of which are visible to the right. Shortly beyond here, go through a gate before crossing the outflow of Loch nan Eun. At this point, you should notice a prominent little crag near Greenstone Point, only several hundred yards away. Make an optional ascent of this crag by way of an easy scramble on the south side. On the top are a cemented cairn and a pole, and it is a fine vantage point for the curious rock architecture all around. There is also a fine view north-east to An Teallach and Beinn Ghobhlach.

After exploring and scrambling on the rock formations around Greenstone Point, turn eastwards, where the character of the walking changes to become less easy and direct. You are now going more 'against the grain' of the underlying rock strata, with more heather and sphagnum moss and several deep inlets to circumvent. One deep inlet has several small dry-stone walls crossing its head.

Beyond Loch an Dun-chairn, it is a good idea to ascend the obvious

Near Greenstone Point

little hill of Druim an Fhasdaidh (52 m), which gives a grand appreciation of the surroundings and the final section back to Mellon Udrigle. Descend the hill eastwards and go round the head of Camas an Lochain. The next little headland can be bypassed by going north of the small lochan. At the next headland, reach two little cairns on a rocky platform with a fine view southwards to the isolated houses of Opinan and to civilisation.

A reasonable path goes round the next cove, and you should aim for the obvious white house at the end of a shallow inlet. At the track near the house, go left, heading for a larger, more modern white house. Go through the first gate on the right, across a field to a second gate, before another field takes you to a third and final gate. This leads to a large, sandy estuary, which you should cross to reach the hill on the opposite side. Climb the grassy hill easily by a path and reach the summit area, containing two cairns several hundred yards apart. There is a fine view across Gruinard Bay to the isolated peak of Beinn Ghobhlach (see Route 70).

Reach the second cairn by way of some boggy ground then descend south-east, passing a freshwater loch on the right-hand side. A final short ascent takes you to the second main hill, with another cairn. This hill gives a glorious bird's-eye view of the sandy beach at Mellon Udrigle, less than a mile to the south. To reach the bay and the end of the walk, simply follow the easy wide grassy path dropping gently down, ignoring any offshoots heading inland. At the beach, cross a small stream past an area of boulders to reach the golden sands of this beautiful hidden corner of Wester Ross. This completes one of the most satisfying circular coastal walks of western Scotland.

Recommended pub: The Old Inn, Gairloch

SCORAIG

The isolated community of Scoraig, situated on a lonely and windswept peninsula between Little Loch Broom and Loch Broom, forms the focus of this beautiful coastal stroll. The walk is on good, dry paths throughout and returns by the same route, though more adventurous alternatives can avoid this if so wished. It is ideal for children.

Distance: 12 miles/19 km (return)
Time: 5–7 hours
OS map: 19

THE NAME SCORAIG IS POSSIBLY OF NORSE ORIGIN, DATING back to around the ninth century, although several Gaelic words, such as *sgorag* or *sgoradh*, meaning a 'waving edge' or the 'forking of peats' respectively, give possible clues to the derivation. Ironically, the settlement's population greatly increased during the Clearances when families were evicted from the glens around Dundonnell and brought to this remote outpost between the two loch Brooms. The population then would have exceeded 300. This viable community was not to last, however, and continued migration over the next century saw its numbers dwindle to just a handful. In 1964, not one person of native descent remained, but four incomers – two English bachelors and a married couple – fought hard to revitalise and reinvent this secluded settlement. Other like-minded latter-day crofters, mainly young people who shunned the rat race and retreated to a more self-sufficient and rewarding way of life, soon joined them to help create a small but industrious microcosm of alternative living.

The steady influx of incomers to Scoraig during the 1970s and '80s attracted much media interest and the community became an icon symbolising the 'Good Life' in this windswept outpost of Gaeldom.

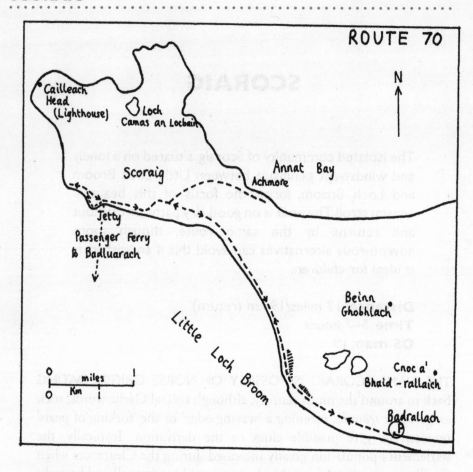

ROUTE 70

Obviously, much hard work, skill, creativity and determination have accompanied this rebirth. Long-abandoned cottages have been rebuilt or repaired, crofts reworked and combined, thousands of trees planted, fruit and vegetables grown, livestock introduced and electricity-generating wind turbines locally built, as well as the numerous other activities required to maintain a self-sufficient community.

Scoraig has its own primary school, and in the early 1980s the Scoraig Teaching Fund, a charitable trust consisting of parents, built a small secondary school, which now has around eight children and two teachers. Prior to this, the secondary-school children were ferried across Little Loch Broom and bussed to Ullapool as weekly boarders. Today, many adults also attend the classes at Scoraig secondary school. The population of Scoraig today is around 80 inhabitants. It should be noted that for any would-be incomers of a religious disposition, there is no church in Scoraig. Nor is there, alas, a pub!

The township has remained remarkably unpolluted from the dubious attractions of the outside world, due mainly to the lack of any connecting motor road. A proposal to build one to the road-head at Badrallach was long ago soundly rejected. Those who wish to visit Scoraig today have only two choices: either cross Little Loch Broom on a boat from Badluarach or walk in from Badrallach (which is the walk described here). Perhaps the relative difficulty in reaching Scoraig helps to promote its peaceful nature and timeless quality of life. In these days of heady environmentalism, Scoraig is viewed by many not as an anachronism but as a working model of our future preservation and redemption.

To reach the start of the walk at Badrallach, take the minor road off the A832 road two miles inland from Dundonnell, at the head of Little Loch Broom. A scenic eight-mile drive on a narrow road with passing places takes you to the parking area at the end of the public road.

Ignore the grassy track on the left and climb the partly tarmacked track on the right, which soon levels off to a pleasant, wide, fine-gravel path high above the coastline. The track is expertly maintained, as it is the only land route into Scoraig, and is suitable for bikes and quad bikes. After about 1.5 miles, the path winds its way round a steep headland, and from here you will gain your first view of the scattered crofts and plantations of your destination. The path literally hugs the cliff-face at one point and is hemmed in between a safety fence on the left and cliff on the right. The steeper parts of the path have been well engineered with flat, slab-like rocks, making the going relatively easy. Look out for seals barking from the sea far below. Beyond the point, the path descends nearer the shoreline and continues across a couple of streams to the deer fence at Rireavach.

Go through the gate and continue along the path as it climbs up to a more substantial vehicle track. You will notice the vast number of trees that have been planted, mainly Scots pine but also alder and rowan. Many of the crofts have their own small wind turbine, unobtrusive and relatively efficient: a world away from the scores of huge, unreliable, heavily subsidised and inefficient monster turbines that litter much of Scotland's beautiful landscape and whose meagre energy offerings are transported south.

A house at Scoraig

Pass the recently constructed lighthouse on the right and the small secondary school beyond before taking a sharp turn left, leading down to a track that runs along to the jetty. There is a pig farm in a wooded area to the right just before the jetty. Beyond the jetty, a grassy path follows the coastline round the little point known as Corran Sgoraig and leads to a small, round house. It is worth continuing on along the coast from here via a grassy path following a fence to reach a prominent rocky knoll. The last house in Scoraig sits in splendid isolation off to the right higher up the hill. From the rocky knoll, you gain a good view of Cailleach Head and the end of the peninsula. This marks the turning point of the walk unless you wish to attempt one of the more ambitious return routes (see below). The views on the return leg are very much dominated by three distinctive mountains: Beinn Ghoblach; Sail Mhor, the steep-sided peak overlooking Scoraig across Little Loch Broom; and the mighty ramparts of An Teallach further distant.

Extension

Fit and adventurous walkers may wish to continue for another 1.5 miles to Cailleach Head, though this is essentially pathless. There is then the option of exploring the wild and little-frequented mini-peninsula north of Loch Camas an Locbain and possibly continuing along the northern coastline at Annat Bay to reach Achmore. A good hill track crosses back over to Scoraig from here, ending just south of the secondary school. This extension is long and arduous, however, and would entail at least another three hours of walking.

In fine, settled weather, a grand alternative to the coast path back to Badrallach is to climb Beinn Ghobhlach by the broad ridge from Rireavach, making a traverse into the big central corrie to avoid steep crags. The smaller summit of Cnoc a' Bhaid-rallaich could also be included before descending steep slopes to Badrallach.

Climbing Beinn Ghobhlach before visiting Scoraig and then returning by the coast path is another option that could be considered.

Recommended pub: The Dundonnell Hotel, Dundonnell

BLUGHASARY TO CULNACRAIG:
THE POSTIE'S PATH

This ancient right of way connecting two isolated communities on the Coigach coast is so called because it was regularly used by the local postman and, although relatively short, it is a consistently demanding but interesting route with some thrilling situations and marvellous views. The walk is essentially linear, although those with the fitness and spare time may wish to consider a return over Ben More Coigach and the path via Meall nan Clachan.

Distance: 6 miles/10 km (linear)
Time: 4–6 hours
OS map: 15

FROM THE MINOR ROAD JUNCTION LEADING TO BLUGHASARY (seven miles north of Ullapool) round to Culnacraig, near Achiltibuie, by road is about twenty-two miles, and if a car is being left at Culnacraig you will therefore have a forty-four-mile round trip to complete before even starting this walk. This road was not tarred until the 1960s and, indeed, the walking route to be described was a more popular route from Achiltibuie to Ullapool until after the Second World War.

It has been said that churchgoers in the seventeenth and eighteenth centuries walked from Culnacraig to the parish church at Clachan, at the head of Loch Broom, but considering this involves a round trip of 50 miles, it seems hard to believe even for the staunchest of Calvinist traditions. In the 1860s a postal service began, and for some 50 years the local 'postie', Kenneth McLennan, walked this route from Ullapool twice a week in all weathers: a truly amazing feat.

Looking at OS Sheet 15 gives a hint of the difficulties and challenges of the walk. The route runs totally 'against the grain' of the land as it

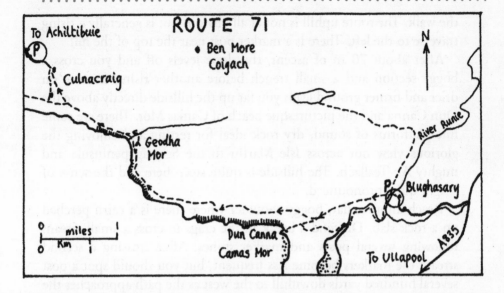

follows a contorted line across narrow spurs, over deep gorges and across streams, so it is virtually impossible to maintain any kind of walking rhythm. The time required is therefore out of all proportion to the relatively short distance covered. For walkers who relish a challenge, all this should spur you on to reach for your boots immediately!

There is a parking area near the bridge over the River Runie, which is situated at the end of a very rough section of track beyond the end of the tarred road at Blughasary. If leaving a car at Culnacraig, the best place to park is at the small parking area several hundred yards before the termination of the tarred road on the left-hand side. This is mainly used for walkers ascending Ben More Coigach.

The car park at Blughasary has an information board and is also the starting point for a short walk to Dun Canna fort, of which there is little left standing. Cross the bridge and note the signpost saying 'Achiltibuie 9 miles'. Take the minor path off to the left immediately after crossing the bridge and ignore the vehicle track following the river. The first mile is slow going, with rocky intrusions and much bog, and the path itself is rather sketchy. Just over a mile from the start, there is a sign directing you uphill to the right, where you should spot some posts and a stone marker with a white chevron. These stone markers are relatively recent and are a regular occurrence throughout the walk. The route uphill is not at all obvious but is generally a rising traverse to the left. There is a marker post near the top of the hill.

After about 70 m of ascent, the slope levels off and you cross a boggy section and a small trench before another rising traverse on drier and firmer ground leads you far up the hillside directly above the Dun Canna and the picturesque beach of Camas Mor. There are some fine platforms of sound, dry rock ideal for resting and enjoying the glorious view out across Isle Martin to the Scoraig peninsula and mighty An Teallach. The hillside is quite steep here and the sense of height quite pronounced.

Reach another flat, boggy shoulder where there is a cairn perched on a rock slab. Descend a break in the crags to cross a small stream following several posts and marker stones. After crossing a second stream the markers become less frequent, but you should spot a post several hundred yards downhill to the west as the path approaches the sea. From here onwards, the path is relatively close to the sea but still a good 50 m above sea level as it clings to the steep hillside with some exposed, sensational situations. There are several short but steep rocky descents more akin to scrambling than walking, and care should be exercised. This section of the route to the rocky chasm of Geodha Mor, literally 'big narrow creek', is possibly the highlight of the walk, possessing a wild and detached feel in awesome surroundings.

As you approach Geodha Mor, the path makes a significant detour upstream of the Garbh Allt (aptly, 'rough stream') to cross it just above a waterfall. It is easy to end up too low here, and a wooden post at shore level is not helpful, as it gives the impression you should go down to shore level to cross the stream! The OS map shows the crossing of the Garbh Allt at a much lower level and was probably the original route.

Once safely across the stream, the path improves significantly, and several parts have been upgraded with the addition of flat flagstones, making for much more rhythmic walking. For the next mile, the path skirts the steep western flanks of Ben More Coigach, or 'the Rock' as it is traditionally known. Gradually, the path moves away from the coast to cross the next major stream, the Allt nan Coisiche ('stream of the traveller' or 'pedestrian'), which has carved out a deep, rocky gorge in the hillside. A post marks the point of crossing, though the descent into the gorge is not immediately obvious. The path descends into the gorge to cross the stream near an attractive little waterfall amongst a canopy of green trees: a peaceful spot. Climb out of the gorge on a more obvious path and continue a short distance until you reach a fork in the path. The left fork leads to the road-end at Achduart and was recently upgraded by local schoolchildren. Ignore this and follow the right fork, which leads past the few cottages of Culnacraig to the end of the public road. The small parking area lies several hundred yards further on, round a couple of bends.

The extremely elongated settlement of Achiltibuie is still another three miles distant, where a welcome pint of beer awaits!

Recommended pub: The Summer Isles Hotel, Achiltibuie

Route 72

RUBHA NA COIGICH

The wild headland of Rubha na Coigich is the northern extremity of the Coigach peninsula and provides the focus of a grand, largely pathless coastal route from the little settlement of Reiff to the beautiful beach at Achnahaird. A complete circuit can be made, beginning and ending at Reiff, but this involves an additional four-mile road walk.

Distance: 8 miles/13 km (linear)
Time: 4–5 hours
OS map: 15

REACH REIFF FROM THE A835 ULLAPOOL ROAD BY TAKING THE Achiltibuie road and then the Achnahaird turn-off. At Reiff, there is limited parking just beyond the last house at the end of the public road.

Cross the outflow of the Loch of Reiff by a bridge and go through a gate to reach a spacious area of undulating hillocks of short grass – a mass of wild flowers in the height of summer. Gradually make your way towards the coast, reaching higher ground at the north end of the freshwater loch. The sea cliffs around this area are a magnet for rock-climbers, the rock being rough and sound Torridonian sandstone.

Descend to the narrow spit of land separating the north end of the loch and the sea before following a vague path round the bay of Camas Eilean Ghlais with its prominent rocky islet, the home of several shags and guillemots. Pass an old fishing cottage and climb steadily to the high point beyond the bay, from where there is a glorious view. Several small knolls are visible from here, all with cairns sitting on immense slabs of Lewisian gneiss. Choose a way through, or over, these knolls, eventually crossing the narrow outflow of Loch na Totaig.

Beyond here is Faochag Bay, which leads directly on to the northern

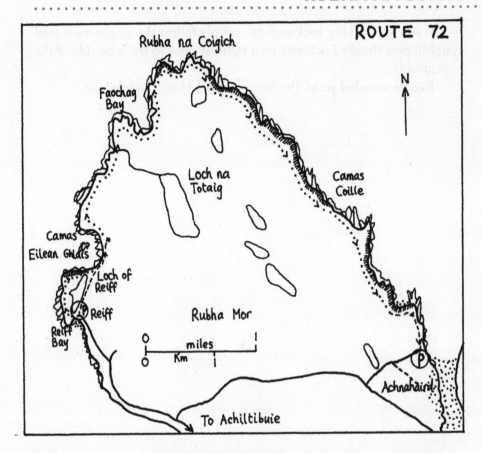

ROUTE 72

tip of the peninsula at Rubha na Coigich. The natural rock architecture here is superb, with dizzying cliffs and broad shelves and ledges, which are home to noisy oystercatchers and gulls. After spending some time on this wild headland, turn south-eastwards to follow the undulating coastline all the way to Achnahaird. The walking on this side of the peninsula is somewhat more arduous on tussocky grass and heather, though it is largely flat until you reach the 88-m hill facing Camas Coille. The view eastwards to the isolated Coigach peaks of Suilven, Cul Mor and Stac Polly is especially fine. Cross a broad area of grass situated further up the hillside, which contains several ruins and inhabited cottages. From this point, a path of sorts leads for the last mile to the road-end and car park at the narrow inlet of Achnahaird Bay, where it is worth spending some time at the picturesque beach. There is a campsite here and the remains of a dun.

If you are walking back to Reiff, simply follow the single-track road uphill past Ruadh Loch and turn right to cross to the west side of the peninsula.

Recommended pub: The Summer Isles Hotel, Achiltibuie

THE POINT OF STOER

A stunning clifftop walk around the wild and lonely peninsula forming the most westerly point of Assynt, the route includes the famous Old Man of Stoer, a classic sea stack, and an ancient dun built on a natural arch. The walk described is a satisfying circular route with scope for variation if so wished.

Distance: 9 miles/14 km (circular)
Time: 4–6 hours
OS map: 15

THE STOER PENINSULA LIES NORTH-WEST OF THE LITTLE HAMLET of Lochinver and can be reached by taking the B869 road, a beautifully scenic drive with many twists and turns. A mile past the village of Stoer, take the minor road to the left past the primary school. A mile beyond here, take a sharp turn left to reach the parking area near the lighthouse after 2.5 miles. This is the start and end point of the walk.

Just beyond a track, there is a sign for the Old Man of Stoer (3 km), which marks the beginning of a grassy path winding its way along the clifftop. Ignore the track and follow this clifftop path. The path is quite popular in the summer months and tends to split into numerous alternatives, some staying very close to the cliff edge and others staying well back. Shortly after setting off, there is a grand retrospective view of the lighthouse perched high on its rocky prominence beyond a wave-battered beach.

The route descends into a grassy gorge, which can be quite wet, before climbing up once again and continuing on past a couple of coves. These contain caves that can be explored depending on the state of the tide but involve steep descents on sometimes slippery grass and rock. At the narrow knife-edge neck of land known as Cirean Geardail (*cirean* is Gaelic for 'crest'), there is a fine first view of the 'Old Man'

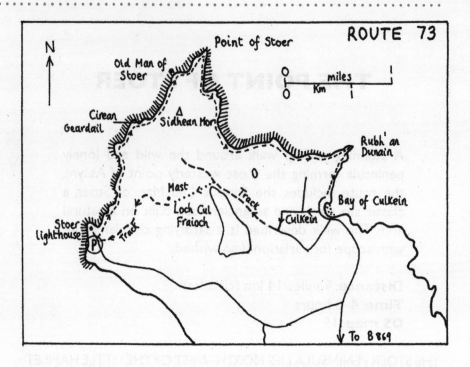

ROUTE 73

standing proud at the end of a curving bastion of cliffs half a mile distant.

From Cirean Geardail, the path climbs steadily higher, skirting the flank of Sidhean Mor, before descending gradually to the vicinity of the Old Man. Several points on the cliff edge offer superb vantage points for this lofty sea stack rising 67 m from its supporting sandstone plinth. Although only half the height of its Orkney cousin, the Old Man of Hoy (see Route 90), it is nevertheless a stirring sight, and it is ascended regularly by rock climbers, who rate it Hard Severe; ironically not that difficult for modern die-hard rock tigers. Reaching the base of the stack is in itself a tricky proposition, and a deep, 8-m-wide channel has to be crossed just to begin the climb.

For the casual car-bound tourist, the Old Man marks the turning point of the walk, but a return from here omits some excellent coastal walking, much of it on reasonable paths. Continue on past the Old Man to turn a small promontory with giddy views down to a churning sea. Cross a fence that runs right across the narrow neck of land forming the Point of Stoer, which is meant to stop sheep from wandering out to the point. The walk out to the tip following the cliff edge is exhilarating, especially on a wild and windy day, when the ravages of the Atlantic swell will send booming and crashing waves onto rocks to explode in a chorus of white surf. Look out for dolphins, porpoises and even whales if the sea is calmer, as these are frequent visitors to the sea off Stoer. Bird-life too, in the form of gulls, guillemots and razorbills, should be evident on the cliff-faces.

The Point of Stoer itself is less than 30 m above the sea, and reaching the true point involves a delicate little traverse along a narrow neck of land, which you may wish to omit!

Continuing round the coast from the point, height is gradually gained once again, and there are some sensational little headlands and rocky promontories before reaching a high, curving line of cliffs enclosing an unnamed bay. A fence runs along the top of these cliffs and a rather boggy path runs to the right of it, so keeping to the left may be preferable.

Beyond the bay, the route gradually descends on drier ground and offers marvellous views out to the mountains of Assynt, with triple-topped Quinag taking pride of place. Eventually, reach the little low-lying headland of Rubh' an Dunain, which is made conspicuous by the presence of a high dry-stone wall crossing the entire headland. Cross the wall by means of a gate standing on a flat plinth of sandstone in the centre of the wall. Continue on a close-cropped grassy sward to the tip of the headland, where the remains of an ancient dun stand on either side of a natural sea arch, itself only visible from a point slightly further east. Cross the arch on a narrow neck to gain a fine grassy platform, which is an ideal rest and vantage point.

Follow the coastline round to the east to view

Old Man of Stoer

the arch and then continue along the coast to the Bay of Culkein, following a wide grassy path to the left of a dry-stone wall. A muddy farm track leads to the little hamlet of Culkein, nestling serenely round the bay.

The return route to the lighthouse uses vehicle tracks and a small section of pathless walking and is now described, though some may prefer a longer road walk. Take the first road to the right, heading uphill away from the bay past a couple of houses, and turn sharp left at the top. After several hundred yards, you will see a vehicle track running off to the right. Follow this track, used for transporting peat, to the large freshwater Loch Cul Fraioch. Ahead, up on a small rise, notice the transmitter mast, which is where you are heading. Beyond the point where the track meets the loch, its state deteriorates abysmally. This is the sign to abandon the track and head west uphill for half a mile to the mast. The going here can be very wet underfoot and a few peat hags have to be negotiated en route. Once at the mast, simply follow the good access track for a mile back to the lighthouse and car park. There is a grand view, in clear weather, of the distinctive Coigach peaks lined up in a row to the south-west: Canisp, Suilven, Cul Mor, Cul Beag and Stac Polly. Near the end of the track there are ruins of a Second World War radar station, one of the remotest in the country. Details of this can be found on an information board at the car park.

HANDA ISLAND: THE WEST CIRCUIT

Handa is an important bird reserve managed by the Scottish Wildlife Trust (SWT) and as such is a sensitive and protected area. The well-established circuit of the western half of the island is on boardwalks and clifftop paths and provides a stunning and unforgettable walk with unique cliffs, sea stacks and a wealth of bird-life.

Distance: 4 miles/6 km (circular)
Time: 2–3 hours
OS map: 9

HANDA ISLAND LIES JUST OFF THE SUTHERLAND COAST AND north of the little hamlet of Scourie, where there is a campsite and hotel. A regular passenger ferry service runs from Tarbet, lying north-east of the island, and is on a first-come, first-served basis: that is, there is no booking. (See the 'Getting to Handa' panel for more information.)

When you arrive on the island, you will be met by an SWT warden, who will take you to the visitor hut, where important information and advice will be given before you set out on the circular walk. It is important that walkers stay on the established trail and walk anticlockwise in order to minimise disturbance to wildlife, such as ground-nesting birds.

From the visitor hut, take the obvious grassy path leading north-west across the interior of the island. This climbs a short hill initially and soon leads to a good boardwalk trail. About a third of the way across the island, you will pass the ruins of an old village where eight families lived until 1848, when the potato famine struck and the islanders emigrated to America. The form of society was not dissimilar to that of St Kilda, where the men had a daily parliament to decide the day's work and the islanders harvested seabirds and eggs.

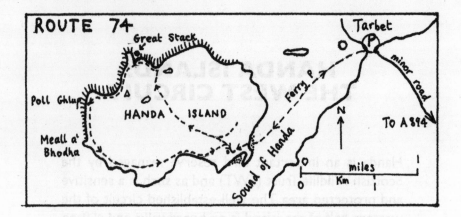

As you approach the cliffs on the north side of the island, prepare to be dive-bombed by Arctic skuas and even great skuas as they protect their territory. Carrying a trekking pole and pointing it up in the air keeps them at a safe distance! After only a mile from the visitor hut, reach the other side of the island at Puffin Bay, where, despite the name, you will probably not see many puffins! Their main stamping ground is the famous Great Stack of Handa, a short distance west of here along the trail.

Handa is composed of Torridonian sandstone, and the horizontal layers on the cliffs, formed by prolonged weathering, provide ideal resting sites for thousands of seabirds, including guillemots, razorbills, kittiwakes and fulmars. At the peak of the breeding season, the onslaught on the senses is an incredible experience. The climax of the walk is undoubtedly the Great Stack, an enormous 115-m-high monolith with a flat grassy top, hosting thousands of guillemots and puffins and separated by a gap of only 24 m from the nearest point of the island, on its west side. Puffins nest in burrows on top of the stack while guillemots utilise every available space on the numerous rock ledges below.

A roped traverse on to the flat top of the stack was made in 1876 and was repeated in 1967 by Tom Patey. The stack was first climbed in 1963 by Hamish MacInnes and party by a Very Severe route on the seaward side, which was reported to be surprisingly bird-free.

The best vantage point for viewing the Great Stack is on the little promontory to the west, where you can gaze across the 20 or so metres

Great Stack of Handa

to its grassy summit. This is a grand spot in which to while away a good half-hour and absorb the unique atmosphere.

Leaving the stack, the path curves round the top of Geodh na Goibhre with its gaunt, sheer cliffs and then downwards to several other outstanding viewpoints. Look out for Poll Ghlup ('the muddy pool'), a collapsed sea cave that has formed a stomach-churning sheer hole in the ground behind the cliff edge.

Further on, the headland known as Meall a' Bhodha is worth a short detour, and if you are lucky you may spot grey seals basking on the lower rocks. The remainder of the walk is almost entirely on a boardwalk and takes you directly back to the start, with one small inland section.

Recommended pub: Scourie Hotel, Scourie

Getting to Handa

The Handa Ferry runs Monday to Saturday from 9 a.m. to 2 p.m. The last return is at 5 p.m. Note that the ferry does not run on Sundays and does not take dogs. For enquiries relating to the ferry, please contact the operators: Roger Tebay (07780 967800) and Paul Murray (07775 625890). Ferry ticket prices include a donation to SWT.

Tel: 07920 468572
Email: handaranger@swt.org.uk

SHEIGRA TO SANDWOOD BAY

The walk along the moorland path to the remote and fabled beach of Sandwood Bay is a magnificent excursion, but this walk involves a more sporting and challenging circular alternative, taking in the dramatic coastal scenery south of the bay and returning by the path. Exceptionally hardy walkers could combine the outward section of this route with Route 76.

Distance: 11 miles/18 km (circular)
Time: 5–7 hours
OS map: 9

THE WALK BEGINS AT THE TINY SETTLEMENT OF BLAIRMORE, which is reached by leaving the A838 at the Rhiconich Hotel and taking the B801 to Kinlochbervie. Here, a minor road turns right, leading in just over three miles to Blairmore, where there is a car park and toilet facilities established by the John Muir Trust, which owns the area.

The signposted track marked 'Sandwood' is your return route. Instead, follow the minor road downhill, turning off just before Sheigra to reach a walled cemetery. Go through a wooden gate just before the cemetery and follow a vague grassy path up to a second gate. Turn left here and gradually climb steeper slopes on a sheep track to reach the cliff edge and the start of the coastal route proper.

A little further on is a dramatic and fascinating example of cliff erosion on a massive scale. Colossal blocks of Lewisian gneiss have sheared away from the main cliff, leaving huge fissures and extensive debris on a grand scale. Just before this spot, you will need to cross a well-built dry-stone wall. Great care should be exercised as you continue onwards, as several large fissures may be partly concealed by heather. Reach a high point at Cnoc an Staca, where there is a cairn.

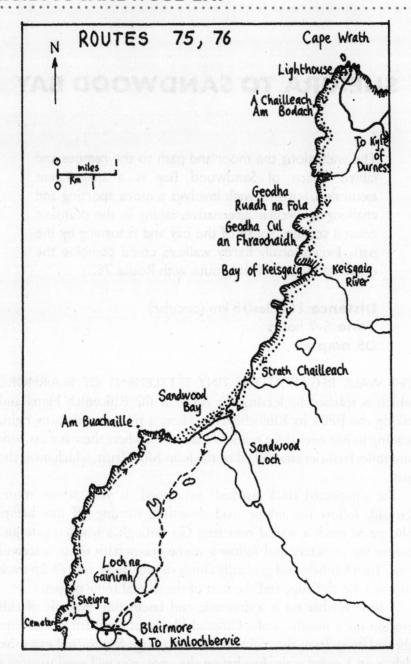

ROUTES 75, 76

N

Cape Wrath

Lighthouse

A' Chailleach
Am Bodach

To Kyle
of
Durness

Geodha
Ruadh na Fola

Geodha Cul
an Fhraochaidh

Bay of Keisgaig

Keisgaig
River

miles

Km

Strath Chailleach

Sandwood
Bay

Am Buachaille

Sandwood
Loch

Loch na
Gainimh

Sheigra

Cemetery

Blairmore
To Kinlochbervie

From here, continue northwards, descending to the left of Loch a'
Chreadha. Several hundred yards beyond here you will need to turn
inland for a short distance, following the top of the cliffs, until you

can descend via a wide grass and heather gully. Turn left, passing another lochan, and begin to climb easy grassy slopes following a fence. This leads up to a delightful mile of easy clifftop wandering, eventually leading down to an obvious flat grassy promontory crossed by a dry-stone wall. The stack of Am Buachaille ('the shepherd' or 'herdsman') is visible from here.

Explore the promontory before continuing round its northern extremity to make a descending traverse into a wide gully. Cross the stream and climb steep, heathery slopes beyond to follow the clifftop once again. Before descending, gradually veer away from the coastline to drop into a wide defile and cross the stream at its base. Make a rising traverse through heather to become established on a good path that hugs the clifftop all the way to the final promontory before Sandwood Bay and a fine view of the stack of Am Buachaille. This sandstone monolith rises nearly 70 m above the waves and was first climbed in 1967 by Tom Patey. You may be able to spot some old rope and slings near the summit.

As you turn the promontory and head east, the first view of Sandwood Bay is absolutely breathtaking. Over a mile and a half of white sand and Atlantic surf is backed by extensive dunes and the deep cobalt-blue of freshwater Sandwood Loch. Lower down, a flat sandstone plinth is a fine spot from which to savour this magnificent sight and soul-piercing desolation.

A good path continues to follow the coastline, above low cliffs, gradually descending to the dunes at the south end of the bay. You will no doubt want to spend some time exploring this wild and beautiful bay before embarking on the return route.

Sandwood is a corruption of the Old Norse *sand-vatn*, meaning 'sand-water', and the bay itself was one of only five UK beauty spots to be included in a list of the world's top fifty beaches compiled by the *Daily Mail's Travel* magazine in 2010. But Sandwood Bay possesses more than just a rare beauty: there is an aura and atmosphere that have captivated many who have sampled its precious delights, and many visitors talk of a 'presence'. Indeed, there is a long history of sightings in the bay, including a red-haired mermaid originally spotted by a shepherd and subsequently by others. Many shipwrecks have helped reinforce stories of a black-bearded sailor who haunts the shore and dunes.

Sandwood Bay's increased popularity over the years have resulted in the John Muir Trust embarking on a serious overhaul of the badly eroded path from Blairmore, and on your return leg the renovation work will be apparent. The path begins in the dunes near the small lochan between Sandwood Loch and the sea and rises up to pass between a small knoll on the left and the steep hill on the right. Initially, this is just a sandy furrow and grass path but soon develops into a well-engineered ash and gravel path complete with drainage channels. You will pass several freshwater lochs on the four-mile route, which is a pleasing contrast to the dramatic cliffs of the outward journey. The path ends at Blairmore and your starting point.

Recommended pub: Rhiconnich Hotel, Rhiconnich

CAPE WRATH TO SANDWOOD BAY AND BLAIRMORE

The walk from the wild and windswept north-western extremity of Britain at Cape Wrath to the iconic and mesmerising beach of Sandwood Bay is quite simply one of the most breathtaking coastal walks in Britain. Reaching Sandwood Bay, however, is not the end of the expedition, as there is still another four miles of inland path and track to walk to reach civilisation at Blairmore. This is for fit and experienced walkers only. This route could be combined with Route 75.

Distance: 13 miles/21 km (linear)
Time: 7–9 hours
OS map: 9

ACCESS TO CAPE WRATH IS NOT STRAIGHTFORWARD AND involves a foot-passenger ferry across the Kyle of Durness before an 11-mile shuttle service by mini-bus to reach the lighthouse at the cape. The ferry starts at the end of a minor road about 2.5 miles south-west of Durness and operates between May and September only. Sailings usually begin around 9.30 a.m. subject to tides, weather and passenger uptake. (See the 'Getting to Cape Wrath' panel for further information.) There is also a Ministry of Defence firing and bombing area east of Cape Wrath, and this may cause delays or even cancellations. Before thinking of going to Cape Wrath, you would be well advised to visit the tourist information centre in Durness, which will supply all the information required. The difficulty of access to Cape Wrath is the main reason why this walk is described from north to south; that is, you will finish in an area relatively easy to access rather than at Cape Wrath.

It should also be noted at this point that following prolonged heavy

Am Buachaille from Sandwood Bay

rain there are three river crossings that may prove problematic, and you would be well advised to tackle this walk after a dry spell of weather.

The area around Cape Wrath Lighthouse, with its dizzying sea cliffs, inlets and stacks, is worth exploring before you begin the long trek south. As you head south along the clifftop, you may just spot the tiny spire of the sea stack known as Am Buachaille at the south end of Sandwood Bay, only seven miles away as the crow flies. The walking is relatively easy on sheep tracks, but beware of patches of long, tussocky grass, heather and peat hags. Pass two dramatic sea stacks, A' Chailleach and Am Bodach ('the Old Woman' and 'the Old Man') about a mile south of the cape.

Continue southwards, descending into the first of many straths and gorges to cross a stream before a short ascent and a level clifftop stroll lead to a more substantial and steep-sided gorge. The stream flowing through this gorge is generally easy to cross, but the descent into the gorge and ascent from it involve some scrabbling on loose dirt and scree, and you may prefer a slight inland detour to avoid the steeper section.

South of the gorge, the cliff scenery improves further as you climb easy slopes past Geodha Ruadh na Fola and up onto a fine little grassy hillock overlooking a rocky bay backed by immense cliffs. Look out for the varied bird-life such as kittiwakes, fulmars, herring gulls and oystercatchers all shrieking and vying for attention.

Round the headland south of this bay to overlook the Bay of Keisgaig. The Keisgaig River, which flows into this bay, is the first river that may be difficult to cross in very wet weather. The best advice in poor conditions is to drop down to its mouth at the bay itself and cross just below a ruined shelter.

Beyond here for the next two miles is a superb clifftop extravaganza as you climb steadily to around 150 m above the pounding Atlantic rollers at Rubh' an t-Socaich Ghlais. A gradual descent of just over a mile brings you to the second major river crossing, at Strath Chailleach. Near its outflow into the sea there are several rocky falls that should prove negotiable, but failing that, a long inland detour may be required.

Less than a mile beyond Strath Chailleach, descend a craggy bluff to finally reach golden sands backed by low dunes. Sandwood Bay is a glorious spot to unwind from the rigours of the last nine miles, but there is still one last river crossing to negotiate, in the form of the outflow from freshwater Sandwood Loch. This is most easily crossed close to the wider, shallower mouth near the sea, and wading barefoot is a refreshing wake-up call for tired feet.

Seton Gordon described Sandwood Bay as 'the most beautiful place on all the west coast of the Scottish mainland' in *Highways and Byways in the West Highlands* and, walking barefoot along the extensive sands with the pounding Atlantic breakers on your right, it is easy to sympathise with this sentiment. Sandwood Bay has had its fair share of legendary and mythical visions, such as several sightings of a red-haired mermaid and the ghost of a bearded shipwrecked mariner.

Off to the right, the sentinel-like Am Buachaille rises nearly 70 m above the waves and was first climbed in 1967. Those walkers whose appetite for more dramatic cliff scenery has still not been whetted may wish to consider continuing along the clifftop to Am Buachaille and then for 3.5 miles to the tiny settlement of Sheigra, half a mile from Blairmore (note that this is Route 75 in reverse).

The quickest route, however, is to follow the grassy path running up behind the dunes leading up to the right of an obvious knoll. This skirts around the south flank of Druim na Buainn, passing three lochans before developing into a proper Land Rover track. This passes to the left of the large Loch na Gainimh before reaching the car park at Blairmore.

Note that if two cars are not available, there is a taxi service allowing you to be driven back to the ferry car park at the Kyle of Durness. For details, enquire at the tourist information centre in Durness or talk to the ferry operator.

Recommended pub: Rhiconnich Hotel, Rhiconnich

Getting to Cape Wrath

There is a foot-passenger ferry service across the Kyle of Durness operating between May and September, although it may be cancelled depending on bad weather, MoD exercises and tidal conditions. Phone the ferry operator, J. Morrison, for details.

Tel: 01971 511246

AN FHARAID

The unique little peninsula of An Fharaid is fabled for its stunning dunescapes, limestone rock scenery and arctic-alpine flora. As such, it has been designated as a European Special Area of Conservation. Its circuit provides relatively easy walking on a beach, dunes, short grass and a tarmac road. Unfortunately, Faraid Head itself is an out-of-bounds Ministry of Defence lookout station. This route is ideal for children, but care will be needed near the cliffs.

Distance: 5 miles/8 km (return)
Time: 3–4 hours
OS map: 9

FARAID HEAD LIES NORTH OF THE VILLAGE OF DURNESS ON THE A838 road. The walk begins at Balnakeil, which lies north-west of Durness along a minor road. There is a car park at Balnakeil Bay, from where there is a grand view of the sandy beach forming the first part of the walk.

Head north along the beach, which has firm sand and is notable for its sunsets. There is also good swimming here. At the far end of the beach, join a tarmac road, which is often difficult to see as it becomes covered in sand during windy conditions. On a really windy day, the sand is whipped up and can sting the eyes and face – be warned! The road leads up into the dramatic, high sand dunes, which are some of the tallest and most mobile in Britain. At an open area at the end of the dune system, leave the road by bearing left to follow a grassy path. This leads out to the cliff edge and eventually the exposed headland at GR 378715.

The *machair* en route to the headland is a haven for wild flowers in the spring, and its lime-rich, sandy soil is ideal for plants such as

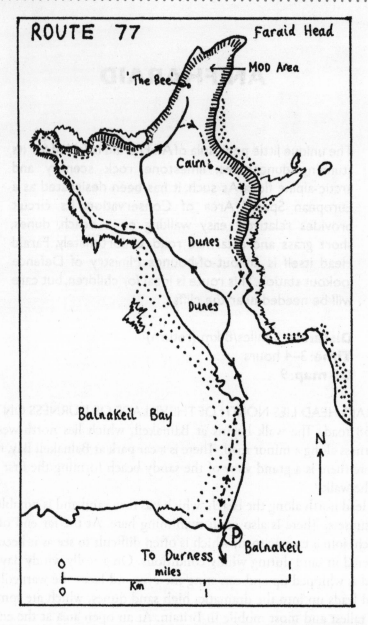

ROUTE 77
Faraid Head
MOD Area
'The Bee'
Cairn
Dunes
Dunes
Balnakeil Bay
N
To Durness
Balnakeil
miles
Km

orchids, gentian, clover, harebell and wild thyme. If you are really lucky, you may spot the rare Scots primrose, a small purple plant with a yellow centre. The cliffs themselves are Durness limestone, in contrast to the more common sandstone that forms much of the north-coast sea cliffs.

Viewpoint cairn, Faraid Head

From the headland, follow the clifftop along the beautiful close-cropped grass until you reach the tarmac road leading uphill to the MoD area. The obvious lookout building with its black-and-yellow chequered base is known locally as 'the Bee'. Turn right at the boundary fence, where a path leads to an excellent viewpoint marked by a cairn on a small knoll. This is a marvellous spot to take a short rest and gain an overall impression of the whole peninsula.

Leave the cairn and continue to follow the clifftop south to the dune system, where a right turn will lead you back to the tarmacked road used earlier. Turn left and head south to reach the beach and the start of the walk. The large building beside the car park is Balnakeil House, built in 1744 and at one time a residence of Clan MacKay. The ruined Balnakeil Church opposite is worth a visit and contains some interesting old graves.

Route 78

STRATHY POINT

The dramatic pointed headland of Strathy Point
provides the focus for a fine, though short, circular
walk taking in magnificent cliff scenery and natural
arches. It is suitable for small children only if they are
closely supervised!

Distance: 2.5 miles/4 km (circular)
Time: 1–2 hours
OS map: 10

STRATHY POINT LIES HALFWAY ALONG THE NORTH COAST OF
Scotland and is one of the narrowest headlands in the country, being
under 300 m wide for over half a kilometre of its length.

The village of Strathy lies ten miles east of Bettyhill, on the A836,
and Strathy Point is three miles north of here. Cars can be driven on
a minor road to a car park almost a mile short of the point itself.
Walk north along the continuing minor road. As the peninsula
narrows on both sides, there is a feeling of approaching the summit
of a sharp peak. Just before the lighthouse, pass a small lochan with
a model lighthouse. Go to the right of the real lighthouse and cross
a narrow rocky neck to reach the very tip of the point – a grand
situation.

The remaining part of the walk can be made as long or as short as
you wish, depending on your inclination to explore the many
promontories and rock formations lying south-west of the point.
Leave the road near the lighthouse entrance gate and follow the cliff
edge. The first promontory conceals a natural arch that is visible on
the approach, but the promontory itself offers a dramatic view of the
lighthouse perched on the edge of the land. Beyond here, you can
explore further prominent rocky fingers pointing northwards, one of
which is so flat and grassy that it would double as a putting green.

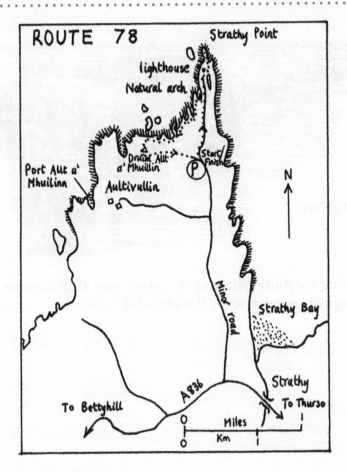

There is no real path along here, but numerous sheep tracks lead the way and care should be taken.

A fence on the left makes a sharp turn inland just north of Druim Allt a' Mhuilinn, and this marks the point of return to the car park. Follow the fence uphill, from where there are marvellous views across to the sandstone cliffs of Orkney. From here, continue to follow the fence as it turns left downhill to a gate. Leave the fence here and walk across heath to reach a second fence and a track leading back to the minor road and car park.

Extension

An obvious extension to the above short walk would entail continuing along the coastline to Port Allt a' Mhuilinn then

Strathy Point

returning via Aultivullin and the minor road that connects with the original approach road. This extended route covers around four miles.

HOLBORN HEAD

This is a satisfying circular walk from Scrabster to the spectacular cliffs at Holborn Head, followed by an airy clifftop stroll and a return by vehicle track. Much of the route is on a well-marked grassy path and is suitable for children provided they are supervised at all times.

Distance: 5 miles/8 km (circular)
Time: 2–3 hours
OS map: 12

SCRABSTER IS THE MAIN FERRY TERMINAL FOR ORKNEY AND LIES just north of Thurso at the end of the A9. Park in the designated parking area on the right, just before the new terminal complex.

Beyond the complex, take the narrow tarmac road that leads uphill and along the coast to Holbornhead Lighthouse. Just before the lighthouse, go through the gate on the left and climb the grassy slope by a fence. Turn right at the end of the fence and follow the obvious grassy path over several stiles and concrete slabs to reach the cliffs at Holborn Head.

The area around Holborn Head is worth exploring, but a word of warning needs to be given. Not far from the cliff edge are deep fissures and blowholes dropping sheer into the thunderous collapsed sea caves far below. In stormy weather, these can be a stirring sight (and sound), and even greater care should be taken in such conditions. These blowholes were mainly formed from thin-layered stratified sandstone, which has also been worn by the relentless action of sea and wind into numerous geos and stacks, such as Clett, a short distance west of Holborn Head.

A shorter variation of the described walk would be to simply return from here by the outward route, but the coastline west of Holborn Head provides grand, airy clifftop walking on close-cropped turf for

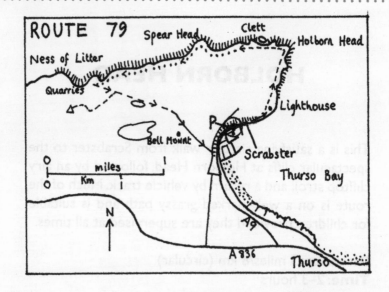

ROUTE 79 — Spear Head, Clett, Holborn Head, Ness of Litter, Quarries, Bell Mount, Lighthouse, Scrabster, Thurso Bay, Thurso, A836, A9. miles, Km, N.

nearly two miles and should not be missed. After observing the great rock stack of Clett, continue pleasantly on a good grass path through two metal gates. Beyond Spear Head, there is a marvellous view along

Holborn Head

the wriggling line of sandstone cliffs to the Ness of Litter, and a plethora of sheep tracks hug the clifftop, giving beautiful, easy walking.

All too soon you will reach the disused slate quarry just before the Ness of Litter, which marks the start of the return route by way of the gravel quarry track. This leads in just under a mile to a wooded area with a house on the left. By this point, you will have noticed a ring-like monument known as Bell Mount on the horizon. It is easily reached from a point just after the house and is worth visiting for the view alone. The monument is known locally as 'the Polo' and is a large, vertical stone ring used in annual festivals held by people in the north to celebrate the Vikings. It is certainly not ancient by any stretch of the imagination!

Continue along the track, which soon develops into a road past a modern estate. At the junction further on, descend a long flight of concrete steps down the steep embankment to reach the main A9 road several hundred yards south of the parking area. Turn left to reach the car park in just a few minutes.

Route 80

DUNNET HEAD

This is the classic walkers' route to the most northerly point on the Scottish mainland and is not for the faint-hearted. The walk alternates from pathless, tussocky terrain to rough sheep tracks on the top of high sea cliffs and is not suitable for younger children.

Distance: 6 miles/10 km (linear)
Time: 3–4 hours
OS map: 12

IT IS A COMMON MISTAKE TO BELIEVE THAT JOHN O'GROATS IS the most northerly point on mainland Britain. In fact, it is beaten fairly and squarely by Dunnet Head, several miles to the west. This point can be reached by car via the B855, but walking there is far more satisfying. The ideal way to tackle the route would be to leave a bike at Dunnet Head to be picked up at the end of the walk. The return cycle is almost all downhill and a glorious finale to the day.

The start of the walk is at Dwarwick Pier, which is reached from the small village of Dunnet on the A836 road nine miles east of Thurso. Turn left onto the B855, where there is a sign for Dunnet Head. Do not take the right-hand turn a few hundred yards further on; instead, continue straight on for a kilometre and turn left at a T-junction. The road ends at a car park near the pier.

Walk west from the pier over a small hill and cross a stile over a fence. The larger hill beyond can be climbed via several different sheep tracks and you may wish to keep close to the edge of the cliff during the ascent. Descend the less steep northern slope past Dwarwick Head to a small bay. The prominent large white house to the right is the House of the Northern Gate, formerly owned by the late Commander and Lady Vyner of Sheffield steel fame. The late Queen Mother was a friend of Lady Vyner, and regular visits to the house instilled a love of

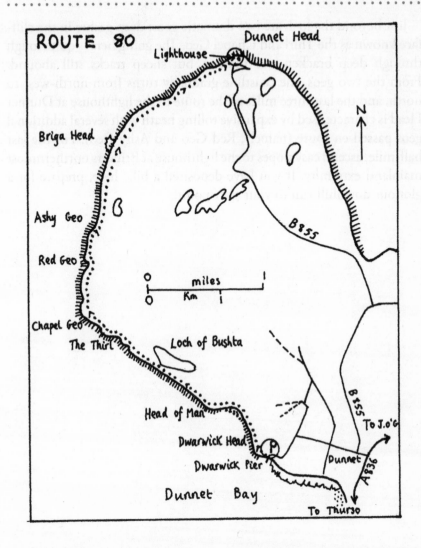

ROUTE 80

Dunnet Head

Lighthouse

Briga Head

Ashy Geo

Red Geo

Chapel Geo

The Thirl

Loch of Bushta

Head of Man

Dwarwick Head

Dwarwick Pier

Dunnet Bay

B855

To J.o'G

Dunnet

To Thurso

N

miles

Km

the area in her, which ultimately led to her buying and renovating what is now known as the Castle of Mey.

Continue onwards up the small hill beyond the bay on a vague path and follow the top of the Old Red Sandstone cliffs, keeping an eye open for gannets, kittiwakes and fulmars, which nest on the numerous ledges. A mile further on, you will pass the freshwater Loch of Bushta, but it will not become visible until you ascend the hill beyond. It is worth making the short detour to observe the loch, especially if you are treated to the sight of red-throated divers, a common occurrence here.

Just beyond the loch are two dramatic geos: deep gashes in the cliff-face known as the Thirl and Chapel Geo. The going here is quite tough through deep bracken and heather, but sheep tracks still abound. From the two geos, the coastline gradually turns from north-west to north, and the last three miles of the route to the lighthouse at Dunnet Head is characterised by expansive rolling heath with several additional geos passed en route (namely, Red Geo and Ashy Geo). For the last half-mile, ascend easy slopes to the lighthouse at Britain's northernmost mainland extremity. If you have deposited a bike here, prepare for a glorious downhill run to your start point!

4

The Outer Isles:

THE OUTER HEBRIDES, ORKNEY AND SHETLAND

NORTH UIST: THE GRENITOTE PENINSULA

The Grenitote peninsula, the most northerly headland of North Uist, also known as the Udal peninsula, is a gnarled, low-lying finger of land stretching for three miles into the blue ocean. It provides a wonderful location for a satisfying circuit on easy tracks, *machair* and flat sandy beaches with great opportunities for bird-watching and archaeology.

Distance: 7 miles/11 km (circular)
Time: 3–5 hours
OS map: 18

THE LITTLE HAMLET OF GRENITOTE IS EASILY REACHED FROM Lochmaddy by taking the A865 road for nine miles. At Grenitote, turn right along a minor road for half a mile to a gravel parking area on the right at the road-end.

Just ahead of the parking area is a tidal stream, but a track goes off to the left, crossing the outflow by a bridge, and this is the recommended start of the walk. This slight inland diversion soon swings back to the coast, going through a gate and back to the sandy beach of Traigh Ear.

Continue to follow the coast for over a mile either on the sand flats or on the grassy track at the top of the beach. On reaching the long, narrow spit of sand and dunes known as Corran Aird a' Mhorain, you should notice a large wooden post marking the point at which the route heads inland through the dunes for a short distance. This post was helpfully placed here by television personality Monty Halls, who spent six months as voluntary ranger in the Uists. This was one of his favourite walks!

The sandy track soon develops into an easy grassy track winding its way northwards towards the high point at Aird a' Mhorain, where you

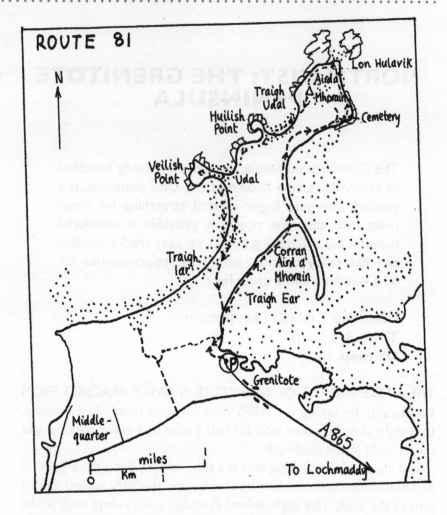

may spot the trig point. Several posts also mark the route, which is fairly obvious. At the point where the track makes a sharp turn left to ascend the high point, leave the track and follow a secondary path round to the right. Just below here, a cross has been carved into a rock wall, possibly to mark a well below it, but no one really knows.

The small path soon leads to an exposed little cemetery which is the traditional burial ground of the MacLeans of Boreray, the island lying a mile or so to the north-east. It is worth spending some time exploring the graves, the last resting place of many clan members.

Continue northwards, following the coast on an easy grass path until you reach 'land's end' at Lon Hulavik, looking out to a tidal

The MacLean cemetery,
Grenitote peninsula

gravel and rock skerry. Gradually turn southwards and begin to follow the west side of the peninsula for about a quarter of a mile before ascending easy grassy slopes to reach the summit trig point of Aird a' Mhorain. Enjoy marvellous views south across the beaches and dunes and also to Boreray.

Leave the trig point on a grassy path that winds its way south towards the dunes backing the small beach of Traigh Udal. Stride along the beach towards the little headland of Huilish at its southern end before heading across the *machair* to the next small beach at Udal. En route, look out for evidence of prehistoric occupation in the form of a midden and a wheelhouse. The midden is basically an ancient rubbish pit and is a mass of rocks interlaced with shells and possibly pieces of pottery.

A small diversion to the hummocky, protruding piece of land at Veilish Point, joined to the main island by a narrow neck of land, is worth it for the view down the next huge beach of Traigh Iar. Just inland from here on a knoll is an excavated site dating from the Bronze Age, which was engulfed by a sandstorm late in the seventeenth century.

The vast, curving, sandy beach of Traigh Iar should be followed for about half a mile, keeping an eye open for Arctic terns and gannets. At a suitable point, climb the high dunes on the left and reach the grassy track through the *machair*. You may be lucky to spot dunlin, plovers and snipes. Also, listen for the snipes' distinctive drumming sound.

This grassy track wanders delightfully through partly cultivated *machair* before making a left bend at a green corrugated-iron shed where the grass becomes a gravel vehicle track. This leads in less than half a mile to the outward route.

A possible extension for those with spare energy and time is to walk the whole length of Traigh Iar and then head south along the sands to the road-end at Middlequarter. Rejoin the A865 and turn left to reach Grenitote and the start of the route.

Recommended pub: Lochmaddy Hotel, Lochmaddy

BERNERAY CIRCUIT

A beautiful and varied walk around Berneray, the main 'stepping-stone' between Harris and North Uist, this route includes the island's high point, at 93 m, and a glorious stravaig along the spacious 3.5-mile West Beach, the longest beach walk in this book.

Distance: 10 miles/16 km (circular)
Time: 5–7 hours
OS map: 18

THE ISLAND OF BERNERAY IS NOW CONNECTED TO NORTH Uist by a causeway built in 1999 and is also the location of the main vehicle ferry to Leverburgh, in Harris. About three miles long and 1.5 miles wide, Berneray's west side is one glorious stretch of shell-sand beach backed by huge dunes and low-lying *machair*. The beach itself has been compared with some Caribbean beaches, but, frankly, there is no comparison: this wins hands down, and, more to the point, it is relatively deserted.

Prince Charles stayed on Berneray for a time in the late 1980s in order to sample simple island life, staying in a typical household and getting his hands dirty by helping out with the farming and fishing. It speaks volumes for the Berneray residents that not a word was breathed about their royal guest to the media, both during his time on the island and on his return home. The prince himself came clean several years later.

Begin the walk at the community centre in Borve, which lies on its own at the end of the minor road south of Borve Hill. The building is clearly recognisable by its red roof and wind turbine. There should be plenty of parking space in front of the building.

Start by walking back up the road to the junction, and turn left to go round the little bay of Poll an Oir ('pond of gold') and then the

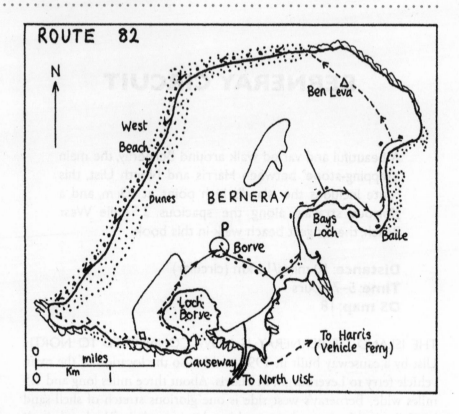

ROUTE 82

N

West
Beach

Dunes

BERNERAY

Ben Leva

Bays
Loch

Baile

P Borve

Loch
Borve

Causeway

miles

Km

To Harris
(Vehicle Ferry)

To North Uist

larger Bays Loch with its scattering of cottages around the rim. Pass the Nurse's Cottage, now a museum and information centre, which you may wish to visit. Further on, there is a seal viewing point with an information board, and if you hang about you should almost certainly spot common seals basking on the rocks.

Continue round Bays Loch, heading slightly inland until you reach a gate and a sign indicating the youth hostel at Baile. From here, a new minor road runs north parallel to the shore, but closer to the shore is a grassy track, which is easier on the feet. Follow the track or road along the flat *machair* for nearly a mile until the public road ends near some new houses. Here you should spot a sign on the left saying 'Berneray Circular Walk' with an arrow pointing diagonally across a field towards the summit of Ben Leva (or Beinn Shleibhe), your next objective.

You will need to cross the fence at this point and head diagonally upwards until you reach a gate and an old cemetery. Several waymarker posts may be evident. Continue upwards on a grassy path to the trig point marking the summit of Ben Leva, where, unsurprisingly, there are superb views to be had.

Descend an easy grassy path north-westwards to reach the end of West Beach and the start of a magnificent three-mile wander along its bleached-white shell-sands. For many, this will be the highlight of the walk, and it is nothing short of a true delight on firm sand, allowing easy, effortless strolling and time to let the mind wander.

About an hour later, you will reach the southern end of the beach on pleasant rolling *machair*, possibly with livestock for company. Pass some old, grassed-over ruins of black houses on the southern shore and a small hillock with a stone ruin on its top. This is known locally as the 'Mound of Skulls' and is possibly an ancient burial mound. The ruin on the top is a much more recent shepherd's lookout hut.

Further on, reach a tall, cemented cairn surrounded by a stone wall with a gate. This was built in 1991 to commemorate Angus MacAskill, who lived on a croft on the site of the cairn in the mid 1800s. His main claim to fame was being a natural giant, standing at 7 ft 9 in., the same height as the cairn. He left Berneray, however, when he was only six years old to emigrate with his family to Nova Scotia, but the islanders clearly considered him famous enough to celebrate him with this cairn.

Just beyond the cairn is a walled burial ground, where a new tarmac road begins. Continue on in the direction of Loch Borve, an almost fully enclosed tidal sea loch that is a magnet for waders and other bird-life. Follow the edge of Loch Borve on a grassy track as it swings round the loch, eventually heading inland to join with the new tarmac road at a bend. You may wish to make a small diversion to a tall standing stone on the small hillock opposite Loch Borve. The tarmac road leads directly back to the community centre and your starting point.

Recommended pub: Lochmaddy Hotel, Lochmaddy

Route 83

ST KILDA: HIRTA CIRCUIT

The circuit, or partial circuit, of Hirta, the largest of the St Kilda group of islands, is without a doubt the most adventurous and uniquely atmospheric walk to be described in this book. Wild, dramatic and uncompromising, it is an expedition unlikely to be repeated in a lifetime and will remain permanently in the memory. Both shorter and longer options are described.

Distance: 3–8 miles/5–13 km (circular)
Time: 3–6 hours
OS map: 18

THE ST KILDA ARCHIPELAGO COMPRISES BRITAIN'S MOST remote islands, lying some 40 miles west of the Outer Hebrides. Born 60 million years ago as a vast volcano, the rim of which defines the south and west coasts of Hirta and also Soay, the islands are mainly composed of granite, gabbro and softer dolerite. The name St Kilda does not refer to a saint but originates from the Old Icelandic *skildar*, meaning 'shields', which could describe the shape of the islands when seen from afar. For around 4,000 years, Hirta was inhabited by a group of islanders small in number but hardy in constitution before being finally evacuated in 1930 amongst a flurry of publicity. Since Hirta's evacuation, St Kilda's public profile has risen and the archipelago is now a National Nature Reserve and has earned the ultimate accolade of being designated a double UNESCO World Heritage Site due to its historical and cultural significance as well as its unique environmental and scenic value. For many, a trip to St Kilda is a lifelong dream and a once-in-a-lifetime experience.

When you arrive on Hirta, you will be met by the warden from the National Trust for Scotland (which owns the whole archipelago), who

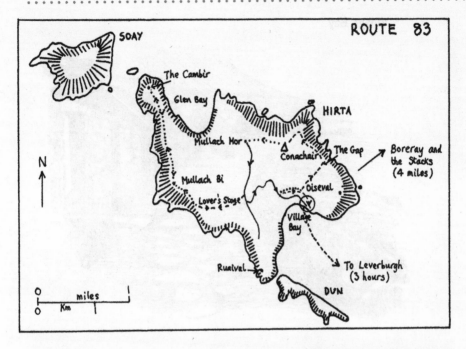

ROUTE 83

might want to know your intentions. Many folk will be content to spend most of their time in and around Village Bay, but a significant few will wish to reach the highest point of the island at Conachair (430 m). For any walker, this is a 'must' and is essentially the first part of the walk round the island.

Begin the walk by heading north-east from Village Bay up into the depression known as An Lag ('the hollow in the north'). To your right is the peak of Oiseval and to your left is Conachair. Dotted all around the hillside are the stone structures known as cleits, which were used by St Kildans to store turf, which then dried and could be used for fuel. In twenty minutes or so you will reach the Gap, the wild and windy defile between Oiseval and Conachair and a grand spot from which to view Boreray and the Stacks, some four miles to the north-east. At this point, you are already 160 m above the crashing waves. The Gap is a grand place to loiter, with the only intent being absorbing the unique atmosphere. Here you have a superb view of Village Bay and of the jagged knife-edge ridge of Dun, a natural breakwater for the bay.

There is the option of heading right here and climbing 130 m up the grassy ridge to Oiseval, but most will opt to go left up the grassy

Village Bay

path to eventually reach Hirta's highest point, Conachair. En route, you are likely to be dive-bombed by great skuas, and a trekking pole is useful for holding above your head. Although less continuously vertical than the Kame on Foula in Shetland or St John's Head on Hoy, the Conachair cliffs are the highest sea cliffs in Britain and have only been climbed from sea level relatively recently (1987). Some 6,000 pairs of fulmars breed on the Conachair cliffs. On a clear day, the view from Conachair is simply awesome and it is possible to make out the Cuillin ridge of Skye, 100 miles distant.

Leave Conachair by its grassy west ridge and head to the spacious summit of Mullach Mor, conspicuous due to the massive radar station perched on its very crest, somewhat out of character in this wild spot. From Mullach Mor, a tarmac road winds its way down to Village Bay, and this would complete a very short part-circuit of the island, taking up to three hours.

Very fit walkers will opt to cross the head of Gleann Mor and attempt to reach the Cambir, the end of the northern peninsula overlooking the island of Soay. Despite the relatively short distance involved, the time taken to get there and back is deceptively long and the route is over very rough and rocky ground. Reaching the dramatic summit of Mullach Bi is a good halfway measure and also gives the chance to see the famous Lover's Stone, which is actually visible from the tarmac road across the head of Gleann Mor. This consists of a huge overhanging slab and is often confused with the Mistress Stone on Ruaival.

Getting to St Kilda

Up until a few years ago, the minimum time taken to reach St Kilda was around eight hours from the Outer Isles, so day trips were simply out of the question. With the phenomenal public interest in St Kilda that has arisen, making available significantly shorter trips was bound to be a clear winner, and it is now possible to reach these remote islands in only three hours by means of a 55-ft motor cruiser from Leverburgh courtesy of Kilda Cruises.

Angus Campbell, Kilda Cruises, 'Heatherlea', West Tarbert,
Isle of Harris, HS3 3BG
Web: www.kildacruises.co.uk
Email: angus@kildacruises.co.uk
Tel: 01859 502060
Mob: 07760 281804

Despite the relatively short journeying time of three hours to St Kilda, the time for the return journey must be taken into account, and so time on Hirta is at a premium. Theoretically, you will have five and a half hours ashore, but in reality you will be lucky to take five hours to complete the walk. Remember also that some time should be allocated for looking round Village Bay. Unless you are extremely fit and fast, a full circuit of Hirta is not a likely proposition, despite the low mileage involved.

From the Lover's Stone, follow the cliff edge on short grass up the steep slopes to reach Mullach Bi, which at 358 m is the highest point on the western cliffs. This is another stupendous viewpoint and Soay is especially well seen from this summit. If time is available, it is worth continuing at least part of the way to the Cambir, but the ridge becomes increasingly rocky, with some unavoidable scrambling at a narrow gap required. Looking across Glen Bay, you will see that there is a long,

The Lover's Stone

tunnel-like natural arch at the Gob na h-Airde headland.

It is doubtful if even a very fast walker will have time to include the southernmost extremity of Ruaival in an already packed itinerary, but this final summit can be reached by returning to the tarmac road by the head of Gleann Mor and following the ridge line south. Note that a true circumnavigation of the island would also involve a steep descent to Glen Bay, but a second visit would probably be required for this excursion.

On the return to Village Bay by the road, take the time to meander through the well-preserved ruins in the Village Street and try to imagine the St Kildans going about their daily life – the children going to school, the men organising their daily 'Parliament', the women tending the crofts – and listen to the ancient stones whispering stories of the past.

Recommended pub: The Anchorage, Leverburgh

HARRIS: CHAIPAVAL AND TOE HEAD

This is unquestionably one of the finest walks in Harris. The view from the summit of Chaipaval on a clear day is unparalleled, with glorious vistas of golden strands, wild hills and magnificent islands, including St Kilda. Chaipaval is not high (365 m) but involves a stiff little climb to the summit.

Distance: 8 miles/13 km (circular)
Time: 4–6 hours
OS map: 18

THE WALK IS SITUATED ENTIRELY ON A SMALL, RUGGED peninsula that is almost a separate island from Harris. It lies in South Harris, four miles north-west of the little coastal hamlet of Leverburgh, just off the A859 Rodel to Tarbert road. Take the minor road to Northton (or Taobh Tuath) and park near the gate at the end of the village. There is only limited space to park here and you may wish to park further back.

Go through the gate and follow a sand and gravel track across the *machair* to a second gate. Beyond this point, the path splits into three. The extreme left fork leads to the southern end of the beautiful beach of Traigh na Cleavaig and the middle option leads to the northern extremity of the same beach. Either of these options will suffice, with the first resulting in a pleasant walk along the sands to the north end of the bay.

From the end of the bay, a pleasant grassy path hugs the coastline rounding another idyllic sandy beach to arrive at a picturesque ruined chapel (Rubh an Teampuill). This was built in the sixteenth century and there is a plaque nearby giving more information. The chapel is an ideal spot for a first rest and an appreciation of the peaceful surroundings.

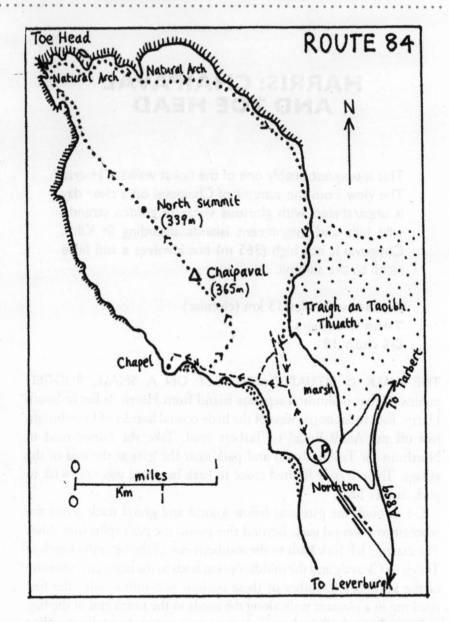

ROUTE 84

Toe Head

Natural Arch

Natural Arch

N

North summit
(339m)

△ Chaipaval
(365m)

Traigh an Taoibh.
Thuath

Chapel

marsh

To Tarbert

P

Northton

A859

To Leverburgh

miles

Km

The hill of Chaipaval can be climbed directly from the vicinity of the chapel, but it is easier to double back along the path for about a quarter of a mile before tackling the steep, heathery slopes to reach the south shoulder. You will need to cross a dry-stone wall en route. Once established on the shoulder, magnificent views reveal themselves in all

Chapel

directions. To the north-east lies the island of Taransay, famous for its use in the BBC series *Castaway 2000*. The wide expanse of the Scarasta sands are spread out to the east, and the *machair* separates Scarasta from the twin beaches above Northton.

The tough little climb levels out to tussocky moorland crowned by a trig point and cairn, where you can enjoy a well-earned rest and more magnificent views. On a clear day, the unmistakable profile of the St Kilda group can be seen some 50 miles to the west. This is a truly stupendous viewpoint and it will be hard to drag yourself onwards for the second part of the walk.

Follow the obvious summit ridge of the hill in a north-westerly direction over an unnamed subsidiary top (339 m) then gradually descend the shoulder on grass and rock terraces. After about one and half miles, you will reach the small lochan just before the hilly prominence of Toe Head at the end of the peninsula. Climb the small hillock and observe the long, narrow, rocky inlet just before Toe Head itself. The immediate area is a beautifully wild and remote spot. From here it is a long way back to the start, and the route essentially follows the coastline round the peninsula in a clockwise direction. There is no obvious path, but it is easier to stick as close to the rocky coastline as possible.

Look out for the natural arch at GR 966946. The arch itself is very close to the land behind it and, from above, the water visible through the narrow gap has the appearance of a blowhole. As you reach the vicinity of the sands at Scarasta, you will have to cross several fences via gates and look out for Highland cattle. Finally, reach a grassy track leading to the gate and your starting point.

Recommended pub: The Anchorage, Leverburgh

HARRIS: SCALPAY CIRCUIT

The picturesque island of Scalpay, close to Tarbert on the south-eastern side of Harris, is the focus of this magnificent walk. Partly on quiet roads and partly following a waymarked route around the island's southern and eastern coast, it is a walk of continuous interest and wonderful views, though it is best reserved for good weather. Although the route is waymarked, it can be quite rough going and boggy in places.

Distance: 6 miles/10 km (circular)
Time: 3–5 hours
OS map: 14

SCALPAY CAN BE REACHED FROM TARBERT BY A MINOR ROAD winding its way along the north shore of East Loch Tarbert, leading to a bridge to the island built in 1998. On reaching the island, take the sign marked 'Village' and park at the community centre, near the fire station at North Harbour.

Leave the community centre and follow the road to the right leading to South Harbour. From here, it is a delightful two-mile walk with wonderful sea views along the road. You will pass idyllic little cottages to reach the road-end at Kennavay, where there is a small parking area.

The waymarked route begins on the left of the road just before the parking area, where you should spot the first yellow-topped waymarker. The view from the west here, across the scattered islands of East Loch Tarbert to the hills beyond, is absolutely stunning. The waymarkers are numbered but not always easy to spot, and there is a confusing section around numbers 6, 7 and 8 where the route appears to double back, descending into a hollow before ascending the opposite side. This is unnecessary, and it is better to go straight ahead into the hollow

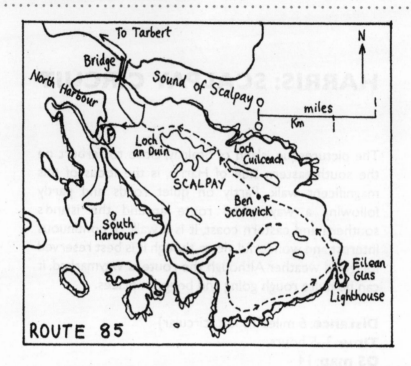

ROUTE 85

to rejoin the posts on the south side near the sea. This avoids a dog-leg and an extra climb.

Follow the markers as the route ascends hillocks and drops into gullies on the south coast. Stop to take in the fine views of Skye and the prominent Shiant Isles to the east. Soon, the Eilean Glas lighthouse comes into view, but there seem to be endless gullies and hummocks to cross until you reach the stone boundary wall. Go through a gate in the boundary wall and head for the small harbour just before the lighthouse buildings. Explore the lighthouse and its environs before continuing the walk.

Leave the lighthouse by the main stone path, which is raised above the surrounding bog for a short distance. There are no waymarkers at this point. Reach a grassy ridge and look down on a well-built stone wall that sits in a hollow stretching to the sea on the right. Up the hill on the opposite side you should spot a marker post, but to reach it you will need to descend and climb the wall at a low point. Climb up to reach the post and several others before descending to an area of peat hags and bog. Markers lead you across this short section before ascending the easy grassy slopes of Ben Scoravick, at 104 m the highest point on Scalpay.

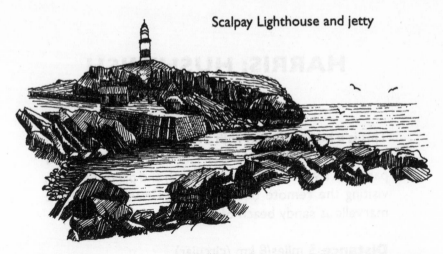

Scalpay Lighthouse and jetty

Unsurprisingly, this is a marvellous viewpoint and an ideal spot for some rest and a bite to eat. Ahead you will see a complex area of knolls and lochans, and somewhere through this terrain lies the next phase of the route. Leave the summit cairn, heading north-west, following the markers as they lead down to Loch Cuilceach, the first of two large lochans, where you may spot a black-throated diver. The route then passes between two knolls to arrive at the south end of the second lochan, Loch an Duin. The marker posts disappear here, but go right past some old wooden pontoons and follow the northern shore of the lochan, where you should pick up the markers once again on higher ground.

At the end of the lochan, head left in front of a white house and pick up a grassy track that should be followed to a metal gate and out onto the road past several houses. Turn left again to reach the village and community centre.

Recommended pub: The Isle of Harris Inn, Tarbert

HARRIS: HUSHINISH

This is a beautiful walk with a real wilderness flavour in this hidden corner of Harris. The route is circular and partly on a well-engineered cliff path and partly pathless, visiting the remote beach at Loch Cravadale and the marvellous sandy beach of Traigh Mheilein.

Distance: 5 miles/8 km (circular)
Time: 3–4 hours
OS map: 13

THE TINY COMMUNITY OF HUSHINISH LIES AT THE END OF THE long and tortuous B887 road on the north side of West Loch Tarbert. There is a small parking area on the right at a toilet block, shortly before the end of the road.

Walk along the road for a hundred yards before turning right up a minor sandy road leading to a small pier. Before reaching the pier, take a grassy path to the right crossing the *machair* and going through a gate. Beyond the gate, the path develops gradually into a good rocky path climbing steadily up the steep western flank of Husival Beag. The view across to the island of Scarp and beyond is breathtaking.

The path traverses around a deep gully high above the sea before rising again slightly, heading inland for the dip between the little knoll of Gresclett and the steep flanks on the right. Ahead, high above the coast, you may discern another path leading to the sandy beach of Traigh Mheilein. This is your return route.

As you approach the *bealach*, the path becomes increasingly sketchy and the descent to the freshwater loch of Loch na Cleavag is on tussocky grass and sphagnum moss. Follow the southern shore of the loch on the indistinct path, heading for the obvious little white isolated cottage of Cravadale, which is heavily boarded up and padlocked – not a bothy! If you are very lucky, you may spot a golden

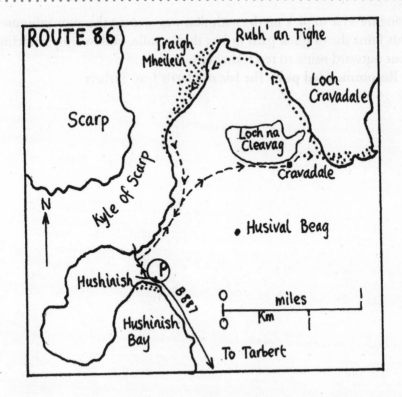

eagle, but it is more likely you will need to settle for a raven or crow.

From the cottage, it is worth swinging round to the right and dropping down to the wild and remote sandy beach at the head of Loch Cravadale, a heavenly spot to while away an hour.

To continue, follow the sheltered western coastline of Loch Cravadale on low-lying grass for about a mile before ascending slightly to pass between a small knoll and grassy slopes near Rubh' an Tighe. Descend gradually south-westwards to reach the broad sandy expanse of Traigh Mheilein, one of the finest beaches in Harris. Stroll along the sands and gaze across the narrow Kyle of Scarp to Scarp itself, a high and rocky island, once the most westerly inhabited British island, following St Kilda's evacuation. The island was abandoned in 1971, but there are holiday cottages that may be rented. In the 1930s, Gerhard Zucker, a German scientist, initiated a post delivery system on Scarp using rockets ('the rocket post'), but it was soon cut short when the first rocket prematurely exploded, scattering mail everywhere!

At the south end of the beach, leave the shore and gradually make a rising traverse to pick up the path that was seen on the outward route. This joins the original path in less than a mile. Follow this, retracing your outward route to reach the start.

Recommended pub: The Isle of Harris Inn, Tarbert

LEWIS: GARENIN TO DALBEG

A fine waymarked walk on the wild north-west coast of Lewis beginning at a unique restored black house village. Though not particularly long, the route involves considerable ascent and descent and possesses the feel of a real wilderness excursion, with much potential for exploration of the many rocky coves and inlets. An extension to Bragar is also briefly described for those walkers with spare energy and time. The walk is best reserved for clear, settled weather.

Distance: 4 miles/6 km (linear)
Time: 3–4 hours
OS map: 8

THE 'WEST COAST WALK' ON LEWIS IS PART OF THE NESS Coastal Trail network of coastal paths, though many, such as this one, are little more than waymarked routes with no genuine path construction.

To reach the start of the walk, turn off the A858 at Carloway Bridge and follow the sign for the Blackhouse Village at Na Gearrannan (Garenin). There is a car park just before the village on the right-hand side.

The village itself provides a fascinating insight into the way of life of a typical crofting township of the 1800s, and you may wish to explore the village in detail before or after your walk. There is a small charge for entering the houses. There is an excellent cafeteria and toilet facilities.

Walk through the village down the hill to a sign and plaque indicating the start of the walk, which goes through a gate and along a grassy path, gently climbing up the hillside. Follow the green and yellow marker posts across the undulating ground to a high point at Aird Mhor ('high headland'), where there is a grand view of the

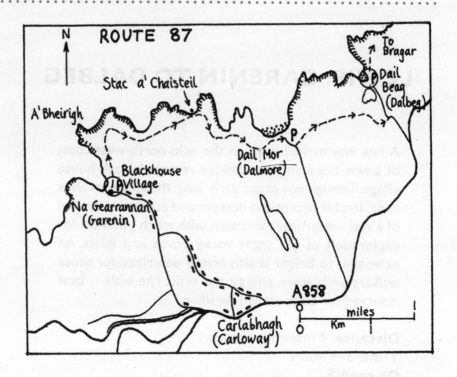

coastline and surrounding islands. A smaller promontory called A' Bheirigh lies west of here and is the site of a prehistoric fort, which you may wish to visit.

From Aird Mhor, descend gradually, following cairns if you lose the marker posts, which tend to go more inland anyway. Reach the small bay of Fibhig, surrounded by cliffs. You should spot old lazy-beds or runrigs, corrugated channels fertilised with seaweed and dung at one time and used for sowing oats and barley. Some of the barley was no doubt used in a nearby whisky still, of which there were at least four!

From here, climb easy grassy slopes to another high point at Aird Mheadhonach, where there are several large cairns. A short distance beyond is an impregnable-looking stack called Stac a' Chaisteil ('castle stack'), which, given that it looks too sheer and steep for anyone to climb and build on, contains the improbable remains of a defensive structure possibly dating from the Iron Age. Like Carloway broch, just south of here on the A858, it had double walls with stone stairs

Stac a' Chaisteil

between. The only way of reaching the stack is by way of a steep 20-ft-high cliff and is not recommended! The cairn standing proud on the summit of the stack is a relatively recent construction.

Climb up to another high point with a cairn before dropping steeply to the bay at Seiligeadh, where there is an old turf wall separating Garenin and Dalmore. There are ruins of three mills on the nearby stream of Allt na Muilne ('the mill burn'). At this point, the 'path' heads inland and climbs to cross a small ridge before zigzagging downwards to the cemetery at Dalmore.

Dalmore is a beautiful sandy bay surrounded by fertile farmland and was home to a thriving settlement up to about 1850, when the people were cleared. On reaching the road, turn right past the parking area and then turn off left between a dry-stone wall and a fence, where the waymarking posts begin once again. Continue uphill between the fences to reach the shoulder of the hill and then walk on down to a boggy area.

The waymarking posts are well inland here and continue over another shoulder following a fence. Just before Dalbeg, the route turns abruptly right following another fence to a stile. Go over the stile and head for a pedestrian bridge through an overgrown area. A final short climb leads to the road. The parking area lies less than half a mile down the road from this point and is the endpoint of the walk.

Extension

This excursion to Bragar involves an additional seven miles of walking, also waymarked, with numerous opportunities to cut short the route if preferred. Generally, the walking is on flatter terrain and the cliff scenery is not as dramatic as in the previous part. The route begins at the end of the road at Dalbeg, where there is an information board.

Just 20 minutes into the walk, at the headland of Aird Bianish, there is a remarkable flat grassy promontory that is rapidly eroding and is a curious feature. At the end of the road that leads to Siabost bho Dheas, look out for a massive blowhole in the ground.

On reaching the wide shingle Bay of Port Mhor Bhragair, follow the minor road from Labost to Bragar to complete the walk. Expect this extension to take between three and four hours.

LEWIS: TOLSTA HEAD

This is a fine walk contrasting a sublime sandy beach and dark, brooding, impressive cliff and sea stack scenery. The route is mostly waymarked but has a distinctive wild feel despite its relatively close proximity to civilisation.

Distance: 6 miles/10 km (circular)
Time: 3–4 hours
OS map: 8

TOLSTA HEAD LIES ON THE EAST SIDE OF LEWIS, NORTH-EAST OF Stornoway, and can be reached from there by taking the B895 road and its continuation on a minor road to the car park at the north end of the magnificent beach at Traigh Mhor ('big beach').

Go through the gate near the toilet block and walk down to the start of the magnificent strand stretching for a mile and a half to the cliffs at Tolsta Head. If you have started early enough, you may be lucky to be walking these sands in splendid isolation. This is an ideal and peaceful leg-stretcher before the more rigorous delights of the clifftop far ahead. Look out for gannets diving into the sea and also turnstones, which flit along the sand. Ahead, there is a dramatic vista of enormous sea stacks and cliffs.

At the end of the beach, climb onto the dunes and then the obvious grassy break leading up to a marker post and sign. The waymarking posts have blue tips and are situated at various intervals round the indented coastline of the headland. There is a path of sorts, but it is largely a sheep track with a fair amount of bog and imagination! Not that there is any chance of getting lost – just follow the coastline.

As you descend into a depression at the rocky cove of Heisgeir, there is a magnificent view back to the long beach of Traigh Mhor with an

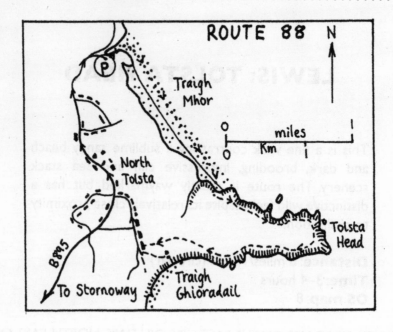

impressive narrow rocky promontory and sea stack in the immediate foreground. This is indeed a place to linger and absorb the unique atmosphere. In summer, underfoot is a colourful array of wild flowers, such as eyebright, buttercups, scabious, sea thrift, bog asphodel and field gentian to name a few.

As you round the tip of the headland at Tolsta Head itself, there is a fine view south to the Eye peninsula and you may spot the lighthouse at Tiumpan Head.

From here, the route continues westwards, back along the southern edge of the headland for a delightful airy mile until you reach a point overlooking a second fine beach called Traigh Ghioradail, another superb vantage point and a place to rest and meditate.

Ahead is a private house and track leading to a minor road, but the waymarked route heads slightly inland near a fence before descending slightly and then rising to follow a grassy path on the far side of the house. The marker posts are there but may be difficult to spot. The path develops into a gravel track just before the road, where you go through a gate and turn right. Follow this minor

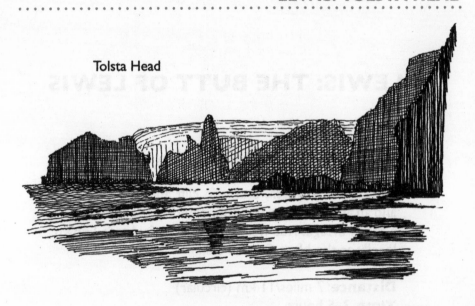

Tolsta Head

road for half a mile to the B895, where you again turn right for just over a mile to reach the car park at Traigh Mhor and the start of the walk.

Route 89

LEWIS: THE BUTT OF LEWIS

This is a beautiful circular walk taking in not only the most northerly point of the Western Isles but also a superb sandy beach, dramatic cliff and stack scenery and an ancient island dun connected to the mainland by a metal bridge. This walk forms part of what is known locally as the Ness Coastal Trail.

Distance: 7 miles/11 km (circular)
Time: 3–5 hours
OS map: 8

THE EXTREME NORTHERN PART OF LEWIS IS KNOWN AS NESS, or more commonly by its Gaelic equivalent, Nis, and road signs from Stornoway to 'the Butt' indicate Port Nis, the small settlement on the east coast, rather than the Butt of Lewis itself. Take the A857 through Suainbost (Swainbost) and Tabost before turning left down a minor road that ends in a mile at a cemetery. Cars can be parked here.

Walk down the grassy path from the cemetery, leading in only a few hundred yards to the marvellous sandy bay of Eoropaidh (Eoropie), backed by high dunes. From here, you should be able to spot a natural arch in the prominent headland to the north. Walk along the sands accompanied by the sight and sound of Atlantic rollers pounding in on the left.

Go through a gate at the north end of the beach and begin to follow a grassy path as it meanders its way around the rugged coastline. Looking back gives a fine view of Eoropaidh Beach and beyond. Wind round the smaller bay of Cunndal and climb gently up to a cairn built on a flat stony area just before a narrow, deep inlet. From around this point, the lighthouse at the Butt of Lewis should be visible.

Continue northwards, where the coastline becomes more indented, rugged and sheer, with the gnarled Lewisian gneiss rock much in

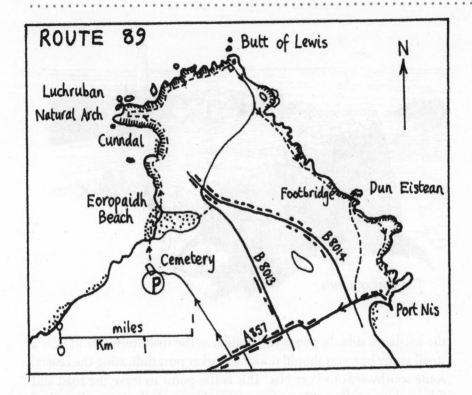

ROUTE 89

Butt of Lewis

N

Luchruban
Natural Arch

Cunndal

Eoropaidh
Beach

Cemetery

Footbridge

Dun Eistean

B8014

B 8013

P

miles

Km

A857

Port Nis

evidence. Pass the tidal rocky islet of Luchruban, which a race of pygmies was believed to inhabit in prehistoric times. The grassy summit of the islet contains the ruins of a chambered structure where small bones were discovered. They were, alas, identified as animal bones.

From here, continue round the numerous inlets and headlands for nearly a mile until you reach the vicinity of the Butt. There is a fine view of the lighthouse to be obtained on a little rocky promontory with three cairns just before you reach the building itself. This is also a good spot from which to observe the vast colonies of seabirds nesting on the cliffs.

The lighthouse, which was automated in 1998, was built in 1862 by Thomas Stevenson, and it is worth spending some time exploring the environs and contemplating the fact that, apart from the tiny islands of Sula Sgeir and Rona far to the north, there is only the restless ocean between here and the Faeroe Islands 200 miles north.

Leave the Butt by the narrow minor road, passing a small lochan on

The Butt of Lewis

the left-hand side. In about half a mile, as the road leads inland near a small sandy bay, you should notice a marker post indicating the coastal route southwards to Port Nis. This is the point to leave the road and follow the coastline using grass paths. Alternatively, if you have had enough, stay on the road until you reach the village of Eoropaidh, where a track leads down to Eoropaidh Beach and the parking area beyond. This is only one and a half miles.

Follow the coast in a south-easterly direction round numerous small coves and little promontories. In a mile, you will reach Dun Eistean, a remarkable little islet with the remains of an old dun on its summit. Long before this, however, you will have no doubt spotted the recently constructed steel pedestrian bridge that now spans the deep chasm separating the island from the mainland. Near the bridge is an information plaque indicating that Dun Eistean was once the island stronghold of Clan Morrison, which dominated North Lewis for many years. In fact, the clan crest has a picture of the original 4m-high defensive tower. Walk across the bridge and wonder how anyone managed to reach this detached rocky outpost in the absence of a bridge.

At the time of writing, a new vehicle track and car park were in the process of being constructed, making access to Dun Eistean considerably easier. For a quick return, follow this track to Port Nis. The described route, however, continues along the coast to pick up a track that descends to the harbour area of Port Nis. From here, simply follow the A857 for just over a mile to the minor road that leads off to the right and to the cemetery car park in another mile. This completes a most satisfying walk.

Route 90

ORKNEY: HOY (RACKWICK TO MOANESS)

The full coastal walk from Rackwick to Moaness must lay claim to being one of the wildest and most dramatic coastal walks in Britain. Taking in the Old Man of Hoy and the highest vertical sea cliff in the UK, at St John's Head, it is a truly awe-inspiring expedition. Shorter variations are possible.

Distance: 10 miles/16 km (linear)
Time: 6–8 hours
OS map: 7

HOY IS THE SECOND-LARGEST OF THE ORKNEY ISLANDS AND BY far the highest and the wildest, its name originating from *há-oy*, the Old Norse for 'high island'. It is also very different in character from the rest of Orkney, being mostly covered in moorland heather and with quite distinctive hills.

Hoy is normally accessed from Houton on Orkney Mainland, where a vehicle roll-on roll-off ferry goes to Lyness, 12 miles from the start of the walk. In the summer months, pre-booking is essential. Alternatively, a small passenger ferry operates from Stromness once daily during summer months, leaving at 7.45 a.m. and arriving at Moaness half an hour later. However, this timetable is subject to variation and it is best to contact the tourist information centre in Stromness for up-to-date information prior to undertaking the walk. For those with plenty of time available, it is possible to walk from Moaness to Rackwick directly on a well-established path through the hills (five miles) and return by the walk to be described, though this would be a very long day.

The majority of people who visit the famous landmark of the Old Man of Hoy do so from the little hamlet of Rackwick, on the west

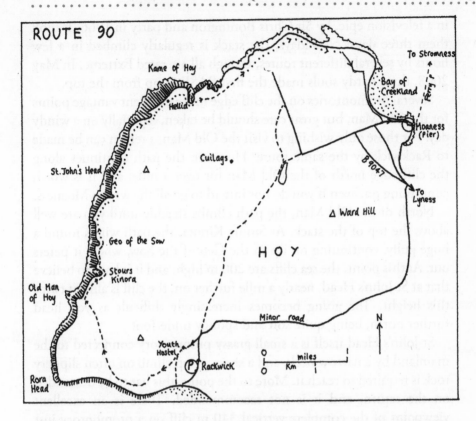

ROUTE 90

coast, and this marks the beginning of the described walk. From the parking area in Rackwick, walk right back up the road and take the left fork, leading to the youth hostel. A vague path runs behind the hostel and soon develops into an established waymarked trail across the hillside. Pass through a kissing gate and follow the peaty path as it winds its way round the southern shoulder of Moor Fea. There is a fine view of Rackwick Bay from here.

At Lang geo, the path heads inland, reaching the vicinity of the Old Man of Hoy in less than a mile. However, it is possible to stick to the coast by heading west to Rora Head and then north to the Old Man on pathless terrain. You should catch your first sight of the Old Man well before you reach the cliff edge, but it is only when you are almost upon it that you are able to appreciate this, the highest sea stack in Europe, in its full dramatic splendour.

The sandstone monolith rises sheer for 137 m and was first climbed, in a television epic, by Sir Chris Bonington and party in 1966. It took them three days! Nowadays, the stack is regularly climbed in a few hours by several different routes, though all are rated Extreme. In May 2008, three hardy souls made the first BASE jump from the top.

Several promontories on the cliff edge make excellent vantage points for the Old Man, but great care should be taken, especially on a windy day. For those only wishing to visit the Old Man, a return can be made to Rackwick by the same route. However, the path continues along the cliff edge north of the Old Man for over a mile, and it is worth continuing on, even if you do not intend to go all the way to Moaness.

North of the Old Man, the path climbs steadily until you are well above the top of the stack. At Stours Kinora, the path winds round a huge gully, continuing on up to the Geo of the Sow, where it peters out. At this point, the sea cliffs are 200 m high, and it is hard to believe that at St John's Head, nearly a mile further on, the cliff is almost twice this height. The going becomes increasingly difficult as you head further north, being quite soft and spongy underfoot.

St John's Head itself is a small grassy promontory connected to the mainland by a narrow neck, and a short, steep climb on often slippery rock is required to reach it. More to the point, this has to be descended on the return, and it is not recommended. There is an excellent viewpoint of the complete vertical 340 m cliff on a promontory just north of here. The Kame on Foula, in Shetland, and Conachair, in St Kilda, are higher but do not involve absolute vertical drops. In 1970, St John's Head was climbed, taking five days to ascend and two days to descend by abseil!

Beyond St John's Head, descend on a vague path and cross a stream before making the ascent to the last high point of the walk, at Hellia,

The Old Man of Hoy

which is 290 m high. From here, there is a fairly steep descent on spongy vegetation past the Kame of Hoy. Make a small detour inland to round a rocky inlet and pick up a path that follows the coast. This is bonxie country and a lookout should be kept for these dive-bombing predators!

The final haul to Moaness can be made by either rigidly adhering to the coastline or picking up the road at Murra and following it for just over two miles to Moaness.

ORKNEY MAINLAND:
THE WEST COAST WALK

The full walk from the Brough of Birsay southwards to Stromness is undoubtedly the classic Orkney coastal walk and involves 20 miles (32 km) of magnificent unspoilt coastline, most of it on exposed and stunning clifftops. The majority of walkers, however, will find this too long for a single day, and the route can be conveniently split in two at the Bay of Skaill, where Skara Brae is situated. However, the following route descriptions highlight the three most popular areas, namely: (a) the Brough of Birsay; (b) Marwick Head; and (c) Yesnaby to the Bay of Skaill.

(a) **Distance**: 1 mile/1.5km (circular)
Time: 1 hour
OS map: 6

(b) **Distance**: 2 miles/3 km (circular)
Time: 1–2 hours
OS map: 6

(c) **Distance**: 5 miles/8 km (linear)
Time: 3–4 hours
OS map: 6

(a) The Brough of Birsay

The Brough of Birsay is a tidal island accessible via a concrete causeway, but it can only be reached for a short period either side of low tide. Its defensible and yet unisolated nature endowed it with a quality unique for human settlement and, indeed, it was occupied from Pictish time

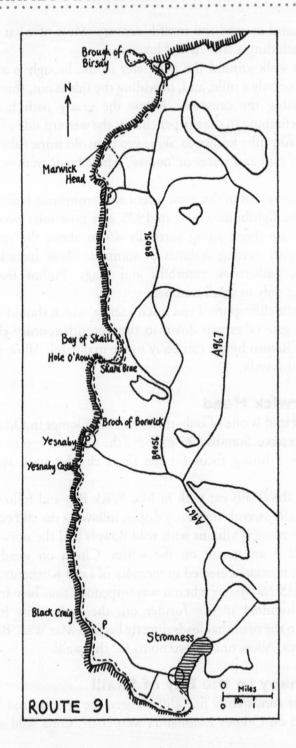

ROUTE 91

right up until around the twelfth century. Most of what remains is Viking, including a church and houses.

A short walk around the perimeter of the brough is a delightful excursion of only a mile, and, providing the tide is out, this is a 'must'. After crossing the causeway, follow the grassy path heading left, gradually climbing to the steeper cliffs at the western side of the island. At the narrow inlet known as Skiba geo is an old stone fisherman's hut with a turf roof and traces of 'nousts', where boats were stored in the winter.

Continue round to the most recent and prominent building on the brough, the lighthouse, built in 1925 and now solar powered. The cliffs here are sheer, rising vertically 45 m above the sea, and are crowded with nesting seabirds in summer. These include fulmars, kittiwakes, guillemots, razorbills and shags. Puffins frequent the brough but only in small numbers.

Follow the clifftop until you reach a fence, which should be adhered to until a gate takes you down to the eleventh-century church and buildings. Return by the causeway to the mainland. Allow one to two hours for this walk.

(b) Marwick Head

Marwick Head is one of only three seabird colonies in Orkney that is an RSPB reserve. Standing 87 m above the sea, with spectacular views, it provides a fitting focus for the short circular walk about to be described.

Park in the RSPB car park in Mar Wick Bay and follow the path that gradually ascends the grassy slopes, following the cliff edge. In late spring, the route is vibrant with wild flowers and the noise and sight of seabirds is an assault on the senses. Climb on steadily to the prominent memorial erected in memory of Lord Kitchener, who died on the HMS *Hampshire* when it was torpedoed near here in 1916.

A few hundred metres further on, the path turns inland and downhill to the road that leads directly back to Mar Wick Bay and the parking area. Allow one to two hours for this walk.

(c) Yesnaby to the Bay of Skaill

In terms of consistently fine cliff scenery, the area around Yesnaby is unequalled on Orkney Mainland's west coast. On a wild and windy

The Kitchener memorial and cliffs,
Marwick Head

day, with the heaving Atlantic swells crashing and exploding onto the Old Red Sandstone cliffs, Yesnaby exudes an elemental, tempestuous ferocity which is truly awe-inspiring.

Yesnaby can be reached by car by a minor road off the B9056, and there is ample parking space at the abandoned Second World War military base once used for gunnery practice. The walk from Yesnaby to the Bay of Skaill is superb on its own but can be enlivened by first turning left and exploring the coastline south as far as Yesnaby Castle, only a mile from Yesnaby itself. The 'Castle' is actually a fine sea stack with a natural arch.

North of Yesnaby, climb the eroded slopes of the Hill of Borwick and continue round into an obvious inlet. Just beyond is the Broch of Borwick, an Iron Age fortified settlement perched dramatically on the edge of a cliff. Severe erosion has destroyed the seaward side of the broch, but the eastern half is well preserved, including the small entrance door. This makes a grand spot for a breather. The view north from here is stunning, with continuous cliffs all the way to Row Head, over a mile away.

About half a mile north of the broch is Ramnageo, one of the longest geos in Orkney. The name originates from 'Raven geo', as its sheer rock walls and relative inaccessibility provide ideal haunts for ravens and other birds. This is another place to linger and another reason why coastal walking shouldn't be rushed.

The walk up to Row Head from here is magnificent, and Yettna geo and the natural arch of Hole o' Row provide more diversions and interest for the inquisitive hiker. The final descent to the beautiful sandy Bay of Skaill is truly delightful and is an ideal end to a classic

Broch of Borwick

coastal walk. The bay itself is a peaceful haven after the more dramatic charms of the clifftop and is the location of Skara Brae. Allow three to four hours for this walk.

ORKNEY MAINLAND: MULL HEAD

This is a spectacular circular walk around Mull Head, in the eastern extremity of Orkney Mainland in the district known as Deerness. The route takes in several points of interest, including the Gloup, the Brough of Deerness and the Covenanters' Memorial.

Distance: 6 miles/10 km (circular)
Time: 3–4 hours
OS map: 6

DEERNESS IS CONNECTED TO THE BULK OF ORKNEY MAINLAND by a thin neck of land only 100 m wide at its narrowest point. The main road (A960) from Kirkwall runs through here, narrowing to the B9050 and arriving at a car park and visitor centre at the start of the walk. The walk is popular and relevant leaflets are available in the visitor centre.

Take the signposted path, which leads directly in just a few minutes to the collapsed sea cave known as the Gloup. This is similar to but more spectacular than other such geological phenomena mentioned in this book, such as the Bullers of Buchan (see Route 14). The Gloup was originally a long, narrow sea cave, which later partially collapsed, leaving an enormous chasm still connected to the sea by an arch.

Turn left after observing the Gloup and follow the broad grassy path along the coastline. It is worth leaving the path at various points to wander nearer the cliff edge and gain a more detailed view of the sandstone cliffs. In just over half a mile, you will reach the Brough of Deerness. In Old Norse, a *brough* is a promontory, almost or entirely detached from the mainland (like the Brough of Birsay – see Route 91), and is often confused with a broch, which is literally a fort. A signpost leads you down new wooden steps to the gap between the

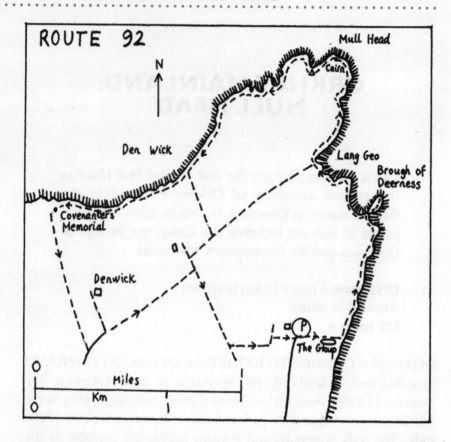

mainland and the brough; then a steep path aided by a chain handrail leads up to the grassy flat top, where there are remains of a small twelfth-century chapel. It is thought that at one time the brough was accessible by a land bridge. Surrounding the chapel are the grassed-over remains of several houses, now thought to have been of a secular rather than an ecclesiastical nature. The brough was a place of pilgrimage from the mid 1600s to around 1860 and is a superb spot to linger on a warm sunny day – but there is still the bulk of the walk to come!

The next point to aim for is Mull Head. The Mull Head Local Nature Reserve constitutes around 400 acres and was designated a reserve in 1993 due to its geological and archaeological interest. The winding route out to Mull Head has duckboarding strategically placed at boggy parts, and there are fine views looking back to the brough. Current low-level grazing by sheep has maintained the natural flora around Mull Head and the area is dominated by ling, bell heather and crowberry, which have disappeared from much of Orkney in recent years. The cairn at Mull Head is a good place for a short rest.

From here, continue along the coastline, paying a short visit to the triangulation point at 48 m height, the highest point of the walk. The tall monument in the far distance is the Covenanters' Memorial and the next main objective. Delightful, easy walking leads around the wide bay of Den Wick, from where a path leads away from the coast back to the start point for those who prefer not to visit the memorial. This shorter option makes for a four-mile-long route.

Cross several minor gorges by wooden footbridges, following the narrow grassy path until it eventually reaches the monument. In December 1679, the ship known as the *Crown of London* foundered on rocks at Scarva Taing, 300 m north-east of the monument. The ship's human cargo was 257 manacled Covenanters who were being transported to the New World for failing to submit to Charles II's Anglican form of worship. The captain refused to allow the prisoners to be released, though a key was passed to them and around 50 escaped, only for many of them to drown: once they had floated to shore on wreckage, they were not allowed to land and were forced back into the sea under the captain's orders.

From the memorial, leave by the gate and follow the fenced grass track for nearly a mile inland to the end of a minor road. Turn left and follow a sign that advises you to use the grassy path running to the side of the private access road to Denwick Farm. Take the second turn-off to the right and follow this track until it emerges near the visitor centre and car park. This completes a highly satisfactory circular walk.

Route 93

ORKNEY: WESTRAY
WEST COAST

This is a truly magnificent linear clifftop walk: wild, remote and uncompromising. The climax of the walk at Noup Head RSPB reserve is second only to St Kilda in terms of the number of breeding seabirds to be found there.

Distance: 6 miles/10 km (linear)
Time: 4–5 hours
OS map: 5

THE WEST WESTRAY CLIFFTOP PATH EXTENDS NORTH FROM the tiny settlement of East Kirbest to the prominent lighthouse on Noup Head and constitutes one of the finest coastal walks in Orkney. It is essentially a linear walk and, other than returning by the same route, a two-car system, taxi or friendly driver will be required. Another option is to leave a car at Noup Head and then cycle the eight miles to East Kirbest, leaving the bike there to retrieve later. This was the option used by the author. A shorter, circular route begins at Noup Head and continues south to just beyond Russa Taing, where a track leads up to Backarass and the road back to Noup Head. This route is around four miles long and takes three to four hours.

Westray is the most north-westerly of the Orkney Islands and can be reached by ferry from Mainland in one and a half hours. At the time of writing, it is easily possible to complete the walk in between the arrival of the morning ferry at 9 a.m. and the departure of the evening ferry at 6 p.m., giving plenty of spare time for an added cycle run and a pint in the Pierowall Hotel!

To reach the start of the walk at East Kirbest, take the B9067 road from Pierowall. After about three and a half miles, turn right at a large house onto a B road, go past some ramshackle cottages and continue

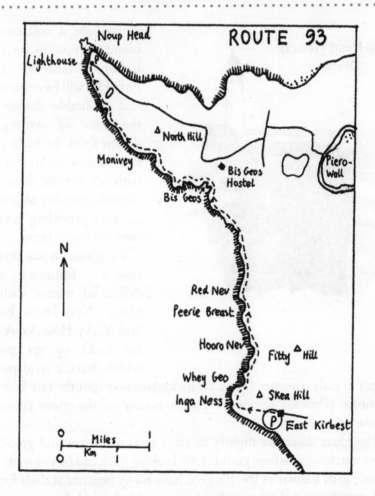

on until a sign appears at a small parking area, which marks the beginning of the route.

The walk is well signposted, with large marker poles leading you past a small farm and over a stile before you become established on the main clifftop trail. The entire path is stiled at various points, and these should be used rather than climbing over fences.

As you round the headland at Inga Ness, the lighthouse at Noup Head suddenly appears, looking surprisingly close but actually still over five miles of glorious walking away. The extraordinary Whey geo provides the first dramatic cliff feature of the day, an enormous inlet where photographic opportunities abound. The route then climbs gradually to the area west of Fitty Hill, the highest point on the island.

Noup Head, Westray, Orkney

If you are a collector of island high points (or, God forbid, Marilyns) then Fitty Hill will be a necessary and profitable detour. At the time of writing, a detour from the main path headed east up to this hill with an electric fence on the left, probably to protect an area providing nesting sites for Arctic terns.

Continue on past myriad coastal features with delightful names such as Hooro Nev, Peerie Breast and Mirky Hole. Look out for thrift or sea pinks, which make a vivid purple carpet in early summer. If you are lucky, you may spot the rare Scottish primrose (*Primula scotica*), a purple variety of the more common yellow primrose.

The route descends slightly to cross several streams and gradually turns north-west, where grand views looking back can be enjoyed. The double geos known as the Bis geos have rocky beaches at their heads, and at each geo a thick rope has been provided to aid descent to these beaches if so wished. Incidentally, the obvious building with the grand conservatory just above these geos is also called Bis Geos and is a recently renovated hostel with cottages, which would provide unique and relatively cheap accommodation if you were staying on the island. Shortly beyond this point is the track that leads back up to the road.

The final two miles from the headland of Russa Taing is undoubtedly the highlight of the walk both in terms of sheer bird numbers and quality of cliff scenery. This is not to be rushed! As you climb up the south-western slopes of North Hill, you are entering the RSPB reserve, where tens of thousands of guillemots and kittiwakes greet you with their raucous cries from every available ledge on the increasingly spectacular cliffs. There are dozens of incredibly photographic vantage points, and it is difficult not to become sidetracked by observing, photographing and just standing and staring at the awesome situations.

There is a dramatic narrow geo at Lawrence's Piece, and higher up at Deil Piece there is a trig point from which excellent views of the lighthouse, just a few hundred metres away, can be obtained. Built in 1898, the lighthouse was the first in Scotland to use mercury flotation in the revolving carriage. It was automated in 1964 and is now powered by 36 solar panels. The lighthouse is a suitable end to a memorable walk.

Recommended pub: Pierowall Hotel, Pierowall

Route 94

SHETLAND: FAIR ISLE CIRCUIT

> Far away across the waters
> Lies the dear land of our birth
> Scattered are her sons and daughters
> So far and wide o'er all the earth
> Barbara Wilson

The complete coastal circuit of Fair Isle is a thrilling, demanding and totally memorable walk. The presence of a road running through the island from north to south enables the walk to be cut short at any point, and several variations are described, depending on time or inclination.

Distance: 11 miles/18 km (circular)
Time: 7–9 hours
OS map: 4

THE TINY JEWEL OF FAIR ISLE, LYING ROUGHLY HALFWAY between Orkney and Shetland, is, like St Kilda, one of those magical islands that all lovers of solitude and remote destinations are sure to visit at least once in a lifetime. Along with Foula, the island boasts Britain's most isolated community, of around only 70 hardy souls.

Intensive study of the island has shown that Neolithic people were probably resident there up to 5,000 years ago, and it contains a remarkable selection of archaeological sites dating from around 3,000 years ago through to more recent times. In particular, there is an Iron Age promontory fort at Landberg and traces of an early Christian church at Kirki geo. The island was peopled by Norse settlers in the ninth century, and most of the place names originate from this time. The name Fair Isle is said to derive from the Old Norse name Fridarey ('the island of peace'), but its isolation would

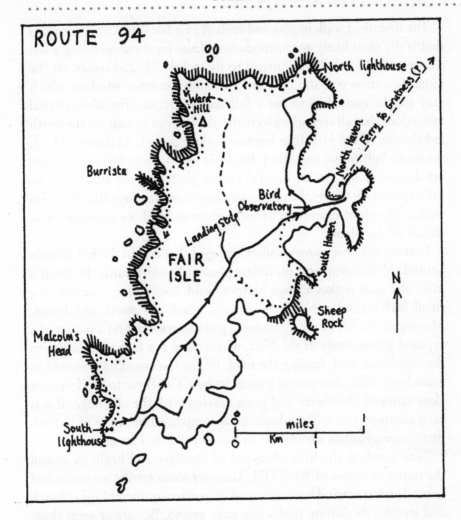

ROUTE 94

North lighthouse (Y)

Ferry to Grutness (Y)

North Haven

Ward Hill

Burrista

Bird Observatory

Landing Strip

South Haven

FAIR ISLE

N

Sheep Rock

Malcolm's Head

miles

Km

South lighthouse

suggest that the alternative derivation of 'far isle' from the Norse *feoer-øy* is more likely.

For centuries, Fair Isle has been an important location for shipping, but its cliff-girt coastline has claimed at least 100 known shipwrecks. In more recent times, the island has become internationally recognised as a significant seabird breeding site, and in 1948 well-respected ornithologist George Waterston fulfilled a life-long dream by establishing the famous bird observatory, providing accommodation for up to 30 visitors from May until October. You are welcome to stay at the bird observatory whether or not you are a 'twitcher'! Fair Isle is owned by the National Trust for Scotland and is now an SSSI.

The described walk begins and ends at Fair Isle Bird Observatory, as that is the most likely accommodation venue for those spending a few days on the island. If you intend to fly to Fair Isle and return on the same day, then you should have a roughly six-hour window, which may not be enough time for a full coastal circuit. The main coastal attractions that all serious walkers should attempt to visit are the north lighthouse, Ward Hill (the island's highest point), Malcolm's Head, the south lighthouse and Sheep Rock. As well as these highlights, there are dozens of sea stacks, natural arches, promontories and geos, the full exploration of which could take more than one day. The described walk is, therefore, essentially a compromise and makes an anticlockwise circuit of the island.

Leaving the observatory, follow the road that climbs the hill directly behind the building and meanders pleasantly northwards. In about a mile, the road makes a huge hairpin bend, continuing onwards to a small lochan and a blowhole. Finally, reach the north lighthouse. Moving to the left of the lighthouse, you can walk out on a path to the exposed promontory of the Nizz, where there is a foghorn. Return to the lighthouse and, leaving the road, follow the coastline downhill in a south-westerly direction to a small lochan. Continue to head west on close-cropped crowberry and grass, staying with the cliff edge. If it is early summer, you will no doubt be accompanied by scores of puffins, their comical antics a source of continuous joy and amusement.

Turn south at the little headland of Dronger and begin to ascend the northern slopes of Ward Hill. There are some terrific sea stacks and natural arches around here, one stack in particular resembling a church and steeple, its sloping roof white with guano. Beware of great skuas as you approach Ward Hill, as they defend their nests with fervent ferocity by dive-bombing intruders – a walking pole is useful for warding off attacks.

At 217 m, Ward Hill is a tremendous viewpoint though somewhat impoverished by the debris of a wartime radar station scattered around the trig point. This is an ideal spot to get a feel for the lie of the land and for a short breather. Far below to the south is the landing strip, which can be reached via a vehicle track curving its way round the north of Ward Hill. For those only wishing to undertake a short walk, this provides a good return route to the observatory, which can be reached in under two miles by track and road.

Harbour and Sheep
Rock, Fair Isle

To continue with the coastal walk, simply head south, staying on the clifftop if possible to avoid bonxie attacks. It should be stressed, however, that the coastline south of Ward Hill is incredibly indented and complex and you will probably not have enough time to explore every nook and cranny. One long, narrow promontory named Burrista is particularly dramatic. A couple of hours should be allowed for the walk from Ward Hill to Malcolm's Head, at the south of the island. Reaching the top of Malcolm's Head, at 107 m, is a 'must' and another superb vantage point.

The next objective from here is the south lighthouse, visible less than a mile away from Malcolm's Head. A pleasant, easy descent southwards leads to an inlet and a low, rocky coastline and the lighthouse beyond. Both of Fair Isle's lighthouses were built by Thomas Stevenson in 1892, and the south one was the last manned lighthouse in Britain.

The route from here follows the road northwards before cutting off to the right after a mile or so to Sheep Rock. However, the more adventurous may wish to stick to the coastline, although it is not as spectacular as the west side. On the road, there is plenty of interest, including a graveyard, museum, kirks and Fair Isle knitwear and craft shops. Note that the road splits into two parallel branches for nearly a mile and not all of the attractions are on the same branch. The museum, kirks and graveyard are on the east; the knitwear and craft shops are on the west.

Getting to Fair Isle

For general information on getting to Fair Isle, it is best to consult the island's website for up-to-date travel information and timetables, but the following gives general guidance for those wishing to pay a visit.

Web: www.fairisle.org.uk

To reach the island by sea, the twelve-passenger *Good Shepherd IV* leaves from Grutness, at the southern tip of Shetland, three times a week in the summer. The journey time is two and a half hours and is often rough, but it is very cheap. You cannot return on the same day, so you would need to book accommodation at the observatory.

Tel: 01595 760363

Alternatively, a 25-minute flight from Tingwall run by Directflight Ltd gives around six hours on the island, which is time enough for a shorter version of the described walk.

Web: www.directflight.co.uk

Tel: 01595 840246

Shortly before the turn-off to the airport, strike off to the right along the side of a dry-stone wall, which climbs steadily to the vicinity of Sheep Rock. This remarkable, almost detached headland rises to 132 m and has four hectares of grass on its sloping summit, which once provided pasture for sheep – hence the name. In St Kilda style, the islanders used to climb the headland with chains and used ropes to raise and lower the sheep! Reaching the top of Sheep Rock should in no way be attempted, as it involves a tricky descent followed by a steep climb on loose and unstable sandstone. Some of the finest of Fair Isle's natural arches lie on the east side of Sheep Rock but can only be seen properly from the sea.

From Sheep Rock, continue round the coast to another little

headland called Goorn before finally reaching the road once again, less than half a mile from the observatory. Those with energy left may consider a short excursion out to the almost separate island of Bu Ness, enclosing the two sheltered harbours of North Haven and South Haven. This latter walk is a pleasant evening stroll.

Recommended pub: The Bird Observatory, Fair Isle

Route 95

heading called Coorin before finally reaching the road once again less than half a mile from the observatory. Those with energy left may consider a short excursion out to the phone Separate island of Fitt... River. This latter walk... Recommended pubs: The Bird Observatory, Fair Isle.

SHETLAND: ST NINIAN'S ISLE CIRCUIT

St Ninian's Isle, once tidal, is now connected to Mainland Shetland by a beautiful and unique shell-sand isthmus or tombolo. The walk across this tombolo combined with a circuit of this entrancing historic island is one of the finest shorter coastal walks in Shetland.

Distance: 3.5 miles/6 km (circular)
Time: 2–3 hours
OS map: 4

ST NINIAN'S ISLE LIES ON THE WEST COAST OF SOUTH MAINLAND and about 18 miles south of Lerwick. To reach the island from the main A970 road, turn off on the B9122 to Bigton and then drive down to the parking area near the shore. Here, there is a fine view looking across the tombolo to St Ninian's Isle. The tombolo is unique as it is the only pure sand tombolo in Great Britain, others being composed of gravel or shingle, such as the one at Fethaland (see Route 99).

From the car park, descend to the beach and wander across the sandy isthmus, with beautiful turquoise water and white waves coming from both sides. Across St Ninian's Bay to the left is a marvellous view out to grassy-topped cliffs leading all the way to Fitful Head. As you approach the island, climb the easy sandy slope and begin a clockwise circuit by contouring round to the head of the little promontory west of St Ninian's Bay. Here, you can gaze across to the offshore skerries of Inns Holm and Coar Holm.

Continue westwards, crossing an old dry-stone wall, and follow the dramatic cliff edge for over half a mile to Longa Berg, which is separated from the stubby sea stack of Sweyn Holm by a sensational narrow channel. Turn northwards from here, climbing a gradual grassy

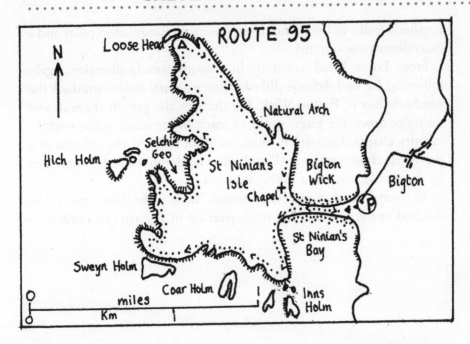

slope to overlook Selchie geo, where you may spot puffins and almost
certainly guillemots.

From Selchie geo, continue to follow the cliff edge northwards for
nearly a mile on good close-cropped grass to Loose Head, the most

Chapel,
St Ninian's Isle

northerly point of the island. Here there is a triangulation pillar and a marvellous view – enjoy!

From Loose Head, continue in a south-easterly direction, again following the well-defined cliff edge past a natural arch to overlook the northerly bay of Bigton Wick. Go through the gate in the wall and meander down the green sward to reach the remains of the twelfth-century chapel. Excavations made in 1958 revealed the remains of a pre-Norse church and some Pictish silver heirlooms probably concealed by the monks prior to a Viking invasion.

To complete this satisfying round, walk right from the ruins, descend to the tombolo and reach your car in a quarter of a mile.

SHETLAND: MOUSA CIRCUIT

This short but varied walk round part of the fascinating island of Mousa not only visits the famous broch but also gives numerous opportunities to spot an abundance of wildlife, including common seals, grey seals, terns, skuas and eiders. It is ideal for children.

Distance: 2 miles/3 km (circular)
Time: 1–3 hours
OS map: 4

MOUSA IS A SMALL ISLAND LYING OFF THE EAST COAST OF South Mainland in Shetland. It is roughly equidistant (14 miles) from Sumburgh Airport and Lerwick. It is justly famous for its 2,000-year-old Iron Age broch, the best preserved in the world, but also for its internationally important wildlife. Mousa is now an RSPB nature reserve and, as such, walking on the island is restricted to certain areas to avoid disturbance to breeding and nesting sites.

On the 15-minute ferry trip, look out for porpoises, seals, otters and, if you are really lucky, killer whales! Once on the island, begin the walk by following the trail marker posts and boardwalks heading south along the coast. The route is an anticlockwise circuit of the central part of the island.

Round a grassy headland and in less than ten minutes the broch will appear across a shingle bay. Built in the Iron Age from local sandstone, it stands over 13 m high and was probably built mainly for defence. Another, less well-preserved broch stands less than a mile away, directly across on Burraland on Shetland Mainland, and both brochs were probably used to guard the entrance to Mousa Sound. The broch is one of around one hundred and twenty built throughout Shetland and its well-preserved status is likely due to its island location.

Entering the broch and gazing upwards gives a startling appreciation

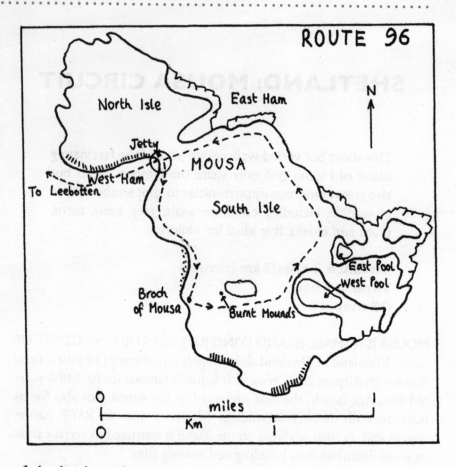

of the height and true antiquity of such an amazingly preserved structure. Climb the internal staircase between the double walls to gain a bird's-eye view of the surroundings. The strange churring noise you may hear in the broch is not from ghosts of the past but from storm petrels, which nest in cavities in the walls.

Leave the broch and follow the trail inland, passing a turf-covered Bronze Age burnt mound, which possibly may have been used for cooking. Near the tidal West Pool, be careful to stick to the marked trail to avoid ground-nesting birds such as eiders and Arctic terns.

The next tidal pool, East Pool, is the best spot for observing seals, which usually congregate on spits of shell-sand, grunting and groaning as they sunbathe. Both types of seal are evident: the short-muzzled common seal and the long-snouted grey seal.

From East Pool, continue north-west along the rocky coastline for

Broch of Mousa

about half a mile to the deep inlet of East Ham. This is a delightful part of the walk, but beware of aerial attacks from skuas and terns.

Finally, head west, following the southern shore of East Ham, and cross the narrow neck of land separating the two parts of Mousa, South Isle and North Isle. This leads directly back to the starting point.

Getting to Mousa

Mousa can be reached by a passenger ferry run by Mousa Boat Trips between mid-April and mid-September. The ferry departs from Leebotten pier, where there is a waiting room with informative displays about Mousa and a toilet. Note that there are no public toilets on Mousa.

Tel: 01950 431367 or 07901 872339

Web: www.mousa.co.uk

Email: info@mousaboattrips.co.uk

SHETLAND: ISLE OF NOSS CIRCUIT

This walk is arguably the finest small-island coastal walk in Britain, not only in terms of awesome cliff and sea stack features but also, and more so, for the vast numbers of seabirds that make their home on the dramatic eastern cliffs. Noss is renowned as one of Europe's finest wildlife sites and boasts the most congested seabird colony in Shetland. This is a walk that will remain in the memory for a long time.

Note that Noss can only be visited between May and August and that the island is closed on Mondays and Thursdays.

Distance: 4 miles/6 km (circular)
Time: 3–4 hours
OS map: 4

THE ISLAND OF NOSS LIES JUST EAST OF THE ISLAND OF BRESSAY, which itself lies only a short distance from Lerwick, the 'capital' of Shetland. If you are based in Lerwick for only a short time and cannot make the long crossing to either Fair Isle or Foula, then Noss is the ideal alternative.

Bressay is only minutes away from Lerwick, and a short three-mile drive takes you to the car park, from where a short walk down a stony track leads to the small jetty. Scottish Natural Heritage (SNH), which manages Noss, operates a small inflatable boat across the 200-m-wide Noss Sound, and the warden, who is resident on the island over the summer, will see you as you walk down the track. If not, then a wave of the hand should ensure that he meets you at the jetty. A red flag flies on the island if the weather is too rough to cross. Call the Noss freephone number, 0800 107 7818, if you are at all concerned about the weather on the day you intend to visit.

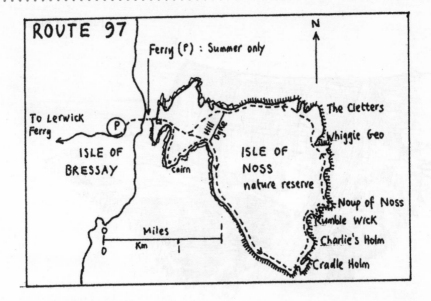

The view of Noss across the sound is one of gentle grassy moorland and belies its real dramatic grandeur, first seen by the Vikings, who approached it by sea from the opposite side and christened it 'Nose', probably because of the similarity of the vast cliff of Noup to a nose.

On arrival at Noss, you will be invited into the small visitor information room, where there is a toilet. The warden will issue you with a SNH leaflet containing a map and much interesting information. You will also be advised to walk round the island in an anticlockwise direction. Note that there is no shop on Noss and you should be self-sufficient as regards food and drink. You are also instructed not to drift into the interior of the island, as the moorland heart is the stronghold of both Arctic and great skuas, which nest on the ground and will aggressively defend their nests with dive-bombing swoops. They rarely make contact, but it is a good idea to wave a stick or walking pole above your head to deter them.

On leaving the information centre, walk round the sandy bay of Nesti Voe and either cut directly across towards the hill dyke or follow the coastline out to the cairn at Turr Ness before doubling back to the vicinity of the hill dyke. As you follow the coastline from here, the land steadily increases in height out past the Point of Hovie, where (if the time of year is right – June to July) you may spot the first of many puffins. From here, the high-rise drama begins to really kick in, and a

Noup of Noss

short distance further on you suddenly come across a yawning chasm between the main cliff and a grass-covered stack called the Holm of Noss, or Cradle Holm. In the seventeenth century, a Foula cragsman engineered a roped crossing to the stack in a box cradle, but he tragically fell and drowned on the return. The contraption was dismantled in 1864 but proved quite a tourist draw in its day, attracting the likes of Sir Walter Scott in 1814.

By now, the tip of the Noup (the island's high point) will be in view, and as you climb slightly higher the sheer immensity of the cliff, stained white with guano, explodes into the senses, as does the cast of tens of thousands of screeching seabirds, the main players in this vast outdoor auditorium of light and sound. The Old Red Sandstone has weathered into myriad horizontal ledges, ideal nesting sites for thousands of gannets, fulmars, kittiwakes and guillemots, which cram themselves into every available space. Closer at hand, you can quietly sit and watch the comical puffins as they enter and leave their clifftop burrows, which they return to year after year after spending the winter at sea. Rounding the great inlet of Rumble Wick, it is all too easy to stop and stare at the constantly changing interplay of cliff, sea and sky and realise that this is what life is all about.

The final haul to the triangulation pillar on the Noup (181 m) is a pleasant grassy stroll following an old dry-stone wall. On a clear day, enjoy a panoramic view of Unst, Fetlar and Mainland and, if you are lucky, Fair Isle and Foula. This is indeed a splendid vantage point – don't miss it!

The highlight of the circuit may now be over, but there is still much of interest yet to come as you wend your way northwards from the Noup still following the dry-stone dyke. The area known as the Cletters, beyond the big inlet of Whiggie geo, is a grand place to stop and offers fine views back to the Noup. The homeward stretch west along North Croo is beautifully relaxing after the excitement of the high cliffs. Cross the Hill Dyke by a stile and follow the signs back to the information centre to complete a unique and unforgettable walk.

Route 98

SHETLAND: MUCKLE ROE

Muckle Roe is one of the most scenic of Shetland's smaller islands and has the added advantage of being connected to Mainland Shetland by a bridge. The complete circumnavigation is around twelve miles, including four miles of road walking, and would be suitable for fit walkers. Described here, however, is the slightly less ambitious and more popular circuit from Little Ayre, which uses a good inland track.

Distance: 8 miles/13 km (circular)
Time: 5–6 hours
OS map: 3

FROM THE A970 ROAD NORTH OF LERWICK, TAKE THE MINOR road at the head of Busta Voe signposted 'Muckle Roe'. Go over the bridge and continue for three miles to the road-end, where there is a small parking space.

Beyond the last house, a good vehicle track climbs steadily north-west, cutting purposefully through the red granite bedrock into a narrow valley between Muckle Field and Mid Field. As you pass the inland loch of Burki Waters, look out for red-throated divers and also golden and grey plovers. Shortly past the loch, the track again becomes squeezed in a narrow defile before opening out into a broad grassy plain.

At this point, the track bends sharply to the left at a large barn, but ignore this and follow a minor path through a gate. This goes directly ahead, passing to the left of an old croft and onto the right bank of Town Loch. Just before a gate at the outflow of Mill Loch, it is worth making a small diversion uphill to explore the ruin of an old water mill, a testament to the human presence that once thrived in this peaceful and beautiful spot.

Return to the path and gate and walk the short distance to the

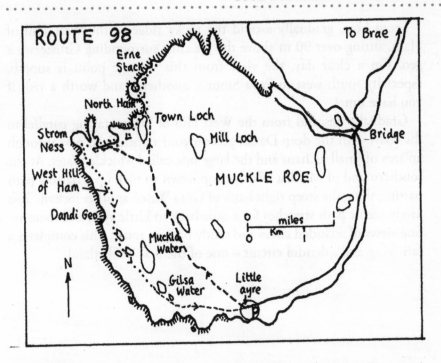

enchanting bay of North Ham, a beautifully sheltered inlet edged with sheer red granite cliffs and a haven for seabirds such as fulmars and shags. This is one of those magical spots where it pays to stand or sit and stare for a while.

At this point, it is worth continuing along the rugged coastline for another half a mile to the island's tallest cliffs at Erne Stack, one of the last nesting sites of sea eagles in Scotland prior to their reintroduction in 1975. Just north of the bay at North Ham is a curious small circular inlet almost completely surrounded by cliffs, also worth exploring.

Return to North Ham and start to follow the deeply indented coastline above Town Loch, with fine retrospective views of the cliffs at North Ham. Between North Ham and the sandy beach of South Ham, there are many inlets and stacks and also a natural arch. At South Ham, there are often seals basking on the rocks, and this is another delectable spot. At the far end of the beach at South Ham, you will see the end of the original track used at the start of the walk. Ignore this and go through a gate taking you out onto the grassy ridge of Strom Ness, where there is a massive, deep geo on the right-hand side.

From here, gradually ascend the rocky ridge of the West Hill of Ham, sitting over 90 m above the sea cliffs surrounding Grusterwick geo. On a clear day, the view from this vantage point is superb, especially south-west to Papa Stour – another island worth a visit if you have time!

Gradually descend from the West Hill of Ham, staying parallel to the coast with the deep Dandi geo on your right. Next, pass through an area of small lochans and the large one called Muckla Water. At the southern end of Muckla Water, drop down to pick up a narrow path passing along the steep right bank of Gilsa Water, another lochan. This lovely scenic path stretches for a mile back to Little ayre, and there are fine views of secluded coves and sandy bays en route. This completes a satisfying and splendid circuit – one of the best in Shetland.

SHETLAND: FETHALAND

A wild and breathtaking walk around Mainland Shetland's exposed northern extremity. This is coastal walking at its sublime best, offering dramatic seascapes, abundant wildlife and a distinctive 'edge-of-the-world' feel.

Distance: 7 miles/11 km (circular)
Time: 3–4 hours
OS map: 1

FETHALAND IS THE NAME GIVEN TO THE REMOTE, GNARLED finger of land at the most northerly point of North Mainland (or Northmavine). Part of it is almost a separate island, being linked to the mainland by a narrow shingle bar. Take the A970 road to North Roe and then to the tiny settlement of Isbister, where the road ends at a gate. There is a small parking area on the right.

Go through the gate and follow the vehicle track northwards, climbing steadily on open moorland and sheep pasture over the shoulder of Lanchestoo, where there is a triangulation pillar. From here, there is a marvellous view of the 'Isle of Fethaland', a verdant green oasis girdled by immense cliffs, with the Ramna Stacks beyond. A short descent takes you down to the Upper Loch of Setter, where, if you are lucky, you may spot a rare red-throated diver, which nest here.

Moving on, continue northwards over broad moorland, following the track past another small lochan skirting the eastern slopes of the Hill of Breibister. Descend gradually past several ruins to the shingle bar separating the Isle of Fethaland from Fethaland. This beautiful narrow spit of rocks and pebbles separates the wild Atlantic from Yell Sound, and on certain days waves can come crashing in on the Atlantic side while the other basks in calm.

Just above the bay are the shells of several buildings, the site of

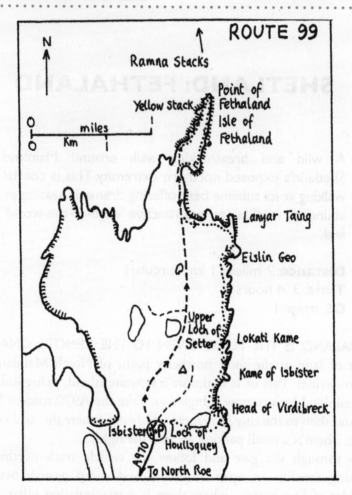

Shetland's largest haaf, a seasonal fishing station that operated until 1904. The word *haaf* is Norse for 'offshore', and such stations were situated near deep water close to the continental shelf. The fishermen who stayed in the huts had a hard life, manning square-sailed boats with six oarsmen and towing seven miles of line with over one thousand baited hooks. Many boats did not make it back, and those that did were pulled up over the flat stones on the beach and berthed in hollows known as nousts, which can also be seen here.

Wander on to the 'island', passing through a gap in a stone wall, and gradually make your way up a grassy path leading out left to the edge of the 50-m-high sea cliffs. The edge of these cliffs forms a fine promenade leading all the way to the lighthouse, where there is a fine

Point of Fethaland

view of Yellow Stack and the Point of Fethaland beyond. At the right time of year, the close-cropped turf at your feet will be a blue carpet of squill. The final few hundred metres out to the point, squeezed in by the pounding sea on both sides, is a sheer delight. Over a mile out to the north lie the Ramna Stacks, a group of small islands and an RSPB reserve. Slightly closer is Gruney Island, with its own lighthouse.

Turn here and follow the east coast, passing several geos. Just past the lighthouse is Cleber geo, where there is an old Viking quarry with a large rock face of soapstone, once excavated for bowls and pots. Once across the shingle spit, follow the outward track for about half a mile before cutting off to the left to follow the eastern coastline southwards to the Kame of Isbister. There is much of interest on this fascinating stretch of rugged coastline, including the protruding finger of Lanyar Taing and the remarkable Eislin geo, a gap in the cliffs coming 100 m inland. Further on is Lokati Kame, where there are remains of a possible Celtic monastic site. The final point of interest is the rocky promontory known as the Kame of Isbister, which is best viewed from the Head of Virdibreck, directly south across a wide bay. From the head, you should spot several grass-covered beehive huts of a medieval monastic site. To return to the start, descend west to the Loch of Houllsquey and follow its southern shore to a track leading directly to Isbister.

Route 100

SHETLAND: UNST (HERMANESS)

This, the most northerly walk in Britain, is a tantalising mix of coastal and moorland walking. The cliff scenery and teeming bird life are an ornithologist's dream, while the view out to Muckle Flugga, the true termination of Britain, is a sight that should be on every walker's list.

Distance: 5 miles/8 km (circular)
Time: 3–5 hours
OS map: 1

HERMANESS IS THE MOST NORTHERLY PENINSULA OF THE MOST northerly inhabited island of Britain, the island of Unst. The area is a bird sanctuary and has been a National Nature Reserve since 1955. The walk begins at the car park near the visitor centre on the west side of Burra Firth.

The footpath heads north from the car park through two gates, climbing steadily and marked by posts topped with green paint. Cross the Burn of Winnaswarta Dale and reach a fork in the track. Ignore the right branch and continue along the left fork, following the burn. The presence of duckboarding at the boggiest parts of the moor is quite welcome, even though it detracts from the wildness of the scene. The moor is populated with golden plovers, wheatears, skylarks and that bully of the skies, the great skua, so it is a good idea to have a walking pole to ward off its aerial attacks.

As you near the cliffs on the west side of Hermaness, prepare for an assault on the senses. You will no doubt hear the sound of thousands of gannets, fulmars, razorbills and kittiwakes, then see the snaking line of vast cliffs rising in endless tiered ledges from the pounding sea, with every available space used. The smell of guano will also fill the air.

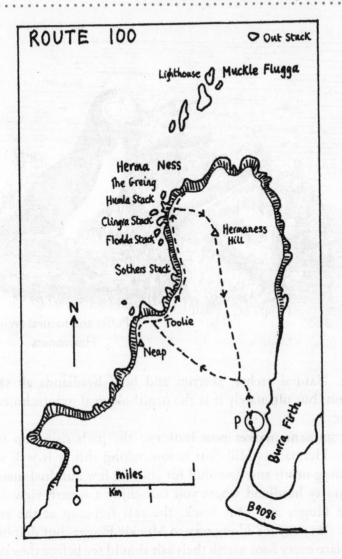

ROUTE 100   ○ Out Stack

Lighthouse ○ Muckle Flugga

Herma Ness
The Greing
Humla Stack
Clingra Stack
Flodda Stack

Hermaness Hill

Sothers Stack

N

Toolie

Neap

P

Burra Firth

miles

Km

B9086

Before turning right to follow the cliff edge, take a diversion left to the top of the Neap and catch your first glimpse of Muckle Flugga, over two miles to the north. If you are walking at the right time of year, there may be scores of puffins at your feet performing their amusing displays.

The walk north along the clifftop is a pure joy on mainly close-cropped grass, and you can venture as near to the cliff edge as you dare. The seascape is incredible, with a plethora of delightfully named sea stacks such as Sothers, Flodda, Clingra, Humla and the

Puffin and natural arch,
Hermaness

Greing. Natural arches, skerries and bold headlands all vie for
attention, but ultimately it is the ornithological pyrotechnics that
win out.

A prominent marker post indicates the path rising up to the
right to Hermaness Hill, but before taking this it is well worth
continuing north and downhill for another few hundred metres to
a flat grassy headland where you can enjoy a superb view out to
Muckle Flugga and Out Stack, the real full-stop at the end of
Britain. They say it's a long way to Muckle Flugga, but despite this
it is a place every Scot worth their salt should see before they shuffle
off to other things.

If you can drag yourself away from this wild and wondrous spot,
return to the post and climb to the top of Hermaness Hill to be greeted
by another marvellous view and the thought that you are presently on
the same latitude as South Greenland (just over 60 degrees north).
Return south along the well-marked path, again, much of it on
boardwalks, for over a mile, until the fork on the path mentioned on
the approach appears. Bear left and follow the waymarked route back
to your car.

Appendix

LONG-DISTANCE COASTAL WALKS
IN SCOTLAND

Though the intention of this book is to describe the hundred best day coastal walks in Scotland, for the sake of completeness, and also because many of the day walks form part of longer-distance routes, the following is a brief summary of the main official long-distance coastal walks in Scotland. The list is by no means comprehensive and omits many shorter walks created mainly by local councils. The routes are described according to the Regions 1 to 4 indicated in the Introduction.

Region I

The John Muir Way

This relatively new route in south-east Scotland has not yet been fully completed but will eventually stretch from Musselburgh, near Edinburgh, to Dunglass, just north of Cockburnspath (the current end point of the Southern Upland Way). It is not a fully coastal route, however, and much of it runs inland on grass paths and tracks. (See Route 2.)

The Fife Coastal Path

This is probably the best known of Scotland's long-distance coastal routes and links the River Forth and River Tay bridges, incorporating some picturesque fishing villages and plenty of history in its 81 miles between North Queensferry and Dundee. (See Routes 4, 6, 7 and 8.)

The Moray Coast Trail

Also known as the Moray Firth Trail, this unfinished walk already runs from Forres to Portsoy, a distance of over 50 miles, and to scattered sections to the east of this. (See Routes 15, 16 and 17.)

The North Sea Trail

The North Sea Trail is an ongoing continental project involving six European countries that share a common North Sea coastline, namely England, Scotland, Norway, Denmark, Germany and the Netherlands. The ultimate intention is to create a continuous series of footpaths around the North Sea coast. The previous three trails are part of this ambitious partnership. For more information log on to www.northseatrail.org

Region 2

The Ayrshire Coastal Path

This is Scotland's newest long-distance walking route and covers 100 miles of the beautifully picturesque Ayrshire coastline from Glenapp, near Ballantrae in the south, to Skelmorlie, north of Largs. The walk is the brainchild of Ayr Rotary Club and in particular James Begg, who has written the official and only guidebook to the route. (See Routes 26 and 27.)

The Arran Coastal Way

This circular walk around the Isle of Arran, in the Firth of Clyde, is sixty-five miles in length, includes two inland options and begins and ends at Brodick. (See Routes 28 and 29.)

Region 3

The North Highland Way

This is, as yet, an idea on the drawing board and may not come to fruition. The intended route would follow the north coast of Scotland from John o'Groats to Cape Wrath and has the backing of several Scottish MPs. Financial support is currently being sought from a number of public agencies. (See Routes 77, 78, 79 and 80.)

A Scottish coastal path – and beyond

With almost 7,000 miles of mainland coastline, Scotland has the potential for the ultimate long-distance walk, and the idea of a Scottish coastal path already has the backing of several MSPs. The 44 routes in this book covering the mainland of Scotland amount to a total distance of less than 500 miles – or less than 7 per cent of the full 7,000 miles. So in a sense this book can only scratch the surface of the enormous potential of Scotland's coastline.

Scotland's core paths network project has already seen the creation of a number of coastal trails (some listed above), covering almost a quarter of the Scottish coastline, and MSP Alasdair Morgan believes that linking them into a single route would be an obvious next step. As he said during a Scottish Parliament debate in February 2009, 'If all the gaps could eventually be filled and the existing paths, plus the missing bits, branded and marketed as a single entity – the Scottish Coastal Path – we would have a tremendous asset.'

There is a huge groundswell of support for this ambitious undertaking, but the practicalities of its implementation, including the vast sums of money required, are a formidable hurdle. Even if and when a Scottish coastal path is completed, the time, effort and money needed to upgrade and maintain it would be considerable. Despite the existence of a traditional right of access to the coast agreed by the Land Reform (Scotland) Act 2003, we may still have to wait many years before a single path around all of the Scottish coastline becomes a reality. Hopefully, this book will help in a small way towards the eventual establishment of what would be a truly striking and groundbreaking natural resource.

A British coastal path

Although this book is only concerned with Scottish coastal walks, the natural corollary of the preceding paragraphs is the implementation of what would be the longest and most challenging walk in the UK: namely, a path around the entire 11,000 miles of mainland Britain – a walk on a truly monumental scale. Several people have already accomplished such a feat, but their total mileage has fallen far short of this figure, owing to inland detours and omissions and so on. If such a path was created, it is doubtful that the total mileage would equate to the above figure, as it relates to a literal adhesion to the shoreline for the entirety of the walk.

Unlike Scotland, England does not yet possess a law enshrining a right of access to all of its coastline, but momentum is increasing, as shown by the passing of the Marine and Coastal Access Act 2009. The Act has the bold and adventurous notion of an English coastal path at its heart, but, as in Scotland, its implementation will take many years.

It is interesting that England already contains what is the longest waymarked trail in the UK: the South West Coast Path, stretching nearly 600 miles from Lyme Regis to Minehead and encompassing a sizeable fraction of the full 3,400 miles of English coastline.

Wales has its very own magnificent waymarked coast route: the Pembrokeshire Coast Path, having a total length of over 180 miles, and progress towards a trail around the 800 miles of Welsh coastline is fully focussed and flying. Indeed, it may only be a few years before its completion, with 2012 being seen as a distinct possibility.

SUGGESTIONS FOR FURTHER READING

Fabian, D.J., Little, G.E. and Williams, D.N., *The Islands of Scotland Including Skye* (Edinburgh: The Scottish Mountaineering Trust, 1989).

Hallewell, Richard, *Walks: Caithness*, Hallewell Pocket Walking Guide (Strathtummel: Hallewell Publications, 2005).

Haswell-Smith, Hamish, *The Scottish Islands* (Edinburgh: Canongate, 1996).

Jones, Rosalind, *Tea with Chrissie: The Story of Burg and Ardmeanach on the Isle of Mull* (Isle of Mull: Craigmore Publishing).

Koch-Osborne, Peter and Koch-Osborne, Rosemary, *Walks: East Sutherland*, Hallewell Pocket Walking Guide (Strathtummel: Hallewell Publications, 2006).

—— and ——, *Walks: West Sutherland*, Hallewell Pocket Walking Guide (Strathtummel: Hallewell Publications, 2006).

Welsh, M., 'Walks on Shetland', *Westmorland Gazette* (1995).

Welsh, M. and Isherwood, C., *Walking Glenfinnan: The Road to the Isles*, Clan Walk Guides 9 (Doune: Clan Books, 2007).

—— and ——, *Walking Orkney*, Clan Walk Guides 6 (Doune: Clan Books, 2007).

—— and ——, *Walking Wester Ross*, Clan Walk Guides 3 (Doune: Clan Books, 2006).

—— and ——, *Walking the Western Isles*, Clan Walk Guides 5 (Doune: Clan Books, 2006).

—— and ——, *Walking the Isles of Islay, Jura and Colonsay*, Clan Walk Guides 8 (Doune: Clan Books, 2005).

Williams, Luke, *Walks: Western Isles*, Hallewell Pocket Walking Guide (Strathtummel: Hallewell Publications, 2007).

Williams, Paul, *Walks: Isle of Mull, Coll and Tiree*, Hallewell Pocket Walking Guide (Strathtummel: Hallewell Publications, 2007).